RELIGION AND SOCIAL CHANGE
IN SOUTHERN AFRICA

ANTHROPOLOGICAL ESSAYS
IN HONOUR OF MONICA WILSON

Religion and Social Change
in Southern Africa

EDITED BY

MICHAEL G. WHISSON

AND

MARTIN WEST

DAVID PHILIP / CAPE TOWN
WITH
REX COLLINGS / LONDON
1975

Rupert Shephard, 1913

FIRST PUBLISHED IN 1975 BY DAVID PHILIP, PUBLISHER
3 SCOTT ROAD, CLAREMONT, CAPE, SOUTH AFRICA
WITH REX COLLINGS LTD., 69 MARYLEBONE HIGH STREET, LONDON
© DAVID PHILIP, PUBLISHER, 1975
ISBN 0 949968 44 7 (DAVID PHILIP)
SBN 901720 99 2 (REX COLLINGS)
TYPESET BY MONOSPOOLS (PTY.) LTD., CAPE TOWN
PRINTED AND BOUND IN SOUTH AFRICA BY
THE RUSTICA PRESS (PTY.) LTD., WYNBERG, CAPE

CONTENTS

vi

CONTENTS

CONTRIBUTORS

A.-I. Berglund, M.A., B.D. (Uppsala), Ph.D. (Cape Town). Director of Theological Education, S.A. Council of Churches, and formerly Lecturer, Lutheran Theological College, Mapumulo. Author of *Zulu Ideas and Symbolism*.

W. P. Carstens, B.A. Hons. (Rhodes), Ph.D. (Cape Town). Professor of Anthropology, University of Toronto, and formerly Lecturer in Social Anthropology, University of Cape Town. Publications include *The Social Structure of a Cape Coloured Reserve*.

W. D. Hammond-Tooke, M.A., Ph.D. (Cape Town). Professor of Social Anthropology, University of the Witwatersrand. Publications include *Bhaca Society* and *Command or Consensus*.

E. J. Krige, M.A., D.Litt. (Rand). Formerly Professor of Social Anthropology, University of Natal. Publications include *The Realm of the Rain Queen* (with J. D. Krige) and *The Social System of the Zulus*.

A. B. M. Mafeje, M.A. (Cape Town), Ph.D. (Cantab.). Professor of Social Anthropology and Sociology of Development, Institute of Social Studies, The Hague, and formerly Head of the Department of Sociology, University of Dar es Salaam. Author (with Monica Wilson) of *Langa*.

C. G. Murray, M.A. (Cantab.). Research Student, University of Cambridge, and formerly Junior Lecturer in Social Anthropology, University of Cape Town.

B. A. Pauw, M.A., B.D. (Stellenbosch), Ph.D. (Cape Town). Professor of Anthropology, University of South Africa. Publications include *Religion in a Tswana Chiefdom*, *The Second Generation*, and *Christianity and Xhosa Tradition*.

A. I. Richards, M.A. (Cantab.), Ph.D. (London). Formerly Reader in Social Anthropology, University of Cambridge. Publications include *Land, Labour and Diet* and *Chisungu*.

H. Sibisi, B.A. (Hons.) (Natal), Ph.D. (Cantab.). Iona Evans-

Pritchard Research Fellow, St. Anne's College, Oxford.

B. G. M. Sundkler, D.Theol., D.D. Professor of Church Mission History, University of Uppsala, and formerly Bishop of Bukoba, Tanzania. Publications include *Bantu Prophets in South Africa* and *The Christian Ministry in Africa*.

V. W. Turner, B.A. (London), Ph.D. (Manchester). Professor of Anthropology, University of Chicago. Publications include *Schism and Continuity in an African Society*, *The Drums of Affliction* and *The Forest of Symbols*.

M. E. West, M.A., Ph.D. (Cape Town). Lecturer in Social Anthropology, University of Cape Town. Author of *Divided Community* and *Bishops and Prophets in a Black City*.

M. G. Whisson, M.A., Ph.D. (Cantab.). Senior Lecturer in Social Anthropology, University of Cape Town. Publications include *Change and Challenge* and *Under the Rug*.

PREFACE

Monica Wilson retired from the Chair of Social Anthropology in the University of Cape Town at the end of 1973. Despite being a very private person, she has commanded the affection and respect of her colleagues and students for a full generation, and the news of her retirement from the university scene, if not from the academic stage, evoked a warm and spontaneous reaction from the scattered community which she has served so well. It was generally felt that a book compiled in her honour should mark the occasion, and after preliminary discussions between Axel-Ivar Berglund, David Hammond-Tooke and the editors it was agreed that the volume should be compiled in what has become 'her' department.

The response to our invitation to contribute to this volume was immediate and positive from a wide range of Monica's colleagues, fellow students and former pupils. In addition to those participating here, there were a number who wished to contribute, but were unable to do so: for reasons of academic specialisation outside the theme of this volume, ill health, or inability to meet the very strict time limits we were compelled to set. We are grateful for their interest and encouragement. We are indebted also to a number of others: Axel-Ivar Berglund assisted in many ways; our publisher David Philip was determined that the quality of technical production should be appropriate to the occasion; and the Editorial Board of the University of Cape Town, together with the Vice-Chancellor, Sir Richard Luyt, who made a generous contribution, made this production possible. We are pleased to record our appreciation to all the foregoing for easing the task of co-ordination.

Grateful acknowledgement is made also to Professor Rupert Shephard for the portrait of Professor Wilson.

The theme of the book suggested itself immediately from Monica Wilson's own contributions to history and social anthropology. The history of her country has been, for her, an abiding concern and the origin of her interest in social anthropology. As is apparent from both *The Analysis of Social Change* (1945) and *The Oxford History of South Africa* (1969, 1971), as well as from that extraordinary, precocious study, *Reaction to Conquest* (1936), history includes for Monica the whole process of human affairs, not merely the chronicles of the mighty. Of her interest in religion and ritual we can add nothing to Audrey Richards's introduction beyond emphasising that Monica has been, to use one of her favourite phrases, both an 'insider' and an 'outsider' in her analyses. As one who has a personal and intuitive experience of religion in addition to a scholarly understanding, she has been unusually well equipped to comprehend and to communicate the meaning and purpose that others have found in their beliefs and rituals. The contributions of Bengt Sundkler and Victor Turner in this volume reflect something of the specifically Christian dimensions of her personal and scholarly interests.

The essays in this tribute have been grouped to reflect some of the dominant themes in Monica's own work. The first five articles deal with the analysis of various aspects of religion and ritual in tradition-ally orientated societies in South Africa. While Hammond-Tooke draws material from Monica's publications on the Pondo in his discussion of Cape Nguni cosmology, much of the inspiration in this group of articles stems from her analyses of Nyakyusa ritual. Berglund and Sibisi contribute discussions of aspects of traditional Zulu beliefs and practices from the viewpoint of outsider and insider respectively. Murray pursues the significance of an acute observation of one of the minutiae of custom in northern Lesotho. Carstens has drawn together material from his own research and from published sources to provide an intriguing analysis of the changing belief system among the remnant of those Khoi peoples who once traversed the greater part of the Cape Province but whose culture seemed, to the casual observer, to have been long since destroyed. Together these writers discuss aspects of all the main groupings of black South African societies which Monica herself introduced to many generations of students in her lectures.

Sundkler provides a shaft of sidelight upon the missionaries who sought to carry the Christian gospel across the Limpopo towards the end of the 19th century. So easily criticised and satirised, so often misunderstood by social anthropologists of later generations, the missionaries not only provided some of the best early published accounts of African societies, they also provided the environment in which Monica's own understanding of her black neighbour matured at Lovedale. Turner complements Sundkler's theme of the restless Christian in his own inimitable way, drawing together his observations of Christian pilgrimages and Central African initiation rites into a single theoretical frame. Both Sundkler and Turner convey something of the urgency which possesses white Christians, whether in their missionary desires to get farther and faster into the frontier or in their wish to participate in 'an accelerator of normal liturgical practice' in the form of a pilgrimage.

The third part chronicles and analyses certain aspects of the Christian and white impacts upon African societies as a process of inter-action. Krige discusses the effect of the European missionary view of appropriate domestic structures upon the Lovedu, drawing upon Monica's own fieldwork for comparative material. Pauw explores the same problem in the domain of religion, discussing the synthesis between universalistic elements of Christianity and the particularistic elements of Xhosa religion against the background of a society under-going an increase in scale. The analysis draws explicitly upon the Wilsons' work for its theoretical inspiration.

In the final two papers the sympathetic and, in the case of Mafeje, · insider's perspective of the process of change takes us far from the white ethnocentric idea that 'change' can be measured in terms of the degree to which 'they' have become like 'us'. Resistance, in as far as it implies a purely negative reaction to alien initiative across all domains of social activity and belief, is clearly inadequate as an explanation of the process. The distinction between cognitive categories, religious beliefs and values, and ritual activities, implicit in Mafeje's analysis and explicit in West's, provides a basis for the discussion of processes of change and interaction which, we hope, will encourage Monica to review some of her own fieldwork material for our future enlighten-ment. Where orthodox structure and function analyses seemed to set forth with the assumption of the 'functionally integrated whole', Mafeje and West suggest that the parts are reassembled with some new elements from the intrusive culture to provide a meaningful framework for thought and action within the part-societies both urban and rural. The novel systems reflect the differing needs and insights of the mem-bers of those dynamic part-societies and merit serious consideration in their own right rather than as the detritus of archaic wholes.

This volume is also, of course, a tribute to Godfrey Wilson. It should not be forgotten that the Nyakyusa corpus was very much a joint effort, and it is highly appropriate that Audrey Richards in her appreciation should record his part in 'one of the most fruitful and happy anthropological marriages I can remember'. The published writings of Monica and Godfrey Wilson are listed at the end of this volume.

Monica has rightly deplored prefaces that pick the plums from the body of the text. Our purpose here can be no more than to reiterate our appreciation to all who have contributed to this tribute to Monica.

MICHAEL G. WHISSON
MARTIN WEST

Department of Social Anthropology
School of African Studies
University of Cape Town

in 1961, in which newer terminologies for descent groups and kinship units were used, and the effects of government legislation during the intervening years described. It was very much an individual contribution when it appeared, for Monica had had none of the training in modern fieldwork methods which students subsequently received. She wrote to me from Pondoland to the Bemba country where I was working at the time and spoke sadly of her intellectual isolation and the lack of stimulus from fellow workers. We had never met and our letters probably took four or five weeks to arrive so it is doubtful whether the correspondence could have helped her much!

In 1933 Monica returned to Cambridge, where she worked for her Ph.D. During this time she attended Malinowski's famous weekly seminar at the London School of Economics, then largely composed of Fellows chosen by the International African Institute from different nationalities and different disciplines to be trained before being sent to Africa. Here they were to work on a special scheme financed by the Rockefeller Foundation for the study of the effects of European culture on African societies. The project certainly sounds naive to modern ears as thus formulated, but it was the first organised drive towards the study of contemporary African peoples and their political and social problems. Moreover the selected areas were to be studied by men and women who had worked together for a year and who had been trained according to one set of anthropological assumptions – those of Malinowski – and the field techniques he had evolved in a remote Melanesian island. This again was an experiment not tried before in England, and the men and women who took part in it formed a brilliant group. They included such names as Gordon Brown, M. Fortes, Hilda Kuper, J. Hofstra, Margery Perham, S. Nadel, K. Oberg, Margaret Read, Gunter Wagner and Godfrey Wilson.

It was there that I first met Monica, then serious, rather silent, and a little aloof but with great charm and the beauty that has never left her. It was at this time that she really came to know her future husband, Godfrey Wilson, then lively, assertive, full of ideas and energy and wholly committed to the new tasks ahead. They were married in 1935 and there began one of the most fruitful and happy anthropological marriages I can remember. Godfrey Wilson came from Oxford with a first in 'Greats' and a philosophical training. Monica was already an experienced ethnographer, her thesis on the Pondo having been accepted for the Cambridge Ph.D. in 1934. Both had fellowships under the International African Institute scheme: he for a general study of the Nyakyusa on the western border of the then Tanganyika, and she for a special investigation on 'The Effects of Christian Missions on the Community'. Godfrey spent from 1935 to 1938 among the Nyakyusa and the neighbouring Ngonde, and Monica, owing to illness, a shorter period of twenty months. Both came back to England in between bouts of fieldwork to work up their material at the L.S.E.

In 1938 Godfrey Wilson accepted the post of first Director of the Rhodes–Livingstone Institute for Social Research, then combined with a museum and sited at Livingstone. Both became deeply interested in the development of this, the first of the local institutes of social research to be set up in British colonial Africa. Godfrey immediately started publication of the Rhodes–Livingstone Papers, which became famous, and together they produced as the second paper in the series, *The Study of Society* (1939), a booklet designed to help district officers who wanted to make studies of African societies. (It must be admitted that such officers would have needed an unusually philosophical turn of mind!)

I visited them from Johannesburg in 1939 and our discussions helped me greatly when I came to start the East African Institute of Social Research attached to the then Makerere College many years later in 1950. Our talks went on in the house and in the car, once as we watched the mystery of the lunar rainbow over Livingstone Falls with the baby Francis (now Senior Lecturer in Economics in the University of Cape Town) asleep in a basket in the back of the car. On that occasion both Monica and I announced our intention of writing a novel or a travel book in our old ages as we felt it so hard to convey the emotional texture of life in an African village within the scope of an anthropological monograph. Godfrey treated our suggestions with the contempt they probably deserved, but in her monographs on the Nyakyusa Monica has surely achieved, at least in part, her ambition of combining a rigidly scientific study with a vivid impression of the quality of village life. Let us hope the novel will come!

Godfrey Wilson wrote five papers on the Nyakyusa and Ngonde before his tragic death whilst serving in the South African army in 1944. He had undertaken a study of an African location at Broken Hill, and to that end visited the Bemba country in 1938 to learn Cibemba as the most useful language for the purpose. Besides this enterprise and the quite heavy work of administering the new institute, both he and Monica were fruitfully engaged on a book in which they attempted to outline their theoretical position, particularly as to the nature of social change, and also to define the terms they meant to use. I have often thought that it would be a most useful practice for young anthropologists to follow and that it would be salutary for them to shut the door of their cupboard of field notebooks, or the lid of the battered tin-box which has followed them round from village to village, and to sit down with some sheets of blank paper to define the terms they meant to use and the ideas that were to dominate their work. I wish I had done so myself.

The Wilsons' book was of course *The Analysis of Social Change* (1945). It was slight in extent but highly condensed and written with elegance. It was based mainly on material drawn from central Africa, from Bunyakyusa, Lubemba, Ngoniland, the Lozi kingdom and what Godfrey called the 'demi-urban' communities of Broken Hill, but data from Pondoland was also used. Its main thesis was that the change from 'primitive' to 'civilised' society was essentially a change of scale: the scale of the social relations in which the people in a community were involved; the proportion of its economic transactions which were limited to the members of this community as compared to those in the world at large; the sum total of the group's empirical or scientific knowledge and the dogma by which it explains the world, again as compared with the more comprehensive and universally valid body of scientific knowledge and beliefs of the wider world. The notion of 'scale' used in the Wilsons' sense was also extended to explain the changes from the emotional expression of the beliefs of the small society in ritual and art forms as compared with those of the more universally accepted world religions and art conventions. The oppositions and maladjustments to be seen in the central African societies of the time were the result, according to the Wilsons, of the conflicts in scale experienced, for instance, by men migrating from their villages to the copper belt. This concept of scale has been redeveloped recently by Monica Wilson in her Scott Holland lectures published as *Religion and the Transformation of Society*. She writes, 'I stand by the arguments set forth in *The Analysis of Social Change* twenty-five years ago.' (Wilson 1971*b*: 12.)

The book made an impact in a year (1945) when anthropology was recovering from its wartime dislocation.[1] I tended to side with Durk-

[1] The animated discussions as to the nature of structure and culture which were characteristic of the post-war years were only just beginning. R. Firth's statement of his theoretical position appeared, as *Elements of Social Organisation*, in 1951, as did Nadel's *Foundations of Social Anthropology*. Evans-Pritchard's concept of structure was of course apparent in his first book on *The Nuer* (1940) but the resultant controversies had not yet taken shape.

heim rather than the Wilsons on the question of scale and did not find useful the complex division of social reality into 'elements', 'forms' and 'aspects' (G. and M. Wilson 1945: 82). I guess that such diagrams often come into being to help the writers clear their own minds rather than as 'do-it-yourself' guides for the reader, but the stimulus of the book was evident. My ancient copy is covered with pencil scribbles and exclamation marks!

Whether or not the division into aspects, elements and conventions proved useful in the writing up of her field material, Monica Wilson certainly based her monographs on the concept of society as a system, but a system that was clearly divided into a series of sub-systems, those of social relationships (social structure in other words), of economic organisation, of values, of dogma and philosophy, of morals and laws. Very important in her work was also the notion of the total ritual pattern of a society. Malinowski's pupils had certainly been drilled into making their field inquiries under such headings, and most of us did so, but when he talked about dogma, for instance, he meant the traditional beliefs associated with a particular institution and necessary for the survival of that institution. For instance the institution of the family and of descent groups depended, according to him, upon the people's theories of procreation and descent. It also depended on the group's empirical knowledge of child-birth, child-rearing and the values and the postulated happenings and tales which formed the mythical charter of, for instance, the clan and the sub-clan.

Monica Wilson, in distinction, tried in *Good Company*, her first book on the Nyakyusa (1951), to describe the total system of this people's social relations, including their chiefship, clan and lineage system and their curious age villages. She then turned to their economic system, their cattle-keeping and banana cultivation; and then to their legal system and methods of enforcing law and order. Lastly, and most important in relation to the subject of the present book, she gives a preliminary outline of the whole set of beliefs which the Nyakyusa hold as to the origin of fortune and misfortune, their dogma of causality in other words. Monica Wilson also attempts to describe the total values system of the people, an idea with which British anthropologists were experimenting at the time, if only to touch their hats to the culture pattern theories then current on the other side of the Atlantic (Richards 1970). Firth (1964: 206ff) has described anthropological attempts in this direction and the many difficulties involved. In *Good Company* Monica Wilson gives a very straightforward account of the virtues and attainments the Nyakyusa admire, but these values are also described as a system and referred to in her subsequent books on ritual.

The notion that the Nyakyusa observe a ritual pattern or a pattern of symbols is implicit in *Good Company*, though it is not developed fully in this book. 'A full analysis of the symbolism of one ritual necessitates a comparison of all the rituals of the society,' she writes in a footnote (Wilson 1951*a*: 26n), so that the idea of the 'ritual pattern' is already there. It became the fundamental notion of the subsequent two monographs, *Rituals of Kinship among the Nyakyusa* (1957) and *Communal Rituals of the Nyakyusa* (1959). Again the symbols are described as another system and not as a list of miscellaneous beliefs. It is this sense of system which seems to me to distinguish *Good Company* from the old-fashioned general monograph. But the handling of such full field data raises problems that anthropologists have not yet solved.

The Wilsons early stated their assumption that studies of ritual must be based on direct observation (G. and M. Wilson 1939: 17). This was an article of faith for my generation but it must plunge the observer into accounts of the infinite variety of ritual performances caused by changes in village composition, local situations and the personality of the performers. The essential elements have almost to be wrestled for. Both the Wilsons were gifted observers, as some of the descriptions of ceremonies quoted from their notebooks show. They witnessed many rites. They attended for instance thirty funerals in whole or in part. I think I only went to four in Lubemba. I do not know whether the death rate in Bunyakyusa was higher; whether two people can achieve more than twice what one can; or whether it was a difference in the 'scale' of transport. I believe the Wilsons had a lorry whereas I was limited to a pushbike!

The Wilsons also attached great importance to the recording and translation of the statements of informants as well as to the publication of case histories. Malinowski had made a cult of 'the native text' and it was the fashion of the time to publish these, part of the anthropologists' struggle to become scientists rather than romantic explorers. The Wilsons' texts are unusually good, both in the way of selected comments such as most anthropologists use, but also, and more characteristically, in the form of long dialogues between the fieldworkers and their informants, and the more formal statements of named men and women. It seems to me to be a real achievement to get such full texts without the use of tape-recorders, which were not then commonly available. Monica has included some of this material in the body of her books and has relegated some to appendices. *Reaction to Conquest* had 34 such pages and *Good Company* as many as 96.

Is the publication of such full data necessary? Does one learn more from witnessing thirty funerals than one? I have certainly attended a great many more than thirty funeral services of the Church of England. Have I learnt more about Christian dogma, ethics, or the structure of British kinship groups by this means? The question is an important one for it is becoming rarer for anthropologists to give such full accounts of their observations or perhaps to attribute so much importance to participant observation.

The answer depends of course on the anthropologist's purpose. The aim of the work may be broadly functional in the sense that the author is interested in the part which ritual plays, say, in expressing and promoting an approved type of social relations, an attitude to a king or a lineage head for instance, or in dealing acceptably with the conflicts within a system of relations as Turner has done. A fieldworker with such a mainly functional approach is also interested in the normative value of rites which by constant repetition can inculcate a particular system of morals, an approved philosophy or a view of the world. He or she may also be concerned to view ritual from an individual point of view and to try to gauge how a member of a particular culture is helped by ritual, whether religious or magical, to deal with emotional crises or disasters. Monica Wilson has adopted this structural–functional approach and therefore the record and the analysis of her direct observations seem to me absolutely necessary. For the student of some of the simpler universal symbols such as oppositions between right and left, north and south, or male and female, it may not be necessary to have such full data. It may also be redundant in the case of anyone in a society in which elaborate mythologies exist and seem to form almost autonomous systems of ideas. This is not so in Bantu Africa, where Monica Wilson's work has been done and is being done. Yet even with this difference of focus some of the younger anthropologists particularly interested in symbolism and mythology, such as Mary Douglas, have felt that richly abundant mythical material should be analysed against a known background of equally rich ethnographic records.[1]

Carefully observed behaviour is surely particularly important in the case of preliterate societies, in which prayers are not committed to paper and where there is no rubric instructing the performers what

[1] See also the views of Nur Yalman, K. O. L. Burridge and others (Richards 1970: 11).

to do, as is provided in our own prayerbooks, for instance 'Then the Minister shall kneel, and say the Lord's Prayer: the people also kneeling and repeating it with him'. Many of the ceremonies observed by Monica Wilson in Bantu societies are very long and complex, taking place over several days or weeks. Informants find it difficult to describe these at all fully, according to my experience (Richards 1956: 135–8). Only attendance at such a ceremony can give the whole pattern of the ritual. I would go on to add that it is only by witnessing at a number of rites in a society of the Nyakyusa type that the anthropologist can gauge the full range of possible variations occurring in societies in which the summoning of people and the collection of food to feed them may be difficult feats of organisation,[1] and alterations in procedure may have to be made. In Bunyakyusa there were also variations in ritual from area to area. It is the range of variations round a single theme which also enables the anthropologist to decide what is absolutely essential in the performance of the rite and what may be omitted. I greatly regret that I was able to attend only one *chisungu*, or girl's initiation rite, in Lubemba. It is these variations in behaviour, in comment, and in the type of the participants, which make the structuralist under Lévi-Strauss's influence so impatient. With very full field data he cannot easily make his model.

Apart from the variability of behaviour in primitive ritual and the flood of comments they produce on the spot, I believe that the emotions of the performers, as they show themselves from time to time in a long rite, tell the observer something which the long narrative of a specialist priest for instance cannot reveal. Since the days of Van Gennep we have accepted the theory that the symbol of a change of social status is often some ritual act like jumping over a fence or a bundle of faggots or whatever it might be. It was only when I watched two Bemba girl initiates trying to jump over a high loop made of two pliable branches that I realised how intensely anxious the mothers were as to whether their daughters would manage the jump. There were frenzied shouts, exclamations, torrents of abuse and whacks on the girls' shins. One of the girls was trembling and in tears, which did not increase her chances (Richards 1956: 138). The emotional scene led me to develop the view that the rite was not simply an expression of change of status, perhaps a magic act designed to 'make the girl grow', but that it was a test, and a very difficult test. If it was passed, it gave assurance to the girl and her relatives that she actually was

[1] These factors were included by Firth under the term 'social organisation'. See particularly Firth (1963).

socially mature. She would be able to behave as an adult with all the new duties which that implied because she had been shown by the successful jump to be adult. There were many rites of separation in the *chisungu* ceremony as in all initiation ritual but this was the only one which was difficult for the candidate to achieve, and which was a real ordeal. Such ideas strike an observer who watches such rites and observes the subsequent behaviour of initiation candidates and their relatives.

Descriptions of emotional behaviour are also very important as another method of underlining what is the essential part of a rite to the performers. At what stage in the ceremony are the participants idling, gossiping or laughing and when are they concentrated, serious, reverent? I have also found descriptive work of this kind revealing in situations of rapid change. I can remember for instance an important communal rite among the Bemba when a senior chief was rolling on his back in obeisance before the royal ancestral shrine while a group of young men returned from a visit to the Zambian copper mines stood with supercilious smiles and even jeered at one point. Monica Wilson herself has made a special study of the differential reactions of Christian and pagan Nyakyusa to traditional rites.

However it is obviously very difficult for an anthropologist to make acceptable generalisations after returning home with such a very full bag of direct observations, case histories and texts. Monica Wilson has been conscious of the difficulty from the start. In acknowledging her debt to Malinowski's 'standard of research' in the opening pages of *Reaction to Conquest* she adds that his standard 'inspires to a constant struggle to get beyond mere description to the analysis of institutions' (Wilson 1936: xviii). In her introduction to *Good Company* she speaks of 'the problem of combining adequate documentation with lucidity and of the difficulty of reaching a balance between the unreadable and the impressionistic' (Wilson 1951a: x). One of Monica Wilson's most effective solutions has been the use of charts to make a preliminary classification of the material. One such occurs in *Good Company*, where a list of the misfortunes attributed by the Nyakyusa to mystical causes is given (Wilson 1951a: 198). Of these afflictions 38 were thought to be due to witchcraft; 23 to the 'breath of men', the righteous indignation mainly felt and expressed by leaders of different communities; 13 to the curse of Christians; 11 to sorcery; and 7 to vengeance magic. One column gives the category of the accused, whether a headman, a neighbour, a wife and so forth, and another gives the category of the accuser. Other columns give the charge brought against the accused, the grounds of suspicion, the method of investigation, and the upshot of the case. This analysis of 92 case histories lists in a convenient form the major Nyakyusa ideas of causality and shows the very large number of misfortunes they attribute to witchcraft. It also illustrates the relationships causing tension in the society whether they be those between co-wives, fathers and sons or neighbours. A similar chart appears in *Rituals of Kinship*, where the author lists 10 incidents in which a sufferer from death, illness or economic failure is held to have been punished by ancestral spirits or 'shades'. The category of the sufferer, a man, woman, child, a son, husband, wife or a younger brother, goes into one column, while their misfortunes, their alleged sins, the category of the injured shade, the method of diagnosis, and the remedy, go into the others (Wilson 1957: 256).

Charts cannot tell everything. Members of the community probably held different views on each incident. But they do make comparison possible between one culture and another, as Monica Wilson showed in the same year in an article called 'Witch Beliefs and Social Structure' (1951*b*), in which she compared the incidence of witchcraft in two societies, the Pondo and the Nyakyusa, which have marked differences in social structure. For me at any rate the analysis of witchcraft cases according to the social category of the accuser and the accused, an examination now regularly made by students of the subject, came from Monica Wilson's work (Richards 1963).

The concept of a symbol pattern is also in itself an abstraction. The anthropologist proceeds from an analysis of many casual remarks as to the meaning of rituals to the longer texts elicited from more thoughtful informants such as Kasitile the rainmaker, described in the three monographs on the Nyakyusa. These texts are very full and Monica Wilson has been accused of basing her whole analysis of Nyakyusa ritual on 'the Nyakyusa translation or interpretation of the symbolism' (Turner 1964: 28). She replied with some spirit in her Scott Holland lectures that she had never been so stupid as to assume that 'the interpretation of even the most self-conscious Nyakyusa, such as Kasitile' could 'reveal the whole truth about Nyakyusa ritual', and indeed she could not reasonably be accused of being so stupid since this sentence comes from *Rituals of Kinship* published in 1957 (Wilson 1957: 4). She adds the firm statement, which has often been quoted since, that '*any analysis not based on some translation of the symbols used by the people of that culture is open to suspicion*' and in this view she is supported by Evans-Pritchard and Firth and probably most of their and my generation.

When she comes to interpreting the ritual, Monica Wilson proceeds by way of the coherent account based on many quotations to deductions based on Radcliffe-Brown's assumption that 'A symbol recurring in a cycle of rituals is likely to have the same significance in each', and the majority of anthropologists writing on ritual have in effect done the same. She then classifies these symbols into the universal, i.e. symbols associated with biological processes such as birth, sex, intercourse and so forth; with meteorological phenomena such as storm and rain; with fire; and with the colours black, white and red, which seem to be universal in Bantu societies and have been so well described by Victor Turner. West African peoples long used to cloth dyed in bright colours, such as blue, may well have associations with these colours in their ritual.

Then there are the symbols arising out of Nyakyusa culture and values, their banana and plantain cultivation, their cattle-raising and their smithing, and there are the animals present in the environment such as the python and the lion, and the differences between the forest land which stands for the male principle and the grasslands for the female. Specially interesting in this culture is the collection of symbols which stand for semen, sex, procreation, and the 'shades' who enforce Nyakyusa morals. But the associations are very complex. The burial ritual has seven different themes and there are as many as ten symbols for sexual intercourse and a great multiplication of other symbolic associations. The list of Nyakyusa symbols is in fact the fullest we probably have for an African society except perhaps that made by Turner for the Ndembu. It is interesting to my mind therefore that the data have hardly been used by students of Lévi-Strauss or any of those writers who are specially interested in looking for universal characteristics of symbolic thinking, such as the classification of natural phenomena into pairs of opposites and the ways in which symbols can be substituted for each other, duplicated or reversed. Is the Nyakyusa material too full to be used in this way and are the comments of individuals too varied? A lot of water has flowed under the bridge since 1957 and it would be stimulating if Monica Wilson could herself try to play the symbol game with her own material.

But she has become more interested of late in problems of philosophy and ethics and in the comparison between the dogma of some of the Bantu peoples with that of world religions such as Christianity. Her Scott Holland lectures would seem to show this. She has in fact been accused of letting her own Christian beliefs affect her judgement in anthropological matters. This seems to me an unreasonable criticism. It is not only that she makes a point of announcing, with typical honesty, when she is speaking as a Christian rather than as an anthropologist, whereas many Marxists, who also have strong views on religion, do not. It seems to me possible that an anthropologist who has never had the experience of believing in a supernatural power nor of feeling the efficacy of ritual may find it difficult to understand the religion of another people. The experience of divinity, so to speak, may give a power of empathy with other believers which is valuable. Perhaps this is the reason why in this secular age there is so much emphasis among anthropological writers on the purely cognitive side of religion and not on the emotional and ethical. Besides, atheism is after all a point of view and with some it is a creed. Why should we not have interpretations of ethnographic data from both types of observer? I think we need them.

Monica has retired to her home on the Hogsback in the Cape Province with the beautiful garden she has made there. It is difficult to think of the School of African Studies without her. In fact I heard a South African scholar say, 'But Monica can't leave! She is an institution!' and indeed she ran that department of the University of Cape Town for twenty-one years. But I am sure she will often be lured away from her mountaintop to visit her friends in other parts of South Africa and in the rest of the world, friends to whom she has always given such generous interest and encouragement. I am also certain that she will go on writing. Anyone who could produce as much work as she has while running a large department, acting for some years as the warden of an African women's hostel at the University of Fort Hare, as well as bringing up two sons, has an energy and a determination which will not let her stop. She will continue to pursue what I have called her distinguished way regardless of anthropological fashions and without pretensions. She once wrote to me that she liked a certain book because it did not 'blow trumpets' and added, 'I do hate books which blow trumpets.' What then are we to do about this book? It is very definitely a trumpet for Monica!

AUDREY RICHARDS

Cambridge

PART 1: BELIEF AND RITUAL

W. D. Hammond-Tooke

THE SYMBOLIC STRUCTURE OF
CAPE NGUNI COSMOLOGY

'Symbolic patterns in the societies that have been studied in Africa all deny chaos, and depict a meaning in life.' (Monica Wilson)

I

The present study is an attempt to answer certain hitherto neglected questions regarding the belief systems of the Cape Nguni.[1] These derive from a change of focus in the approach to traditional cosmology, which sees belief and ritual primarily as expressive of social relations, to a more specific *cultural* approach along the lines suggested by Horton (1962), Geertz (1966) and Spiro (1966). After all, whatever the sociological functions of the beliefs may be, the belief system of any people has a particular form and makes use of certain concepts and symbols. The questions arise: why these forms, why these symbols? What are the Cape Nguni trying to say in their rituals? And why do they say it in just this way? Why are, for instance, certain plants and colours used in rituals, why are cattle and beer important elements, why do the beliefs in witch familiars take the form they do, why the belief in the 'people of the river' (*abantu bomlambo*), and so on? Surely the explanation of the system of belief (the 'theology') in its own terms is as important a part of understanding as the until recently dominant approach that sees it purely as an epiphenomenon of social structure? The point of departure of this essay is the suggestion of Robin Horton (1962) that an important (although not the only) aspect

[1] The Cape Nguni are a congeries of chiefdoms, stretching from the Natal border to the Fish River, Cape Province, and speaking dialects of the Xhosa language. They are patrilineal, pastoral-hoe-culturists and present a general picture of cultural uniformity. They include the Xhosa, Thembu, Mpondo, Mpondomise, Bhaca, Xesibe, Bomvana, Hlubi, Zizi and Bhele chiefdom clusters (Hammond-Tooke 1965). My own field-notes refer to Mpondomise, Bhaca and Xhosa (Dushane). Professor Wilson's contributions to Cape Nguni studies are a lasting monument.

of all belief systems is an attempt at explanation and that the pattern of gods and spirits not only 'reflects' the structuring of the social system but supplies men with interpretive models illuminatory of existential puzzles. As Geertz put it, men turn to religion at the boundaries of their intellectual comprehension (they cannot tolerate the uncanny with its threat of chaos), at the limits of their powers of endurance and at the limits of their moral insights. This study is not essentially concerned with rituals as such but involves a fresh look at Cape Nguni conceptual formulations as to superempirical beings (the diacritical sign of all 'religious' beliefs) in an endeavour to ascertain the structure of the symbolic thought patterns. In this my debt to the insights of Lévi-Strauss and Mary Douglas will be apparent.

II

The first point at issue is whether or not one can talk of a Cape Nguni belief *system*. Is there a sense in which the various conceptualisations about the superempirical interlock and support one another? If we take the belief in superhuman intelligences as our criterion we find that it can be divided into four apparently disparate domains: the Supreme Being, ancestors, River People and witches. Although differing greatly in nature they all have certain things in common – they are not human (although some derive from human beings), they are invisible, and all in some way are connected with animals. If we accept Horton's suggestion that belief in spirit beings is not arbitrary, but fulfils important explanatory functions, the question arises, what are these beings explaining? The question of whether or not there is a system in the strict sense is an open one at this stage, but it seems worthwhile to push the search for consistency as far as it will go.

The Supreme Being

Traditionally the Cape Nguni believed in a Supreme Being (*uDali*, *uQamatha*) but, as among all South African Bantu-speaking peoples, he was a *deus otiosus* to whom no rituals were directed. His transcendence was invoked to explain the phenomenon of creation, but that is about all. There is no evidence that he was thought to be the ground of all being, like the Nuer *Kwoth*, nor can the ancestors or other spirits be thought of as his refractions. Significantly, there is little in Cape Nguni ·thought of the fatalism that seems to inhere in Nuer-type monotheism. The Nuer saying, when calamity befalls, '*thile me lele*, which means that nothing can be done about it because it is the will of

God and therefore beyond man's control' (Evans-Pritchard 1956:13), is foreign to them. Their religious system is essentially manipulative. Nor is *uThixo*, as he is called today, in any sense hierarchically related to the other spirits. Some informants, influenced by Christian concepts, sometimes maintain that one can approach *uThixo* through the medium of the ancestors, but this is almost certainly not part of traditional thought. If, as Horton suggests (1971), the concept of a Supreme Being reflects interest in and awareness of the macrocosm, this God-conceptualised macrocosm was not, for the Cape Nguni, the chiefdom. If one can talk at all of 'tribal religion' it must refer to the ancestral shades of departed chiefs – and is thus firmly rooted in the particular social structure. Neither is there evidence that the Cape Nguni Supreme Being was conceived of as ruling the 'nations' (Sotho, San, Khoi, other chiefdoms) with whom particular chiefdoms came into contact, nor of his being a tribal god like the Hebrew Yahweh, jealous of his people. Cape Nguni cosmologies were essentially microcosmic. In that the question of a first cause arose, the concept of Supreme Being coped with it adequately: the lack of any ritual or feared sanctions prevented the issue from being a live one. Perhaps, despite the disclaimer above, in a sense the concept of *Thixo* can be looked upon as a personalisation of *chance*. Chance is ruled out in the logic of witch-caused or ancestrally caused misfortune, but there is some evidence that reference to *uThixo* is used as a last resort at the limits of man's explanatory powers.

The Supreme Being was apparently but loosely integrated into the cosmological system.

Ancestral shades

The effective spirits in Cape Nguni world views are the ancestors. The nature of the ancestral shades is well known (Hammond-Tooke 1974*b*). They, like their classical counterparts, are identified with the breath (*umphefumlo*) which symbolises the life principle and, as Tylor pointed out long ago, provide an economical explanatory theory for the phenomena of dreams, trance and death. But this 'soul' is not itself an ancestral spirit. It has to undergo a rite of passage, in the *ukubuyisa* ritual, that incorporates it into the category of shades (*iminyanya, amathongo*). My Mpondomise informants, as always, were not entirely clear as to its nature or location, or whether it could be sacrificed to during the period between interment and incorporation, but the consensus was that it could not. Death is a necessary but not sufficient cause of ancestorhood: another is the presence of descendants to commemorate one in ritual. Not everyone, then, becomes a shade, and the attainment of this status is in effect a statement of one's structural position at nodal points of lineage segmentation. There does not seem to be the belief that the unincorporated dead become ghosts (cf. the Edo, Bradbury 1966).

In this respect the Mpondomise appear to differ from other Cape Nguni. Whereas it has been reported from among the Xhosa, Mfengu and Mpondo that the important ancestors are those of the minimal lineage segment (the deceased father, grandfather, and perhaps great-grandfather of the sufferer), the Mpondomise take great pains to emphasise that lineage ancestors form an undifferentiated whole and must be worshipped as such. Thus, at the invocation (*nqula*) at ritual killings, the officiant avoids mentioning segment ancestors by name and calls instead on the group as a whole to come and partake of the feast. Invocations, in fact, tend to be to a selection of *clan* ancestors, with perhaps the name of the lineage founder included, as in' . . . and you, people of so-and-so' (Hammond-Tooke 1968: 40–1). From a structural point of view what seems to be stressed is the integrity of the lineage *as a whole*, in contrast to the more 'domestic' cult of other Cape Nguni.[1] And yet there is an ambiguity here because the ancestors as a whole are sometimes referred to as *abantu bekhaya* (people of the home). The problem of involvement with ancestors remote on the lineage genealogy, and thus unknown to the worshipper, is explained thus in the words of an Mpondomise informant:

Amongst the ancestors who appear in dreams some are known and some are unknown. Those who are unknown are those who died long ago before the person they visit was born. Those who are recognised in dreams are those who died during the lifetime of the living. When they visit a person they do so as *abantu* [people, i.e. they assume a human form]. It is easy to recognise them when they are in this form. But even the unknown ones make them-selves known somehow. The way they come will always indicate whether they are ancestors or not. Usually they come for meat or beer.

Ancestors communicate through dreams to their descendants, and such visitations are almost invariably occasioned by neglect of custom, typically those classified as *ukulungisa umzi* ('to make the homestead right'); they thus, presumably, give rise to feelings of guilt, or at least to a consciousness of blameworthiness; the kind of guilt experienced

---

[1] Raum (1973: 533, n. 14) states that two of his main Zulu informants, Chief Gatsha Buthelezi and Princess Magogo, denied that personal names of their ancestors were mentioned at a sacrifice. The 'people' guess from clues in the praises which ancestor is meant.

by the Nuer towards neglect of *Kwoth* in their very different religious system. Misfortune, too, can be sent by the shades and this (and the possible guilt) can only be assuaged by piacular sacrifices involving the immolation of an ox or goat.

Witches

It seems that the Cape Nguni witch belief system is unique in southern Africa for the elaboration of its ideas about familiars. Whereas among other groups familiars are typically animals (in natural or mystical form), all Cape Nguni conceive of them as mythical monsters that bear little resemblance to anything in the real world, except that most have an alternative appearance in the form of snakes (see below).[1] Thus among Sotho and Venda the hyena, snake, owl and polecat are all selected as were-animals. Even the Zulu, so close in language and culture to the Cape Nguni, have strictly zooform familiars. Jenkinson (1882: 116) and Owen (Cory 1926: 58) independently list (civet) cats, panthers, 'wolves' (hyenas), jackals and owls as the main Zulu familiars in the mid-19th century, and Callaway (1868: 349–52) suggests, quoting Zulu informants, that the concept of *uthikoloshe* (see below) was introduced to the Zulu from the Cape 'for among the Amazulu there is no Utikoloshe' (p. 349). He bases his argument partly on the opinion of informants and partly on the 'many Kxosisms' used by them.[2] The same is true of the South Sotho, who have adopted *uthikoloshe* under the name *thokolosi*. Within the Xhosa-speaking group it is impossible to determine the point of origin of this witch myth in any one chiefdom cluster: certainly we have evidence that Xhosa, Thembu, Mpondo, Mfengu, Bhaca and Mpondomise operate with identical belief systems, although it is possible that the targets of witchcraft accusations may differ slightly between groups (Hammond-Tooke 1970).

Witch beliefs quite clearly provide, with aspects of the ancestor cult and the cult of the River People, an explanatory theory of evil and misfortune. The fact that most witches are believed to be women (also true for the Zulu, Berglund 1972: 438) has been explained as a product of the contradictory perceptions by men of woman's disadvantaged role in social life, which gives rise (it is suggested) to guilt feelings and the casting of woman in the role of a witch in an idea system that postulates witch activity as the result of envy and hostility. The

[1] An exception is the baboon.
[2] I am indebted for the above three references to A.-I. Berglund's thesis 'Zulu Ideas and Symbolism', pp. 482–3.

sexuality of the familiars *uthikoloshe* and *impundulu*, and the dis-
solving forms of *ichanti* and *umamlambo*, are also possibly due to
perceptions of contradictions in traditional constructs of reality and
attempts to resolve them (Hammond-Tooke 1974*a*).

The form of Cape Nguni familiars has been described in detail by
Professor Wilson (Hunter 1936: 276–90) and others (Soga 1931;
Hammond-Tooke 1962, 1974*a*). Briefly they fall into four categories.
Two (*uthikoloshe* and *impundulu*) are highly sexual in nature. *Uthikoloshe* is a small, hairy man with an enormous penis, while *impundulu*
(or *intaka yezulu*, the lightning-bird) can appear in the form of a
beautiful young man. Witches are believed to have sexual intercourse
with these familiars. The second category contains two snakes that
have the power to change shape (*ichanti* and *umamlambo*), while the
third and fourth include the baboon and the zombie-like *isithunzela*,
or resurrected corpse. It is perhaps significant that both these latter
are ambiguous in that, in Douglas's terms (Douglas 1966), they
confuse categories: the baboon is an animal but is also very man-like,
while the *isithunzela* is *both* living *and* dead.

Witches themselves can change shape and, although actual men
and women, they are in some ways not quite human.

People of the river

A third group of beings believed in by apparently all Cape Nguni,
except the Mpondo, are the so-called 'people of the river' (*abantu
besemlanjeni, abantu bomlambo*). I have recorded the belief among the
Mpondomise, Thembu, Mfengu and the Xhosa of the Ciskei, as has
Monica Wilson for the latter two groups (Hunter 1936: 488, 538;
Wilson *et al.* 1952: 190–1). The River People are believed to live in
the deep pools of certain rivers, where, in the words of an Mpondomise
informant, 'they have beautifully built homesteads where they keep
their dark-coloured herds of cattle. They are definitely not ancestors,'
a point which is borne out by the Mfengu of Keiskammahoek (Wilson
et al. 1952: 191n.), although some informants, in some Xhosa groups,
equate the River People with ancestors (Hunter 1936: 488, 538).
Although certain clans are especially associated with the River People,
others maintain that 'Everyone has people of his home in the water.
The people of the river are a combination of all the clans we find on
earth. They are not ancestors but people living there.' There seems to
be no dogma as to how the River People originated. They appear to
be *sui generis*. Some informants say they are fair, with long hair.

There is a close association, however, between the River People and humans, an association which has both its positive and negative sides, for the River People's influence can be both baleful and benevolent. On the good side they play a vital part in the initiation of diviners (again with the exception of the Mpondo, see Hunter 1936: 321n.). I have recorded from both Mpondomise and Bhaca (Hammond-Tooke 1962: 313–14) diviners' detailed accounts of their being called into deep pools where they have been met by a snake and given instructions and the symbolic white stone, indicative of their new status. So at this level there is some connection with the tutelary ancestors. Also beneficent is the belief that River People are closely associated with rain; at marriages of members of the specially associated clans (e.g. Mlambo and Dlomo clans of the Mpondomise and the Ngqosini clan of the Xhosa) rain is sure to fall.

On the other hand the River People are dangerous because they can send an illness called *umlambo*, characterised by pains and the swelling of the body 'as with water' and 'heaviness' (*nzima*). Sometimes the sickness is preceded by dreams of drowning: to dream of dirty water means that the River People are angry. Some state that *umlambo* can also be caused by walking over the spoor of a snake (*umamlambo*?). Such an illness might be diagnosed as having been sent by the River People. They also cause drownings by calling a person to them: 'They do not really intend to kill him. They call a person because they like him.'

A specific ritual (*ukuhlwayelela*) is required in a case of *umlambo*, entailing sacrifice at a pool where the River People are known to live. This consists of the floating out onto the surface of the pool of small grass baskets (*iingobozi*) containing small amounts of sorghum, rolled tobacco, pumpkin seeds, white beads and a calabash of beer (Ngqosini clan of the Xhosa; see also De Jager and Gitywa 1963). These eventually fill with water, and they sink, having been taken by the River People.

If they call (*biza*) a person into the water they keep him at their home for one or two days and, if those of his home do not bring an offering in the form of a dark beast, they kill him and let him float to the surface. Cattle should be driven into the water where he disappeared. One of the beasts sinks and the victim comes to the surface alive. The victim may not be able to remember all that happened, but he will always talk of the kindness of the River People and their beautiful country where not a drop of water falls. (Mpondomise)

A variant was recorded in 1960 by a student of mine, A. C. Campbell, from the Grahamstown area. It is said that the River People are really animals (*izilo*). The chief of these animals (*inkosi yomlambo*) is a crocodile (*ngwenye*), whose name is taboo to those suffering from *umlambo*. The crocodile lurks in the reeds and becomes enraged when he sees people, and he who sees him falls sick with *umlambo*. Monica Wilson records that the crocodile is believed by the Ciskei Xhosa to be the messenger of the people of the river (Hunter 1936: 488). Xhosa stoutly maintain, against all evidence, that crocodiles are still found in the small rivers of the Ciskei (see also Soga 1931: 197). In Keiskammahoek some speak of a 'dog of the river' (*inja yomlambo*, probably the otter), who causes drownings by calling people to join the River People (Wilson *et al.* 1952: 190).

The Mpondo have an analogous ritual associated with specific clans. Sacrifices (*ukunikela emlanjeni*) of meat and/or blood are made at certain pools, which rise up and take the offering left on the river bank (Hunter 1936: 256–64). The pool itself rises up and takes the offering or 'a big black snake appears. If it lies on its back with its stomach upwards it is a sign that the *amathongo* [shades] are angry ... If the snake does not lie on its back, they kill.' Krige records a strikingly similar belief among the Zulu. 'If an *iThongo* [snake] lies on its back, it is a cause of alarm, for this means that something will happen to the village' (Krige 1936: 286, see also Cook 1930: 124–5). We shall come back to the problem of snakes later.

Here we seem to have to do with a strong preoccupation with rivers, particularly deep, silent pools, and with animals and birds associated with water. Apart from the River People and their messengers the crocodile and otter – both ambiguous animals which have the appearance of land animals but live in water – two birds are singled out as being of ill-omen. The hamerkop, or *uthekhwane* (*Scopus umbretta*), which frequents shallow water in the vicinity of trees or low cliffs and builds a large dome-shaped nest, with interlaced sticks and reeds (like an old-styled hut?), is closely associated with water. The semi-terrestrial ground hornbill, or *intsikizi* (*Bucorvus cafer*), was formerly hunted in time of drought and thrown, bound, into a deep pool to bring rain (Soga 1931: 199).[1] It is also perhaps significant that most of the witch familiars have associations with rivers and water; indeed Soga refers to them as 'water-sprites'. *Uthikoloshe* is said to live in dongas and on the banks of rivers, 'We see him by the river, a little hairy man'; 'If you smear a blade of grass with Thikoloshe fat, it will travel upstream' (Hunter 1936: 276). Hunter also quotes the story

[1] Zulu 'heaven-herds' kill the hamerkop and ground hornbill for anti-lightning medicine (Raum 1973: 237).

of the poisoned *uthikoloshe* who is claimed to have said, 'Don't bury me beside the river or it will rain and never stop' (p. 281). *Impundulu* (or *intaka yezulu*, the lightning-bird) is not so explicitly associated with the river, but there is the obviously close connection between lightning and rain and 'to dream of a river, or of green fields, or of pumpkins, is equivalent of dreaming of an *izulu*' (p. 285). The riverine nature of *ichanti* and *umamlambo* is clear: the first is 'a snake which lives in rivers' (p. 286), and the very name *umamlambo* means literally 'mother of the river'. In the Ciskei *umamlambo* is sometimes said to be one of the River People (Wilson *et al.* 1952: 190). Mpondo say that the water iguana (*Varinus niloticus*) is the servant of *ichanti* and *uthikoloshe*, 'fetching firewood for them, smearing their huts, and clapping for them when they want to dance' (Hunter 1936: 387). The reference here is to the fact that the iguana plasters its hole under the water. The only non-water familiar is the baboon – the ambiguous half-man, half-animal.

III

Animal categories

Wild animals are no longer present to any extent in the country of the Cape Nguni. Hunter (1936: 96) lists 'a few bush buck and blue buck, a monkey or two, some wild cats and birds' in Pondoland of the 1930s, to which may be added baboons in the mountains, jackals, hares and rodents and a variety of snakes. The python (prominent in Zulu symbolism) is unknown, and Pondoland is the southern boundary of the deadly mamba. But before contact with whites the country was full of game. Stephen Kay lists elephant, rhinoceros, hippopotamus, lion, leopard, zebra, jackal, hyena, many types of buck, and game birds.[1] Skins of lion and leopard, and hide and tusks of elephant, rhinoceros and hippo, were the perquisites of chiefs, and among the southern chiefdoms the chief's capital was marked by an elephant's tail attached to a pole. Throughout the area the symbol of executive authority was a leopard's tail, attached to a spear, carried by the court messenger (*umsila*). With this history of experience of close relationship with wild fauna one would expect some incorporation of animals into the symbolic system, although, unlike the position among the Sotho peoples, there is no evidence of totemism.

The Cape Nguni are essentially pastoralists, and the symbolic status of cattle (*iinkomo*) is well documented. There is an extensive

[1] Quoted by Hunter 1936: 95n.

descriptive vocabulary based on horn formation and colour. Soga lists seven horn terms and twenty-four colour terms among the Xhosa (Soga 1931: 386–8) and Hunter states that the Mpondo have at least fifty-seven different terms describing marking, and five describing horns. Men and cattle live in a symbiotic relationship, oxen have praise names and they are the appropriate blood sacrifice to the ancestors. Like men they are threatened by *umlaza*, the ritual impurity associated with women's fertility (Hunter 1936: 46–7; Hammond-Tooke 1962: 69–70). The indigenous African goat (*imbuzi*), the other traditional domestic animal, is also an acceptable offering and, significantly also subject to *umlaza*, but goats are not praised (Hunter 1936: 71). The ritual animals are essentially the category of traditional acceptable food animals, and represent the category of edible animals *par excellence*. In a very definite sense they are also part of human society, as opposed to extra-societal nature. The other domestic animals found today – horses, pigs, sheep (*amagusha*) and poultry – are all recent importations and have not been incorporated into the symbolic system.

The animals of bush and grassland form other categories. As we have seen, there was formerly a large variety of these. McLaren's dictionary lists the Xhosa names of two species of monkey and one of baboon, twenty varieties of carnivore (ranging from lion and leopard to hyena, hunting-dog, otter and muishond), sixteen antelopes (e.g. gnu, oribi, bushbuck, eland), two species of zebra, elephant, rhinoceros, hippo, buffalo, and a number of hares and rodents, eighty in all (McLaren 1944: 217–18). But within this taxonomic system there are only three higher order categories. Flesh-eating animals are called collectively *amaramncwa*, antelopes are called *iinyamakazi* (the class of edible wild animals; *inyama*=meat) and the class of domestic animals is *imifuyo*. There does not appear to be any higher order taxonomy for the other animals.[1]

This singling out of the three categories seems to be significant. *Amaramncwa*, *iinyamakazi* and *imifuyo* are homologous with the tripartite spatial categories of forest (*ihlati*), grassland (*ithafa*) and homestead (*umzi*) in the series:

forest . . . . grassland . . . . homestead
(carnivores)   (antelope)   (cattle/goats)

[1] There is strong evidence that the Cape Nguni have a much less elaborate animal taxonomic system than the Sotho, which would support Professor Wilson's comment, 'One can hardly escape the conclusion that the ancient Sotho rituals reflect the life of a people for whom hunting was more important than cattle-keeping' (Wilson 1969: 162).

Each of these spatial categories is the focus of strong affective disposi-
tions. The forest (there are patches of indigenous bush in the eastward-
facing mountain ravines and in the valleys of the broken coastal strip)
is a place of awe and danger. It is in the forests that witches secrete
the fearsome *isithunzela* ('zombie') and it is from the forest that much
of the material of herbalists and sorcerers is obtained. Forests are
often the venues for gatherings of witches, the Gwadana forest in
Kentani being notorious throughout the Transkei and Ciskei (Hammond-Tooke 1970: 28). At the other end of the scale the homestead
provides the model for human society, for the Cape Nguni have no
true village life, being settled in scattered homesteads. It is the homestead which provides the stage on which the social life of the individual
is played, and the social and ritual centre is the cattle byre. Forest and
homestead represent the opposition nature/culture. The associated
animals, too, reflect this polarity. Lévi-Strauss (1964) has stressed the
crucial role of food in the progress from nature to culture. Forest
animals are all inedible, they are the forbidden food *par excellence*,
while cattle and goats represent the category of acceptable food
animals, tamed to domesticity.

The grassland and its antelope fauna mediate between these two
extremes. The very term *iinyamakazi* means literally 'big meat', but
it is wild meat and, as such, partakes of the dangers of the wild, the
extra-societal. Its use must be approached circumspectly, and there is
evidence, unfortunately lacking in detail, of this. Communal hunting
was accompanied by ritual. Among both the Mpondo, in the north
of the Cape Nguni area, and the Xhosa in the south (and possibly
among all Cape Nguni) a young girl (Xhosa *umxobisi*) sat in the cattle
byre all the time the hunters were away and had to ritually pierce
the eye of the slain antelope, on their return, *in the byre*. This would
seem to symbolise a quite explicit attempt to 'domesticate' the wild
meat and assimilate it to the acceptable meat of cattle. It would be
instructive to know whether a special part was set aside for the ancestors, as in the dedication of the *intsonyama* (Bhaca *imbethfu*) (Hunter
1936: 249; Hammond-Tooke 1962: 50). A connection between slaying
an antelope and the ancestral spirits is explicitly recorded for the
Mpondo: 'At the moment when a man killed he shouted praises of
his ancestors' (Hunter 1936: 95), as in a ritual killing.[1] During a hunt
the game was *hlonipha*'d (respected), in that it was never described as
'fat' by the usual name for fat (Soga 1931: 377).

[1] Raum records for the Zulu that game is occasionally 'treated like a sacrifice'
(Raum 1973: 250).

But, if *iinyamakazi* in a sense mediate between forest and homestead through the hunt, there is also a direct relationship between forest and homestead. Some people, especially diviners, have a special ritual relationship with some of the *amaramncwa*, who in this context are called *amatyala* (singular *ityala*) among the Mpondo, and *izilo* (singular *isilo*) among, for instance, the Mpondomise. Mantshawe, a Mpondomise diviner, told me:

Every person has an *isilo* of his home. They are the same *izilo* as the ones found in the forest, i.e. elephants [*?oobade*, Xhosa *indlovu*], lions, leopards, jackals, baboons, and so on. There are also river animals (*izilo zomlambo*) such as crocodiles and hippo. The *isilo* looks after a person and protects him from danger. When a person is ill the *isilo* will come to help him. They help diviners, but they also help ordinary people. They can come as dreams, or as ideas in the mind. *Izilo* of the home are very important and it is necessary that something should be slaughtered for them at times. Normally your *isilo* will not attack you, even if you come across it in the forest. Even if you do not notice it at first it will make you realise that it is present. You must then move off.

This close association between ordinary humans and wild animals has not been recorded for other Cape Nguni groups. What is well established is their association with diviners and, through them, with the ancestral shades. Mantshawe, a diviner herself, described graphically her first contact with her *izilo* (she had more than one):

For some time as a child I had been unwell in the mind. One day we went to bathe in the deepest pool of the Qalethethe stream. As we were swimming I suddenly felt myself being drawn down into the depths of the pool. At the bottom I came to a place where there was no water at all. I saw a gate before me and there met a diviner. Before me were two four-legged animals. I did not know their names, but I knew that they were my guardians, my *izilo zomlambo*.

From February to November I lived alone in the darkest part of the forest. I avoided human contact, living on wild fruit and roots. I became fat and healthy. One night I was wakened by barking and saw a jackal circling the bush in which I was sleeping. I then knew that the jackal was one of my main *izilo*. I went to sleep, and woke up with a baboon lying next to me. Thus the jackal and baboon are the two most important animals to me.

One day I became hungry and went to an *umgwenye* tree [Kafir plum, *Odina caffra*] to get some wild fruit. I found it very difficult to look up into the tree – something told me not to – so I collected only the fallen fruit. I ate the fruit and slept. In my sleep I was shown what was in the tree. It was a leopard (*ingwe*). It did not want me to look up as it did not want our eyes to meet. It is one of the animals of my home.

Among the Mpondo the diviners' animal is called *ityala* (Hunter

1936: 323). The relationship to the animal is an individual one: members of the same clan 'see' different animals. A diviner and her relatives *hlonipha* her *ityala* by not killing it, eating it or mentioning its name. Hunter explicitly identifies the *ityala* with an ancestral shade: 'An *ityala* is an *ithongo* which takes the shape of a wild animal' (p. 321).

But the animal that most frequently appears in the symbolic structure is the snake. The ancestors (occasionally) appear as snakes, the *isilo* of the Mpondomise can be a snake (members of the Mpondomise royal clan have a special relationship with the Majola snake), the familiars *ichanti* and *umamlambo* are essentially snakes, despite their changeableness, as is the *inyoka yabafazi* ('snake of women') sent to bite children (Hunter 1936: 285). Finally the river itself, as we have seen, can appear as a snake (Mpondo), or harbour the snakes which teach the diviners their craft (Mpondomise, Bhaca, Xhosa).

The question to which we must now turn is: why all these animals? Recent research has tended to show that animals, in the classic aphorism of Lévi-Strauss (1969: 162), are 'good to think', that they are used as a sort of symbolic calculus to make statements about existential reality. As Berger (1971) puts it: 'Animals supply examples for the mind as well as food for the body. They carry not only loads but principles.' This has been cogently demonstrated by such writers as Douglas (1957), Tambiah (1969), Rigby (1971), Bulmer (1967), Willis (1974) and the Stratherns (1968), among others.

IV

The symbolic structure

We have spoken of the opposition forest/homestead and its expression (and mediation) through the animal classificatory taxa of *amaramncwa*, *iinyamakazi* and *imifuyo*. But the symbolic code is more complex than this. The ambiguity of the grassland contains also the potent symbol of water, especially rivers and pools, so that the structural opposition is rather:

forest . . . . water . . . . homestead
(river)

Rivers tend to take their rise in the relic forests of the mountains, and flow through the grassland (and past homesteads), thus mediating even more clearly between the two.

Homologous to this is a sequence of spirit beings, namely:

familiars............River People................shades

Associated with each spirit being is a constellation of elements, which can be projected onto the following schema:

	Nature..........mediation..........Culture		
EVALUATIVE	wild	marginal	domestic
	bad	ambiguous	good
	−	−/+	+

LEVELS			
spirit beings	FAMILIARS	RIVER PEOPLE [umamlambo ?/shades ?] − +	SHADES
spatial	forest	'veld' [river/grassland]	homestead
human	witch	diviner	moral man
ethical	unmerited misfortune	fortuity	merited misfortune
social	individualism	structural freedom	societas
sexual[1]	forbidden evil sex (witches with familiars)	foreplay between unmarried adults in the veld	sanctioned marital relations
animal	ferocious wild animals (inedible)	animals of the River People [crocodile/cattle etc.] − +	cattle, goats (edible)

[1] I am indebted for this suggestion to Mr. R. Palmer of the University of Cape Town. He writes (personal communication): 'Transmission of power between witches and familiars is via the sex act and is associated with evil, the forest and the individual. Moral man enjoys full sex relations in the homestead. Opposition is mediated by the ambiguous. Unmarried initiates are neither fully adult (married) nor children (initiated); they are sexually experienced and make pair bonds, yet do not penetrate; hence these sexual relations take place neither in the homestead nor the forest, but in the veld.'

This arrangement obviously needs explication and justification: the rest of the essay will attempt to do this.[1]

From the evidence presented above there is clearly no difficulty about the opposition of the wild, represented by the forest, and the warm, nurturing sphere of human society, the homestead. Although few wild animals exist today, the folk myth populates the forest with lions, leopards, elephants and other fierce animals; the homestead is just as clearly the home of cattle, with their close relationship to man. There is, indeed, almost an identification of man and ox, in that both are at risk from the *umlaza* ritual pollution. Forest and homestead are clearly separated spatially and are strongly valued, negatively and positively respectively. Witches clearly symbolise the essence of evil, whereas the shades are the epitome of good. Both witches and shades can cause illness and misfortune, but there is a crucial difference between the two. Ancestrally-sent misfortune is always due to neglect of custom and as such is merited. Witch-caused misfortune is frequently the product of unmotivated envy and malice. The opposition is fundamental and the elements unequivocal.

But when we turn to the River People this clearness of conceptualisation vanishes. We are immediately precipitated into an area of ambiguity. The River People live under the water, but visitors to them emerge from the river *dry*; they cause drownings, but sometimes this is unintentional; they own 'beautiful herds', which interbreed with humans' cattle, but they also live in paradoxical association with the crocodile, iguana and otter (essentially animals of the wild); they can be dangerous and malevolent (the familiar *umamlambo* is somehow associated with them), but some think that they are ancestors. There is obviously an uncertainty as to classification here. It is not clear whether punishment by the River People is merited or not.

---

[1] An account of the steps in my thinking about the problem might go some way to countering a possible criticism of arbitrariness in this schema. The central question was: why the River People? What role do they play in the idea system? Impressed by the insights provided in other ethnographical areas by an approach through an examination of animal taxonomies (particularly as there was obviously a close association between animals and all three groups of 'spirits'), I examined the Cape Nguni system of classification and was presented with the fact of only three higher order taxa, *amaramncwa*, *iinyamakazi* and *imifuyo*. Immediately it struck me that this classification coincided with a spatial one, which also seemed to accord with the three classes of 'spirit beings' – familiars, River People and shades. It was a short step to linking this with human 'associates' of the spirits. Up to this point the classification developed out of the empirical data. The 'ethical' and 'social' levels are obviously not so clearly derived, but reflect my interpretation of the 'meaning' of the code. The columns must, of course, be treated as totalities.

But these three constructs, which between them structure the cosmological systems of the Cape Nguni, are themselves mediated between. Man and nature are in continual relationship, and this relationship is symbolically expressed. Man can influence the River People by the sacrifice of an ox (and other things), and the River People communicate with man through their 'messengers', the crocodile, leguaan and otter, ambiguously apt to fulfil this role. Cattle, of course, are the prime mediatory offering to the shades – and even, some say, the wild and dangerous *amaramncwa* can assist man through the *isilo* (Mpondomise *ityala*). In all this the office of diviner is pivotal. Not only do diviners interpret the universe, but they participate in all three areas. Based on the homestead, they receive instruction from the River People and enjoy the tutelary mentorship of the *amaramncwa*.

I began this paper by asking whether one could detect a system, a structure, in Cape Nguni cosmologies. I suggest that there is no doubt that one can. I also asked: why all these animals? It seems clear that the animals are used as potent symbols to conceptualise the constructs and the mediations between them. Ferocious animals symbolise the wildness of untamed nature, the patient ox the centrality of the cattle byre as the home of the shades, and the ambiguous water animals the relationship between the two.

But what are the Cape Nguni 'saying' in this symbolic code? In a structural study such as this, the primary object is to demonstrate structure, the 'fit' between the series of homologues, and not to seek 'explanation' in any causal or functional sense. But the system must be looked at as a code in a system of communication, and the question arises: what is being communicated?

It is suggested that the essence of the message is nothing less than an attempt to mediate between two polarities that lie at the basis of all social life: the opposition and tension between the importance of group involvement (*societas*) and the human tendency towards individualism. This is surely a basic problem in all societies, the much-discussed opposition between Individual and Society. The societal aspect is especially strong among the Cape Nguni, who have a highly developed system of descent groups (Hammond-Tooke 1968). As we have seen, the Mpondomise, in particular, stress the importance of lineage solidarity, and descent group loyalty is a basic moral injunction. The solidarity of descent group members is symbolised on the cosmological plane by the close association of the lineage dead with the living – the shades (*amathongo, iminyanya*) are also 'people' (*abantu abadala*), and the object of lineage rituals is to stress this link by means of the mediatory ox.[1]

On the other hand the witch represents the negation of this loyalty. As Philip Mayer puts it (1954: 17), the witch is the enemy within the gates, who attacks typically kinsmen and neighbours. The witch is the image of rampant individualism, the negation of social man. This is symbolically expressed by locating him outside society, in the extreme spatial location of the forest, among the fierce wild animals whose inedibility contrasts with the edibility of the domestic animals of homestead and byre. The familiars work singly (usually), in secret, and are singly distinguished, unlike the shades, who are typically thought of as a collectivity (the term for shade is seldom, if ever, used in the singular).

This contrast between shade/familiar points up what is perhaps the main aspect of Cape Nguni cosmological systems. Unlike some other African religious systems (for example, the Nyakyusa), there does not appear to be a strong emphasis on fertility. Rather is there a strong interest in the explanation of and dealing with misfortune, especially illness (is this perhaps why healing is so important in independent churches in South Africa?), and the two poles, familiar and ancestor, are the two prime explanatory causes of misfortune. This is why the functionary closest to the shades, the diviner, has as her chief role to determine through a trance state the provenance of sickness and misfortune. But the message is paradoxically transposed. It is *merited* misfortune that is meted out by the ancestors for *individualistic* behaviour (neglect of descent group ritual), and *unmerited* misfortune that comes from *social* involvement. (It is the very living together in contiguous homesteads that generates the tensions that result in witch activity.) Those familiar with Lévi-Strauss's theories will not be surprised at this paradox.

But all human society involves both individualism and *societas*, both nature and culture, and the two poles are mediated by the ambiguous image of the River People, on the construct level, and by the office of the diviner on the social level. The very ambiguity and lack of classification of the elements in the River People syndrome shadows the uneasiness in the tension between individualism and *societas*.

---

[1] Note that 'mediation' is used in two different senses. In the general argument presented here the main mediation is between paradigmatic constructs (Berger and Luckman 1972; Ardener 1971) of the wild and domestic, through the ambiguous construct of the River People. In sacrifice the ox is a symbol of mediation in the *process* of man's reconciliation with the shades.

The River People are a community, but can be represented by the *itshologu* (Hunter 1936: 263), in the form of a snake; they are both good and bad (sometimes by mistake); and the misfortune that they cause has about it an element of fortuitousness, the uncalculated, the morally neutral and ambivalent. In the animal code this is symbolised by the co-existence of both edible and inedible animals.

And the person most closely associated with the River People is the diviner, significantly both the most important 'religious' functionary and also the one least 'structurally' determined. Diviners are called to the profession by their *maternal* ancestors, but their influence. unlike that of the lineage 'priest', is not tied to fellow lineage members. They are free to roam, and collect around themselves not a congregation but a clientele. They are essentially 'good' in that they work closely with the shades, but they are also adept in the medicines of witches and sorcerers. Diviners, typically women, are permitted to carry a spear, symbol of maleness (the few male diviners wear skirts). In the divining situation their role is quite explicitly to mediate in the cosmic battle between the forest and the homestead.

V

In conclusion I should like to return to the use of the tail of elephant and leopard (and also the leopard-skin) as symbols of chieftainship. Why should it be that chiefs are associated with wild animals, with all their associations of evil and witchcraft?

It may be, of course, that sympathetic magic is at work here: the powerful and fierce wild animals convey courage and power. But it is interesting to reflect that chiefs occupy a special place in Cape Nguni social structure. They are individuals, but they also represent in their persons society itself. Chiefs are, in a sense, the tribe made concrete: tribes are called by the very names of chiefs. These animal pelts are royal insignia and represent essentially the mystical aspects of chieftainship rather than the executive, for, while Cape Nguni chiefs play little active part in decision-making (Hammond-Tooke 1969), they possess the quality of *isithunzi* (shadow), an aura of fearsomeness and malevolent charisma, that sets them apart from ordinary people. Could it be that chiefs are in a mediatory position in the above schema? Diviners, too, have this quality of *isithunzi* (if to a much lesser degree) and it is perhaps significant that the roles of chief and diviner are never confused.[1] Such a mediation (if it occurs) would seem to take place in two different modes, however. With the diviner it is reflected in what I have called 'structural freedom'; with the chief it inheres in an actual *identification* of the two poles, individualism and *societas*.

[1] The only recorded exception is the Xhosa chief Gcaleka (Soga 1930: 142–5). Mr. John Perry informs me that Sotho chiefs are also accorded ambiguous reference. Chiefs are greeted both as *Dikgomo morena!* (literally cattle chief) and *Sebata-morena!* (literally carnivorous, wild beast, chief), or even more significantly, as *Dikgomo-sebata!*

A.-I. Berglund

HEAVEN-HERDS: A STUDY IN
ZULU SYMBOLISM

[Monica Wilson has underlined the importance of being sensitive to men's own interpretations of the symbols and expressions they use. For it is from their point of view that the use of language, colour, sounds and actions becomes logical and acceptable. Further, sensitivity towards men's self-assessment eliminates many inaccuracies. This study of three men's evaluations of their tools of operation is dedicated to an honoured and much-respected South African scholar who, throughout her life and work, has set an example in her respect for human beings and her scholarly approach.]

Defining heaven-herds

The term 'heaven-herds' describes those men in Zulu society who are believed to be able to protect people, animals, homes and fields from the danger of violent storms. In Zulu referred to as *abelusi bezulu* (heaven-herds) and *izinyanga zezulu* (literally the experts on the sky), they are approached with much awe and great respect.

Unlike diviners, whose calling and subsequent training are very closely related to the shades, the heaven-herds do not have relationships with the shades as far as their duties in regard to the sky are concerned. Theoretically, anybody can become a heaven-herd. But in practice it is required that a candidate be able to refer to some occasion when he narrowly escaped being struck by lightning or has seen lightning enter a house or otherwise can prove that the sky has allowed him to become a heaven-herd. Laduma Madela, one of the heaven-herds described in this contribution, said that he often dreamt about *uMvelingqangi*, the Lord-of-the-Sky, particularly during the summer season when he was frequently called upon to protect people. It was claimed that the Lord-of-the-Sky revealed his activities to the heaven-herd through his dreams. But Madela very strongly dissociated himself from any thought that dreams would be a means of calling to office as is the case with diviners. One of the other heaven-herds said that he dreamt very seldom, and the third claimed that he never ever dreamt about the Lord-of-the-Sky: 'How can I dream of one who is so far away? He is in the sky. We are here. How can I dream of him, I being here? Perhaps the other two [heaven-herds] live on high mountains. That may be the reason for their being able to dream [about him].'

Heaven-herds are emphatically and very consciously associated with herding. Three important details in people's thinking pertaining to heaven-herds underline this fact. Firstly, no woman can become a heaven-herd, for 'where have women been seen tending cattle? Is not the heaven-herd an *umalusi* (herdsman), tending the sky as a herdsman looks after cattle? So how can a heaven-herd be a woman?' Secondly, irrespective of his age, a heaven-herd is always referred to as a boy, *umfana*. 'It is boys who are the keepers of the cattle. That is why we call the heaven-herds *abafana*. To the sky they are only just boys. That is all they are.' Laduma Madela emphasised that the term *umfana* must always be understood in relation to the sky. He accepted the term as one of respect towards the sky, although he admitted that to present-day Zulu men *umfana* is, in one sense, a humiliating term of address. 'The sky is very old. It is a sign of respect if someone who is old is attended to by a boy. So people are honouring the sky when they call me *umfana*. It is also an honour to me. To be a servant (*inceku*) of the aged is a sign of trustworthiness.' Lastly, each heaven-herd is given a stick of *umuNka* (*Maerua angoliensis*) which he uses in his practice in the same way that herdsmen use their sticks in driving cattle. A heaven-herd is also equipped with a flute of reed (*umtshingo*) on which he blows when driving away storms. 'The sound of *umtshingo* is the same as when the boys whistle on cattle. The only difference is that *umtshingo* is more dignified. That is the only difference. But the sound is the same.'

Thunder and lightning

Zulu attribute all thunder and lightning to the Lord-of-the-Sky. Thunder is of two kinds: male thunder, which is not dreaded although looked upon with awe and deep respect, and female thunder, which is very much feared.

Male thunder is characterised by the long, drawn-out and deep thunder that is not accompanied with lightning and hail but frequently followed by good rainfall. Male thunder, known as *elenduna*, is also spoken of as 'the playing of the sky' and refers to a jocular mood which the sky is believed to be enjoying at that time. 'When this kind of thunder is frequent, people say, "The sky is good this year because he [the Lord-of-the-Sky] is just making noise and not destroying." That is what is said that year. They say it because there is just noise and no lightning and hail.'

Female thunder, called *elesifazane*, is the sudden cracking thunder accompanied by forked lightning and heavy downfalls and frequently hail. Forked lightning and the sudden cracks of thunder are like 'the tongue of an angry woman who speaks fearful things, saying unexpectedly such things that one did not think would be spoken by her. But the woman speaks thus because she is angry. Anger causes people to speak evil, smiting this way and that with their tongues.'

Violent and dramatic thunderstorms are attributed to the anger or the bad temper of the Lord-of-the-Sky. 'When he appears in this manner, it is fearful because he is angry. He seeks to destroy somewhere. Sometimes he approaches the one whom he wants [to take], sometimes he is like an angry man who simply destroys everywhere. So wherever this kind of violent thunder occurs, you will hear of some evil [having taken place] somewhere. Sometimes among people, sometimes in the fields, sometimes among the animals. Somewhere the fire [lightning] will have caused damage.' People who have been killed by lightning are believed to be taken by the Lord-of-the-Sky. They are buried nearby, with the right-hand finger protruding above the earth 'so that people may see where he has gone'.

Throughout Zululand attention is focused on lightning during storms. It is the absence of lightning, in the first instance, that makes male thunder less feared than the female. In female thunder it is not the crack of thunder as such that is frightening. It is the lightning that brings about the crack. Common opinion has it that lightning is the instrument through which the Lord-of-the-Sky expresses his anger or bad temper. Hail and expected drought after heavy downpours of rain are side-effects and results of the activities of lightning. Hence the great fear of lightning and the particular attention given it in a heaven-herd's practice.

Lightning is generally believed to be a bird, *inyoni yezulu* (literally, the bird of heaven), sent to the earth by the Lord-of-the-Sky. Others, though not many, believe that lightning is a ball of fire brought to earth by a bird and sent by the Lord-of-the-Sky. Yet another view is that lightning is a bird, but that the bird is fire. '. . . the fire that comes from above is in the shape of a bird. Birds come from the sky. That is why the Lord-of-the-Sky has chosen this animal to be the carrier of his fire. The fire and the bird are one thing.'

Inyoni yezulu is said to be a hen. One of the reasons for its coming down to earth is to lay its eggs. On these occasions it is described as sweeping down over the earth, preferably over the tops of flat hills and mountains. In order to reduce its great speed it digs its beak or its toes into the earth and digs up a long furrow. 'Where the furrow ends, there its eggs are to be found.' Forked lightning is said to occur when the bird intends laying eggs and, in order to confuse the heaven-herds who seek the eggs, the bird 'dives down this way and that, so that they [the heaven-herds] do not find the eggs, not knowing where it came down'.

A man from the Dundee district, who was a novice to a heaven-herd, described his encounter with lightning thus:

We were all gathered in the hut when suddenly the door was opened violently and lightning came in, taking this one and that one. All fell to the ground. But I stood up because of medicine I had taken and because I sought to defend the homestead with the medicines. I was holding them in my hand. So I stood up. Looking, I perceived the thing [lightning]. It was frightening to behold, and it moved very quickly. Yet I saw it clearly. It was a bird. The feathers were white, in flame. The beak and the legs were red with fire. And the tail was something different, similar to burning green or the colour of the sky. It ran quickly, saying nothing, simply grasping those whom it was taking. Then it touched the grass [thatching] with its fire. It disappeared through the door again. When it had left, there was somebody who shouted. So we hurried out of the hut, leaving those whom it had taken.

(Two children and an old woman were killed by lightning on this occasion and they were referred to as having been taken by the lightning-bird.)

Thunderclouds are believed to be the hiding-place of the lightning-bird.

When the bird is sent [to earth] by the Lord-of-the-Sky it enters these clouds. It tells the clouds to carry it to a certain place. When they arrive at that place the clouds stop. They come closer to the earth by lowering themselves over that place. Then the bird prepares to fly down. When its time has come and it has seen the place where it is to do its work, it suddenly leaves the hiding-place, goes to that place with great speed, does its thing and then goes to its place of security [the clouds] again. There it hides, until it departs to do work again.

The heaven-herds

Zulu heaven-herds of standing are few and far between. In this contribution three distinguished heaven-herds will be described. (Other heaven-herds in Zululand are known, but they are of a popular kind and not as renowned as the three described.) Laduma Madela, whose home is situated on the slopes of the impressive Ceza mountain (between Mahlabathini and Vryheid), insists that his name be mentioned when writing about him. Besides being a renowned heaven-herd, Madela is a blacksmith, a herbalist and, to a lesser extent, a diviner. In one sense Madela is not always representative of general Zulu beliefs, for his very lively intellect sparks off his own creative thinking, vision and imagination. He also allows his views to be influenced by the outside world, and what he hears and experiences becomes part-and-parcel of his life and thinking. On the other hand he is a conservative Zulu traditionalist. He has insights into Zulu history, thought-patterns, rituals and customs which a great many people envy. His home is strictly Zulu, his wives are carefully instructed to live as tradition and custom required, and his children likewise.

X lives north-east of Kranskop, overlooking the Tugela valley. From his home one can see into Zululand, the valley of the Tugela and the country beyond the river. His home is surrounded by very stony land, and the houses comprising the homestead are all built of stone, with the exception of his private hut. His own dwelling is built in traditional Zulu fashion. Immediately behind the homestead the land rises steeply to a mountain peak on the top of which is a place of prayer. People in great need, who have decided to approach the Lord-of-the-Sky directly, dress in white and, preferably on Thursdays or Sundays, climb the mountain and pray on the peak. The place of prayer on the mountain is called *isiguqo* (literally, kneeling-place). It is a round opening (radius of about 1½ metres) from which stones have been removed, except for ten stones painted white with whitewash arranged in a heap in the middle of the opening. X claims that he prays and meditates regularly in the *isiguqo*.

X receives clients from the whole Tugela valley, from beyond the valley in Zululand and from the whole farming area between Pietermaritzburg, Greytown and Pomeroy. Once a year he makes himself available to people in the Eshowe district. He claims that he also travels to the Port Shepstone area to treat homesteads against lightning, but that he goes to this part of Natal only when called upon to do so and when assured that his fees and travel costs will be met.

W lives at the foot of a well-known high mountain in the Louwsburg–Ngwibi district of northern Natal. His homestead is on white farmland. But he has reached an agreement with the farmer owning the land, which releases him from the otherwise compulsory labour on the farm. W's eldest son works on the farm, but does so as an ordinary tenant. He does not substitute for his father who pays the farmer a handsome rental. W claims that he treats the farmer's buildings regularly in early summer, as well as having a very large number of people seeking his services from the northern districts of Natal. Unlike his neighbours, W can afford to have four wives. He has nineteen children.

The homestead is surrounded by great blocks of granite stone, and W's private hut has one of these protruding out of the ground immediately to the right of the doorway. W attaches much importance to the presence of these stones, saying that 'he [the Lord-of-the-Sky] has put them there. He has certain things attached to the stones. That is why he often sends his fire to those stones. It [the fire, i.e. lightning-bird] comes frequently to the stones to fetch the things that he wants it to fetch.' People do not live near W's homestead for fear of the lightning which, it is claimed, often strikes the mountain underneath which W lives. W himself claims that he has seen 'the bird of the King' frequently, and has on two occasions been able to obtain feathers from it.

None of the three heaven-herds are in any way related to each other, although two of them have married within the same clan (the wives had no apparent knowledge of each other). Living far apart, the heaven-herds maintain that they have never met, although each admits to having knowledge of the others' whereabouts and activities. Nothing indicates any sense of competition or envy among them. Precisely because there is no apparent contact between the three men, a study of them gives interesting insights into the mechanics and understanding of symbols in Zulu society.

The ingredients of medicine

All three heaven-herds prepare medicines outside their homesteads, in a secluded spot called *isolo* or *iziko lezulu* (literally, the hearth of the sky). All three are emphatic that medicine ought to be prepared in the shadow of a tree or on an overcast day 'so that the sky does not see what we do'. W stresses that medicines must be prepared 'in a cool place', and because homesteads are the abodes of menstruating, pregnant and/or suckling women, these are 'hot' places and therefore unsuitable. 'These medicines must be cool. They cannot be prepared in a hot place, because their power will be crippled. That is why they must be prepared in a cool place. That is a place where there are not hot people.' All three are equally convinced that no medicine prepared in anger will be useful, for 'angry people are hot people'. X said that if medicine is prepared in anger, the product would work the opposite way, attracting lightning rather than removing it. 'The anger of the heaven-herd (*umalusi*) will just cause increased anger with the sky.'

Herbalists operate with a vast amount of material in the preparation of their medicines. But heaven-herds claim that of the various ingredients possible in the preparation of their particular medicine, only ten must be used on any given mixture. Laduma Madela was most emphatic on this point, and returned to the importance of the figure ten again and again. Said Madela, 'As there are ten fingers which make a complete handful and enable a man to work efficiently [literally, completely, fully], likewise there must be ten fingers in the medicine. Then they can work together to a full protection against the sky.' X and W agreed that there must be only ten ingredients but gave no definite reason for this number. However, both accepted Madela's explanation as valid.

Heaven-herds do not use the plural form for medicine (*imiti*) when speaking about their mixtures. They agree that the composition of their medicine varies depending on the choice of the ten ingredients. But the product of the ten ingredients is always *umuti*, not *imiti*. 'The medicine (*umuti*) has only one work, that of cooling the anger of the sky and of asking it to go elsewhere. This one work is done by one medicine. That is why we speak simply of *umuti*. Again it is of respect for the heavens. We say *amazulu* [plural form of *izulu*], paying our respects to it. So our medicine cannot be honoured if the heavens are honoured.' (Madela).

A most important ingredient, and consequently one most keenly sought after, is the fat of *inyoni yezulu* or *impundulu*. Madela and W described in great detail to what pains they had gone to obtain the bird, the risks involved, and the manner in which the bird had been destroyed in order to obtain the much desired fat. X was so secretive on this particular issue that he said, 'I promise you that I will tell you nearly anything you would like to know. But this thing I cannot speak of. It is too fearful. It cannot be spoken of. Please, friend, do not hurt me by asking more of this thing. It is too fearful.'

Laduma Madela claims to have killed *inyoni yezulu* and obtained so much fat from it that it was sufficient for several years after the incident.

When I saw the clouds of the bird coming, I climbed up Ceza mountain and waited there. The bird knew that I was there. I had told *uMvelingqangi* that I would meet it there. So it flew this way and that, going up and down, and looking for a way to deceive me. But the egg was pressing, so at last it came down. When it stopped at the end of the furrow, then it just sat down for a while. It laid three eggs. When it had laid the third egg, I was on it with this stick (*umunka*), beating it on the head and everywhere until it fell down. Then I cut its throat so that the blood might come out on top of the hill, knowing that other birds would come to look for their friend. Then it became cool. When it was cold I went home with it. I carried it in this bag . . . . Yes, all the years from then to 1966 I used the fat of the one bird. It was very fat, even the eggs were surrounded by fat. But in 1967 I killed *impundulu*. That is the same as *inyoni yomlilo*. . . . The bird was so fat because there [in the sky] it lacks nothing. There is no hunger (*indlala*) there. Food is plentiful.

The medicine may further contain the fat of *umonya* (*Python sebae*, Natal rock snake), *imbulu* (*Varanus albigolaris*, large land iguana), *imbila* (*Hyrax capensis*, the common rock-rabbit), and that of a black sheep. If the horns of the sheep are perfectly black and curved, they are used as containers of the ready medicine.

Medicine for the sky must be kept in black horns. The black is the same as the black of the clouds. The black horns say to the sky, 'Black things which carry the bird [i.e. dark clouds].' Here there is nothing but darkness. There is no good to be had here. So just go to another place where you can find white and beautiful things. But here in this place are only black things. So just go to another place. That is what the black says. . . . The curved horns say, 'Just turn away nicely, as these horns are turned. Just turn to another place where there is whiteness.' That is what the curved horns say.

Whilst fat represents wellbeing and prosperity with all the heaven-herds, black fat is a symbol of destroyed prosperity. Madela said that black fat indicates to the sky that if it were to carry out its evil intention to destroy, the result would only be evil, 'as this medicine is evil because the goodness of fat has become black'. X and W agreed that black fat stands for destruction, but their application of the symbol was a little different. They claimed that the anger of the Lord-of-the-Sky would be averted and turned aside by evil, implying that one evil is driven out by another. Hence the absolute need to have black fat, i.e. fat blackened by adding soot or finely crushed dark stone chippings, or by crushing coal into dust and adding this to the fat (W).

The Python is regarded as 'the animal of the sky'.

If it is used in medicines, the sky will recognise its animal, saying, 'No, this is painful. I cannot hurt people as they have hurt this my animal.' Again, this animal is slow to anger. So if the fat of this animal is used, the heaven-herd is saying, 'Excuse me, Lord. Just regard this thing of yours that is slow to anger. Why is it that you do not resemble it and take away your anger? Instead, be like it and let your great heat [anger] just become cool.' That is what is said of this animal.

The iguana is generally accepted as being the most unafraid of animals, and therefore medicine containing it makes people unafraid. The novice referred to above claimed that it was the fat of iguana that made him fearless when lightning entered the hut in which he was sitting. Black sheep are partly 'like the black clouds' (thunder clouds), partly the opposite of lightning, which is described as being white, and partly silent. In the first case 'black drives away black', and in the two latter 'the lightning fears the blackness and it fears the silence. That is why it does not crack, being frightened by the silence of the animal of silence' (the sheep). Fat (and frequently also skin) of a rock-rabbit is used because 'this animal always hides when it rains. So the sky does not agree with it. If it is in the medicine, the sky will not send rain because there is the animal that does not agree with rain.'

Further possible animal ingredients are skin of an otter, *umanzini* (*Lutra capensis*), feathers of a peacock, and flesh of a tortoise, *ufudu*. Common belief has it that the tortoise, when angry, spouts water upwards, especially when a thunder-storm is approaching. Madela claimed that the only occasion when the tortoise becomes angry is when the sky prepares 'to do the thing of its own anger'. 'So the medicine with this animal in it says to the storm, "Go the other way. Let your anger go the same way as the anger of the tortoise." Then the lightning goes upwards and does not come downwards.' Peacocks are claimed to be the birds of kings, eaten by them only as delicacies. X said, 'So the King in the sky is given this bird in the medicine to make him happy, removing his anger. If his anger is removed, then he will not send the fire-bird (*inyoni yomlilo*) to cause havoc among us. That is why this bird is put into the medicine.' X and W said that the skin of otter is used 'because the otter is fearful in its smell, especially the skin.' The smell of the skin would, in other words, drive off the sky. Madela, on the other hand, claimed that he used the skin of a black cat as a substitute for the otter, simply because it smells, adding that 'cats fear rain'. Asked why he did not simply leave out the other skin and not substitute it, he replied, 'How then do I have the hands full?' (How do I obtain the ten ingredients?)

Popular vegetable ingredients are the crushed stem of the thunder-tree, *umunka*, and the crushed bulb of the common red Ifafa lily, *impingizana encane ebomvu* (*Cyrtanthus stenenthus liliaceae*). Describing the thunder-tree, X said, 'It is white inside the bark, just as heaven is white [light] inside with no darkness.' His description made it quite clear that there are parallels between the tree and a human-being. When its thorns are broken off, a red sap emerges. 'This is the blood. It comes out as blood comes out of a human being. . . . That is the tree that he [the Lord-of-the-Sky] himself planted on earth. It is his tree.' Madela spoke of *umunka* as being the 'tree of life' referred to in Genesis.

Because of its symbolic relationships with humans, the presence of *umunka* in the medicine is equated with the presence of human flesh. 'So when we add this tree to the medicine which is the mixture for the sky, we are putting in a human. That is what we are doing. It is because we fear that he [the Lord-of-the-Sky] sends the bird to fetch a human being. With this medicine we say to the bird, "No, bird of the sky, just remain peaceful. Do not cause troubles. Just look at this medicine. Is it not medicine containing a man? Is it not medicine having the thing made by the one who sent you? Just look at it nicely. In this medicine you will find the thing [a human being] you are seeking." That is what we say about this tree of which you are asking, the tree of humanity (*umuthi wobuntu*).'

The Ifafa lily blooms when the grass has been burnt, and hence is closely associated with fire. Describing its symbolic significance, X said, 'If it is used in medicine, the sky sees that this place has already been burnt. So there is nothing more to burn. Then the sky goes elsewhere with its fire [lightning]. It does not strike where the medicine of this plant has been used.'

Symbols and medicines

Over and above the ingredients described above, the three heaven-herds claim that two symbols must be added to the ingredients in order to make the medicine efficient. The symbols are the sound of thunder and the flash of lightning. All three heaven-herds are convinced that the symbol for lightning must be white. Two of them had a symbol for lightning (one a spark and the other a reflection of the rays of the sun), and a separate symbol for the white of lightning. The third combined the symbols for lightning and for white into one (a squirt of milk).

With Laduma Madela the symbol typifying the sound of thunder is very important, and he spent considerable time describing difficulties he encountered in obtaining the symbol. The sound is symbolised by the wing-feathers of *ingqungqulu*, the Bateleur eagle (*Terathopius ecaudatus*), because, when the bird flies, it produces a noise 'that is the sound of the bird of the sky when it comes down from the clouds onto the earth. This sound is in its wing-feathers. That is why I have the feathers in the medicine.'

In comparison with the emphasis Madela gives to the symbol typifying the sound of thunder, the role it plays in X's composition of medicine is quite insignificant. Yet it is very clearly there. But with X a difficulty arises in the combination of the symbol for the sound of thunder with the spark symbolising lightning. X is adamant that the two must be produced at the same time. X symbolises the sound by that of one granite stone being thrown against another.

W prepares medicine under the shadow of a large thorntree growing next to one of the blocks of stone so numerous where he lives. When he wishes to have the sound of thunder symbolised, he instructs either his novice or one of his sons to smite the surface of the rock next to his *iziko lezulu*. Once while listening, I was astonished by the volume of the sound produced, for a common herding-stick beaten against a solid piece of rock could hardly produce a very audible sound. But on closer inspection of both the stick and the rock, I found that a piece of white string, with three pieces of lead attached, was tied to the tip of the stick. When the stick was applied to the rock, the novice or the son made the lead pieces hit an empty pilchard-tin so well fitted into a crack in the rock as to be not easily seen. The continuation of the crack downwards into the rock served as a resonance cavity, adding greatly to the sound produced by the tin.

X produces his symbol for lightning by throwing one granite stone onto another until a spark is clearly visible. It is the spark that symbolises the flash of lightning. X says that it is not difficult to produce the noise that typifies the sound of thunder, nor the spark that is the symbol of lightning. His difficulty arises when he cannot obtain both at the same time. 'The spark must be produced at the same time as the sound is heard. If this does not happen, I must throw again.' (X was emphatic that not every sound produced by the clash of one stone on another was acceptable. There had to be a typical and characteristic sound, accompanied by the smell of sulphur.) On one occasion when X allowed me to attend, he threw one big boulder onto another no fewer than 27 times before he produced satisfactory results.

Madela produces a symbol for lightning by flicking a reflection of the sun's rays over his medicine for a fraction of a second, and immediately returning the mirror he has used into his pocket. I was impressed by the swiftness and the accuracy with which he fulfilled his task, and said so to him. He replied, 'That is what lightning is like. It is very quick. You do not know of it before it has been and gone. It strikes exactly where it wants to. That is why this lightning [the reflection] must be fast and accurate. If it were not so, the medicine would be too slow to work. It must also be fast in its working.'

W's symbol for lightning is a squirt of milk from a pure white cow. He illustrated how he made use of the symbol. The bowl of various ingredients was placed on the ground underneath the udder of the cow and a squirt of milk was drawn from the cow. Milked with an experienced hand, the squirt was collected in the middle of the bowl. 'It [the squirt of milk] comes from above, like lightning. It comes straight, like lightning. It is white, like lightning. Even the cow is white, like the sky [the interior of the sky is believed by W to be wholly white]. So it is clear that the milk from this cow is lightning. That is how I work with this white cow.' (W claimed that the milk produced by the cow would be used by himself only. Anybody else who ate curds from milk of the white cow would become seriously ill.) W gave no great importance to the symbol itself, but elaborated on the great price he had paid for the animal and the great pains he was taking to have it cared for properly.

Madela and X have symbols which typify the white of lightning. Madela uses the fat of *ingqungqulu*, which he claims is the whitest of all the various fats used by heaven-herds, and a white ore obtained from the Nqathi range, where lightning is claimed to strike more often than elsewhere in Zululand. According to Madela both ingredients are very difficult to obtain (the white ore must be fetched from the range during a violent storm), and both are of great importance. X symbolises white with ash obtained by burning dried Ifafa lily bulbs and leaves. 'This is the flower of the black of fire [i.e. this flower grows where the grass has been burnt and before the new grass has grown up]. So its ash, which is white, is what the sky requires in the treatment of the fire from it [lightning]. Just look at the whiteness of the ash. Is it not white? Yet it comes from black [ash of the burnt grass].' X said that the ash was important in the preparation of medicine, but did not greatly emphasise its importance.

Findings and conclusion

The various ingredients used by the heaven-herds in their preparation of medicine fall into two clear categories.

First, there are those ingredients which come from materia and animals and have been chosen because ideas and symbols associated with the ingredients make the heaven-herd's medicine logical. The emphasis lies in the ingredient because it is accepted and understood in a particular way by both the heaven-herd and the society he serves. The ingredient brings to mind ideas and thought-patterns that are relevant to the duty of a heaven-herd, and therefore fits into his practice in a logical and acceptable manner. It is not only the experts who know, for example, that because the python is associated with the sky, therefore a python's fat would be among the ingredients of a heaven-herd's medicine. It was an ordinary Zulu farmer who said, 'I will call upon a heaven-herd who I know mixes python fat in the medicine, because then I am convinced that the heavens will be cooled.' He was referring to the idea that pythons stand for slowness in anger and are therefore regarded as 'cool'.

Secondly, the required symbol far outweighs in importance the materia or the sound typifying the symbol. Once the required symbol has been identified and defined, the materia or sound which will contain the symbol is chosen by the individual heaven-herd. It is evident that how the medicine is blackened is not important. What is important is that the medicine indeed be black; hence blackening by charring or by adding soot or crushed chips from black stones. Evidence shows how important it is to have symbols typifying lightning and the sound of thunder. But whether lightning be symbolised by a squirt of milk or a flash of reflected sunlight or by wing-feathers of an eagle is not of great importance. When I confronted the various heaven-herds with the corresponding symbols used by their colleagues, they accepted one another's interpretations ·without hesitation. The typification of the symbols made sense to them.

It is quite clear that, in a society such as that of the Zulu, symbols appear relatively similar, though not necessarily identical. This also applies to details such as numbers and exact wording, for example the ten ingredients and the use of the singular form for medicine.

Indeed, examination of the three heaven-herds' ingredients revealed a relatively wide variety of materia used in the composition of the medicine, but an amazing similarity in thought-patterns and in what it was considered essential to symbolise.

Symbols and their use are based on the principle of association. Similar behaviour, things, sounds and colours are associated with each other in the sense that they are believed to act against each other. They are thought to be antagonistic *because* they are similar. The blackness of the medicine prepared by the heaven-herds is antagonistic to the anger of the sky, the white symbols typifying the white of lightning act against the white of lightning, the symbols depicting the sound of thunder are opposed to the sounds of a violent storm, the frown of the heaven-herd in attempting to avert a storm acts against the 'anger' of the sky.

But the reverse of the antagonistic association is also true. Because certain colours, actions and sounds are similar and therefore associated with each other, they are believed to produce the same effects. In this sense they are sympathetic. X, who produced a symbol for lightning by throwing one heavy boulder against another, said that the 27 times he had to pick up the heavy stone and throw it onto the other before he was satisfied with the result, was related to the strenuous task of controlling the anger of the sky. No medicine prepared without the symbols for lightning, the sound of thunder and the blackness of the clouds during a violent storm would be efficient.

Heaven-herds show two other interesting aspects of symbolism. There appear to be symbols of identity and symbols of 'convincing'. The heaven-bird appears to be a kind of identity with the sky, as is the python ('the animal of the sky') and the *umunka* stick. One of the heaven-herds went out of his way to emphasise how important it was that the crushed branch of *umunka* should be an ingredient, for 'if it is not in the medicine, the bird will surely take a human (*umuntu*). But if this branch is in the medicine the bird will not fetch anybody because there is already a man in the medicine.' One identifies, in a sense, oneself with the ultimate aim of the sky in sending the bird to the earth, i.e. 'to fetch somebody'.

I have used the term 'convincing' to describe a type of symbol because it was used by one of the heaven-herds (W). Asked to explain the usefulness of the feathers of the peacock in the preparation of medicine, he replied, 'A great man is only convinced (*ukuvumisa*) through food. Only when his favourite food has been placed before him is he convinced of what one is trying to get across to him. Whilst he eats the thing of his desire, you speak convincing him of the thing in your heart. You will speak until you have overcome [convinced] him (*uzokuluma uze umehlule*). That is what we do with this bird of his [the Lord-of-the-Sky's] desire. Whilst this is the bird of delicacy, the other things in the medicine are the one that convince (*ahlula*) him that what he is doing is bad. The ones that speak about evil are all the other things that are in the medicine. But the peacock convinces. Again, *umunka* is just giving him what he is looking for. That is what I mean when I say that the peacock is there to convince him.'

Harriet Sibisi

THE PLACE OF SPIRIT POSSESSION IN ZULU COSMOLOGY

Spirit possession among the Nguni-speaking peoples of South Africa is a subject that has received a great deal of attention in anthropological literature. Bryant (1949, 1970), Junod (1927), Sundkler (1961), Krige (1936), Hunter (1936), Kohler (1941), Loudon (1959, 1965), Hammond-Tooke (1962), Laubscher (1937), Lee (1969) and Marwick (1966) have all drawn attention to different facets of this social and religious phenomenon, and one wonders if there is anything more to be said. My contribution, therefore, will attempt to deepen our understanding of the subject by casting new light on the old ideas and underlining certain aspects.[1]

The meaning of spirit

I begin by giving a brief description of what the Zulu people described as 'old' or 'traditional' forms of spirit possession. To understand this we must first examine ideas regarding the supernatural world.

It is believed that the Supreme Being, or God (*uMvelingqangi*), lives up above (*ezulwini*) along with the Goddess often referred to as the 'Princess of the Sky' (*inkosazana yezulu*). The spirits of the deceased live down below, hence they are often referred to as 'those of below' (*abaphansi*). Both the deities who live above are remote and are rarely invoked. The ancestors are more concerned with the day-to-day lives of the living.

The 'world below' is thought of as divided into three sectors – that of the unborn spirits, that of the recently deceased spirits, and that of the ancestors. When a woman conceives, the biological event is said to be in conjunction with the entry of the spirit from the sector of the unborn. Each baby during the first year of its life has a sacrifice

[1] My first-hand contact with the ideas of spirit possession was mainly between 1963 and 1971, when I lived intermittently among the Nyuswa/Zulu of Botha's Hill in Natal.

(*imbeleko*) performed for it, whereby the baby is placed under the protection of the parents' ancestors. Through this sacrifice a child is given not only a social status[1] by being made a child of a definite set of parents, but also a ticket of passage which enables it to complete the cycle of life. What this means is that, if a child dies before the first sacrifice is performed, the spirit is said to return to the sector of the unborn. But, if sacrifice has been performed, the spirit will go through the processes that will enable it to join the body of ancestors. (For Swazi beliefs, see Marwick 1966: 232.)

The expectation, or rather the ideal, is that a person grows up to maturity, marries, has children and dies of old age. The deceased who has had the essential first sacrifice does not, however, join the body of ancestral spirits directly. Soon after death the spirit is said to be in a place of 'wilderness' (*endle*), 'in an in-between state' (*esithubeni*), and is believed to be lonely and unhappy. The period of isolation depends on the social status of the deceased: if married, about a year; if unmarried and adult, about six months; and if a baby or a child, about three months. During this period the chief mourner observes mourning behaviour. Ideally at the end of this period a sacrifice is performed to integrate the spirit with the rest of the ancestral spirits. This leads to the desired full status of spiritual being which empowers the spirit to bless or punish descendants.

The passage of the spirit from the world below to this world, and vice versa, is effected through married women. When a woman conceives, such a transference is made, and when death occurs the chief mourner is always a married woman, mourning the death of her husband, her children, her mother-in-law or her daughter-in-law. In this way she is associated with death in a special way: she can be said to be 'mother of birth and death'. However, as a wife and mother she is an outsider in her husband's lineage group, and in this position she is associated with spiritual beings that are powerless – the unborn spirit and the spirit of the recently deceased – both of which have not reached a completed spiritual state.

Traditional spirit possession

The spirits that are said to possess a diviner (*isangoma*) are not the unborn or the recently deceased, but they are those that have reached

[1] Through the first sacrifice an adoption of a child may be effected; e.g. an illegitimate child of a daughter is placed under the protection of her mother's ancestors. Such a child then becomes the child of its maternal grandparents and calls them mother and father while its biological mother becomes a sister.

the completed state of spiritual being. They return as ancestors to this world through their daughters (not through their wives, mothers or daughters-in-law). The diviner is possessed principally by the spirits of her own descent group, not her husband's. Divination is a woman's thing; if a man becomes possessed he becomes a transvestite, as he is playing the role of a daughter rather than that of a son. The special and very close contact with the spirits is reserved for women only. Women are marginal and can thus fulfil the important social role of forming a bridge between the two worlds.

During possession, the spirits are believed to 'ride' on the shoulders of the possessed and to speak or whisper to her. She hears voices and in this way receives her clairvoyant powers. As a diviner she avoids unclean situations and uses white symbols to emphasise her purity and her special association with the purity of the ancestral spirits.

Indiki possession

At the turn of the century a new type of possession was experienced in Natal and Zululand. This is known as *indiki*.[1] Bryant wrote about its outbreak in 1911 among the Zulu, and Junod reported the same thing among the Thonga in Moçambique in 1913. Both reported it as a new form of spirit possession. Today it is often regarded as a form of possession particularly associated with industrial workers.

The *indiki* is believed to be a spirit of a deceased person, a spirit which never underwent integration with the body of other spirits. People from countries outside South Africa who come to work in the mines may become *indiki* if they die in the country. Their families never know of their death and therefore perform none of the rituals necessary to place the spirit in its proper position in the spirit world. Such spirits in their desperation wander about and become a menace to the local people. They may possess them and cause illness. *Indiki* is therefore a male spirit (usually only one) who enters a person and resides in the chest. The person becomes deranged and manifests this by crying in a deep bellowing voice and speaking in a foreign language usually identified as one of the languages spoken by people in the north.

The treatment, which is always given by a diviner who was herself once possessed by *indiki*, involves a period of initiation into the spirit cult, of three months or less. During this period the treatment attempts to exorcise the alien spirit and replace it with the ancestral male spirit,

[1] The meaning of the term is not known. It is widely used in many language groups in southern Africa where the same type of possession occurs.

which would protect the patient from future attacks. The *indiki* initiate uses red emetics to eject the alien spirit, and white emetics to arouse her own spirit. Such emetics are used on alternate days during the whole period of initiation. In addition to red emetics the *indiki* initiate wears red symbols, such as a red wrapper around her waist or a red scarf (a red cap, for a man). Because her own ancestor is to be persuaded to possess her and supersede the alien spirit, she behaves like the traditional neophyte – she withdraws from society, observes various forms of abstinence, wears white strips of goat's skin across her chest, wears skin wristlets and inflated goat bladders, all of which are derived from sacrificial goats, slaughtered to induce possession by her male ancestor. In addition she sings, dances and works herself into ecstasy. The main difference between the *indiki* initiate and the traditional initiate is that the former attempts to arouse her spirit in order to regain her health, with no intention of becoming a fully-fledged diviner for the rest of her life. Her possession is consciously induced whereas the ancestors of the traditional neophyte choose to possess her even against her will. She is a 'chosen one', chosen by the good spirits for the benefit of society, while the *indiki* is primarily chosen by an alien which she views as a bad spirit and which must be superseded by the good ancestral spirit for her protection.

The treatment results in a spirit cult membership which gradually lapses with the passage of time or is strengthened by additional forms of accepted possession. If she belongs to an independent sect which practises an ecstatic type of worship, such an *indiki*[1] may promote powers of prophecy and healing; or she may be possessed in the traditional way by ancestral spirits and become a fully-fledged diviner who will have special ability in treating *indiki* patients.

Indiki has caused concern about the safety of infants in an environment made more dangerous by these alien spirits. This has given rise to a new method of treating newborn babies to protect them from the effects of such alien spirits. The treatment purports to arouse the baby's male ancestor (to raise *indiki* – *ukukhuphula indiki*) to take special care of it until it has passed through the dangerous stage of babyhood. Such treatment is performed only by diviners and not by ethno-doctors (*izinyanga*). The treatment, usually discontinued after a year or eighteen months, is known as *igobongo*, because the red and white medicines are prepared in two separate gourds (*amagobongo*). These emetics are used on alternate days.

[1] Even when the alien spirit – the *indiki* – is thrown out and replaced by an ancestral spirit, the patient is still referred to as *indiki*.

Ufufunyane,[1] *or izizwe possession*

Both Bryant and Junod wrote on the sudden spread of *indiki* possession, but made no mention of *ufufunyane*, which is another form of spirit possession. This suggests that *ufufunyane* is a much later concept and it is indeed usually associated with the late 1920s and 1930s. It is also said to have been introduced into South Africa by people who live to the north.

Whereas *indiki* is contracted by chance, *ufufunyane* is primarily due to sorcery, although chance is not ruled out as a secondary cause. A sorcerer is said to include soil from the various graves, and ants from the graveyard, in his harmful concoction. In this way the spirits of the dead are said to be captured and controlled by the sorcerer. The harmful concoction may be placed in the path of the victim, who becomes sick through contact with it.

A person with *ufufunyane* in its worst form usually appears mentally deranged. She becomes hysterical, weeps uncontrollably, throws herself on the ground, tears off her clothes, runs around in a frenzy and usually attempts to commit suicide. She reacts violently and aggressively to those who try to calm her. The patient is said to be possessed by a horde of spirits from different racial groups. Usually there may be thousands of Indians or whites, some hundreds of Sotho or Zulu spirits. The treatment may be given by any of the ethno-practitioners – either a diviner (*isangoma*) or ethno-doctor (*iyanga*). The treatment is calculated to force the spirits out of the patient. When such spirits have been exorcised they roam the countryside in small bands and may attach themselves to people who are not sufficiently fortified against them. This is chance possession and the attack is less violent, or may manifest itself in some form of neurosis or mental confusion.

Ufufunyane spirit possession does not lead to any cult membership. It does not give any diagnostic or healing powers. Some ethno-practitioners in treating *ufufunyane* install benign spirits. These are not the patient's ancestral spirits, but spirits controlled by the ethno-practitioner. They are referred to as the army (*amabutho*) installed to protect and defend the patient against malign spirits.

There is an ailment of babies connected with *ufufunyane* – malformation of the placenta, known as *ipleti* (a Zulu-ised form of the English word 'plate'). A normal placenta is said to be shaped like a clenched

[1] The dictionary translation of *ufufunyane* by Doke and Vilakazi is: 'Rapidly spreading disease which causes delirium and insanity; type of brain disease, mania, hysteria.'

fist while a malformed placenta is flat and has the circumference of a dinner plate. *Ipleti* is said to have affected babies born in the late 1930s and after. Many elderly women claim that only the children they had in that period had *ipleti*, while those born before then had normal placentae.

There are two ways in which *ipleti* is caused. Firstly, if the mother suffers from *ufufunyane* even in its mild form, her baby would be born with *ipleti*. Secondly, midwives bury such malformed placentae along the main pathways, and it is possible for a pregnant woman to step over one and catch the same condition.

In treating spirit possession certain symbolic medicines are used which are characterised by their colour – black, red or white. The power attributed to these medicines differs. Black and red stand equivocally for bad and good. Black, however, has more dangerous and bad attributes than good ones, while red is almost equally good and bad with some leaning towards goodness. White is unequivocally good – it stands for purity, life, peace and all things desired.

For this reason only white symbols (for example white emetics and frequent ablution with white medicines) are used by diviners to promote their state of purity, while red emetics are followed by white emetics for the *indiki* possessed. The red medicines are calculated to take out the alien spirit and strengthen the patient against future attacks, while the white medicines are used to regain good health. In the cases of the *ufufunyane* patients, or babies with malformed placentae (*ipleti*), black medicines are used to throw out the spirits or to correct the effects of the malformed placentae. Such black medicines are followed by white medicines to facilitate the return to good health.

Analysis

There are several things that we learn from this brief account. I will summarise them as follows:

The notion of evil brought about by spirit possession in the case of *indiki* or *ufufunyane* is conceptualised as violation of the principle of patriliny. A spirit that takes possession indiscriminately outside the patrilineal descent principle is thus regarded as evil. The evil is inherent not so much in the spirit itself but in confusing the categories. In other words spirits within their proper place have no evil connotations. They acquire these only when they intrude. The intrusion is dramatically emphasised by the very nature of possession, in that the alien spirit actually takes 'possession' of the patient by residing within and superseding the identity of the patient, who becomes a husk that houses a spirit speaking in its own voice from within her.

What is illuminating is that in social life the possession by such alien spirits is associated with the changing social circumstances.

For instance, let us consider *indiki* possession in a situation where the development of the mines necessitates the recruitment of miners from alien cultures north of South Africa. Such men come to work for long stretches of time without their families. The danger of intrusion into the family life of the indigenous peoples can be seen when relationships develop between such alien men and the wives, sisters and daughters of the Zulu men. Such unions constitute a threat to the stability of the society, not only because of differences in culture, but also because miners are likely to return to their homes when their contracts expire, leaving their Zulu wives and children behind. In this way an element of disorder is introduced. It is significant that in treating an *indiki* possession an endeavour is made to replace the alien spirit with a male ancestor. This suggests emphasis on the rejection of the alien male, and replacement with the native male. In other words this symbolises the desired pattern of behaviour.

Ufufunyane possession represents yet another dimension of social relations. As the industries flourished, the towns developed. This meant further intrusions of peoples from overseas – particularly after the depression in Europe following the first world war. With increasing mobility and intensifying migratory labour, contacts between peoples of various racial groups grew day by day. A Zulu became a threat to another Zulu as each competed for jobs, housing, land and economic security. The feeling of insecurity grew, and Indians and whites were seen as formidable forces bent on the disruption of the equilibrium of Zulu society. I suggest that the millions or thousands of spirits of various races that are believed to possess an *ufufunyane* sufferer and show their presence by violent aggression, hysteria or threat of suicide, indicate the social disorder which has led to many forms of social deprivation of the indigenous peoples in an unequal society.

There is a subtle discrimination in treatment which is significant. The traditional possession, which is good and desired, is promoted by white medication; the *indiki*, which is not so good, is treated with red and white symbols; and *ufufunyane*, which is thoroughly bad, is treated with black and white medication. The grading of the evil-spirit possessions signifies the intensity of the social malady which I suggest is represented by such evil-possession.

There is yet another important difference between traditional spirit possession and the new form of possession. In the former there are relatively few people who become diviners – indeed diviners have to go through a long-drawn-out process. Possession of this type is gradual. In the latter, however, possession is sudden and may even assume the form of an epidemic in a given area. The epidemic nature and the element of sudden attack strongly point to the association of new forms of possession with stresses and strains which may be experienced by people as a group at a particular point in time.

It would be naive to imagine that the possessed consider themselves as expressing the above sociological notions. The philosophers of the society have interpreted the manifestations of such deviant behaviour in a way that lends itself to sociological analysis. These are the diviners and ethno-doctors, whose function it is to understand the various types of illness, explain the new ones and find relevant treatment.

What has emerged in this presentation is that there are various levels of spirit possession. On the one hand there is the traditional, morally acceptable, spirit possession of the diviners (*izangoma*); on the other hand the evil, undesirable and unacceptable possession of the *ufufu-nyane* type. In addition to these there are the 'in-between' forms of possession which may begin as evil and be developed to be morally acceptable, those of the *indiki* type.

There is yet another form of possession which I have not men-tioned up to now, the temporary possession experienced by the faithful during worship in the Zionist or Pentecostal sects. Possession in this category is not as continuous as with other forms of possession. However, a prophet (or prophetess) in such a sect may be thought of as being in continuous contact with the Spirit, in which case his (or her) role is seen as more or less identical with that of a diviner.

It is important to distinguish between the various levels of posses-sion in order to understand the meaning of spirit possession. For instance the people possessed by good spirits often belong to the priestly class (diviners, prophets). Whereas in some societies the 'calling' to the priesthood is reserved for men, in other societies such a 'calling' is reserved for women. Looked at in this light such women (who are the diviners among the Zulu) are playing a role which is set for them by the society for its own benefit. They are not primarily looking for outlets in an unequal, male-dominated society, as is suggested by many anthropologists, for example Gluckman (1955), Hammond-Tooke (1962), and Lee (1969).

In attaining the status of a diviner, a candidate or neophyte goes through various phases of experience such as abstinence from various

pleasurable things (drinks, smoking, sexual intercourse, certain foods),
withdrawal from society, observance of silence, avoidance of unclean
situations such as contact with death, ecstatic singing and dancing. All
such ascetic abstinence is calculated to achieve a desired contact with
the sacred realm, a practice found in many religions in one way or
another, as part of a priestly behaviour pattern.

Possession by alien spirits (*ufufunyane*), diametrically opposed to
possession by ancestral spirits, can be linked with psychogenic
disorder, as Loudon (1965, 1959), Lee (1969) and Lewis (1971) point
out. This form of possession seems to be an aftermath of colonialism
related to intrusions by alien peoples into a culture or society as a
result of a higher degree of mobility in an industrial era.

However, I believe that Lewis's interpretation of this type of possession overstresses its relationship to the weak and the deprived. He
sees it mainly as a means used by the weak to gain certain favours from
the strong; such as in a wife/husband relationship where the spirit
possessing the wife may want a new dress or good food. Although this
may be true up to a point, it is nevertheless not the central explanation of
evil-possession by alien spirits. I see the notions of alien-spirit possession as closely related to the extreme form of depression or nervous
breakdown which may be coupled with hysteria and suicidal tendencies.

Depression of this nature is not only typical of peoples of Southern
Africa or East Africa, but the manner of handling various forms of
mental disturbance differs from society to society. In Britain, for
instance, it is reported that about two hundred babies are bashed to
death every year by their parents, and more are incapacitated for life.
Some of the parents courageous enough to appear on British television
tell a tale of extreme depression, hysteria and suicidal tendencies;
symptoms which in many ways match those of *ufufunyane* patients.
But in Britain more often than not, such people are expected to 'pull
themselves together' and 'cope with their lives' (sometimes with the
help of tranquillisers). The onus is usually on the depressive person
to try to cope in the first instance, and the appropriate treatment is
often given only when the condition is advanced – perhaps even as
far as the baby-bashing stage.

The Zulu handle such mentally disturbed people so that they do
not feel responsible for their condition; they are not made to feel that
anything is wrong with their minds, but merely that they are victims
of external forces – the intruding alien spirits – which must be removed.
The patient gets the support, sympathy and attention that depressed
people often long for.

Because *ufufunyane* patients, if provoked or annoyed, are believed to be susceptible to *ufufunyane* attacks after recovery, those around them must take special care to avoid situations that might make *ufufunyane* recur. Whisson (1964) reports the same notion among the Luo of East Africa, where the patient, although pronounced fit, is treated with respect and consideration lest the dreaded affliction recur.

If we accept that spirit possession of the *ufufunyane* type is symptomatic of various forms of extreme depression or nervous breakdown, such precautions become understandable, as people who have experienced such mental confusion become vulnerable in situations of stress and strain. They must exercise caution and avoid situations of anxiety or strenuous mental exertion.

What I am suggesting is that the notion of evil-spirit possession among the Zulu is used as an idiom to handle the escalating incidence of psychoneurosis[1] often associated with failure to cope with the changing way of life in colonial and post-colonial industrial society.

The diviners and ethno-doctors in interpreting such mental disturbances as *ufufunyane* or *indiki* do not only recognise them as derived from the social insecurity of a particular individual but also realise how the new disruptive social forces could threaten the very existence and continuity of Zulu society as a distinct entity. Hence prophylactic measures must be taken at a mystical level of treatment to reassure the people that their young are protected.

[1] The Zulu distinguish between different levels of mental disorder. For instance, a schizophrenic person is said to be mad (*uhlanya*) and not possessed by any spirits. An epileptic suffers from *isithuthwane*, an incurable condition. He is not possessed by the spirits. Some people may suffer from a form of hysteria, *umhayizo*, whereby they weep aloud uncontrollably and are not necessarily possessed, if they do not show other symptoms of mental confusion.

Colin Murray

SEX, SMOKING AND THE SHADES:
A SOTHO SYMBOLIC IDIOM

Introduction

An old Mosotho woman will approach a young boy, saying, 'Make me smoke,' or she calls him, 'Come, man, I want to smoke.' She touches his penis, holds her finger to her nose, sniffs vigorously and sneezes violently, exclaiming, 'Strong, this tobacco!' The exegesis of this is invariably *hohodisa ngwana*, making the child grow, so that his sex will be strong and vigorous. 'When a woman behaves in this way she is showing the child that tomorrow he will be a man, he should use his *kwae*, he should use it in the matter of life.'

Such behaviour is described by informants simply as a game, yet it nicely encapsulates two themes which recur in everyday observation of Sotho village life.[1] On the one hand, the common reference of the word for tobacco (*kwae*) to penis, such that there is a constant potential ambiguity in ordinary speech, and a metaphorical equivalence between smoking and the sexual act; on the other hand, by extension perhaps, the association of smoking – in particular the inhalation of snuff[2] – with the process of physical maturation. In my view the latter is one reflection of obligatory relations between senior kin and junior kin, relations which are maintained in perpetuity through the moral

[1] This material derives from a period of fieldwork amounting to eighteen months during 1972–4, spent in a village in northern Lesotho. My experience thus relates to a small area within the southern Sotho linguistic group, and for comparative convenience I use the 1959 Republic of South Africa orthography although this differs from the official orthography used in Lesotho. I wish to acknowledge generous financial support under the Anglo American Advanced Research Fellowship scheme. And I am grateful to Rick Huntington and to the editors for their comments on an earlier draft of this essay.

[2] A minor problem of translation recurs throughout the essay. The phrase *hotsuba kwae*, 'to smoke tobacco', is applied to taking snuff through the nose and taking it by mouth, as well as to pipe- and cigarette-smoking. It should be understood that 'smoking' here includes the inhalation of snuff through the nose and indeed, in the contexts I discuss, specifically connotes this technique.

authority of the shades. My interest in exploring these themes derives from what I take to be the two most important aspects of Monica Wilson's work on ritual and symbolism: the one substantive, her vivid illustration, above all among the Nyakyusa, of the connection between fertility and the shades – neatly summed up in the idiom 'the semen and the shade are brothers' (Wilson 1957: 205, 230; 1971: 31); the other methodological, the view which she forcibly expressed in the well-known quotation, 'any analysis not based on some translation of the symbols used by people of the culture is open to suspicion' (1957: 6). As a small tribute to a teacher whose inspiration and guidance I have always found sympathetic and constructive, this essay is an attempt to apply her methodological rigour to one of her favourite ethnographic themes. I do so in a cultural context in which I found virtually no articulation of an explicit association between sex and the shades.[1] It follows that the 'problem' of the essay – one which recurs in Monica Wilson's writing – is the question of how the anthropologist may set about interpretation beyond indigenous exegesis. Few would quarrel with her insistence that 'The symbolism of another society must be translated systematically not guessed at' (1971b: 54).

Ancestors depend on their living descendants for recognition, while the living depend on their ancestors for their very existence. Control of procreative power is thus a fundamental concern in societies where the dead retain their moral authority over the living. The philosophical aspect of this 'ineluctable' interdependence has been beautifully analysed by Fortes (1961); while the material aspect, in my view, is vividly illuminated in Monica Wilson's work. Ancestors, or shades in her usage, are crucially incorporated in the world of the living not simply as a reflection of belief in a system of morality; they are also significant protagonists in the action contexts of everyday life. The richness of Wilson's data reveals the pragmatic importance of maintaining proper relations with the shades. Their concerns are earthy and intimate: they are present, for example, in every sexual act (Wilson 1957: 112–13); and Nyakyusa ritual endeavours to achieve a separation from the dangerous contagion of their 'filth'.

My specific stimulus for this essay was her Nyakyusa work which led me to seek a connection between sex and the shades among the Sotho. Precisely because the connection was intuitive and because

---

[1] When pressed on the matter, informants typically respond, with mild surprise since it is self-evident, that *Modimo* (God) and the *badimo* (shades) are present in everything a person does. Conception of a child, as any successful enterprise, thus depends on their goodwill, but I have not been able to record more specific statements.

comparably rich exegesis was not available to me, it seemed essential to apply her own methodological prescription: to be sceptical of any interpretation which did not have some support from indigenous statement. The symbolism of tobacco was, on the face of it, an unlikely mediator. Yet the strength of the case seems to me to lie in the fact that the evidence is neither esoteric nor confined to ritual specialists; indeed I would argue that the association through tobacco operates at what Wilson would describe as the 'less conscious' (1971*b*: 54) level precisely because of the pervasive triviality of its manifestations in Sotho culture. The generality and repetition of, for instance, the grandmother's game make it irrelevant for Basotho to articulate elaborate rationalisation of it. As Mary Douglas has remarked (1968 and *passim*), the categories of everyday experience may reveal underlying symbolic ideas of association and manipulation. And categories of thought which remain implicit for the actors must be made explicit by the anthropologist if he is to do justice to the problem of translation.

Evidence

Attempts to establish the meanings of *kwae* elicit three answers: firstly tobacco; secondly the sheep slaughtered when a bride first arrives at her husband's home; thirdly the *hlonepho* (respect) alternative for penis. If only for reasons of modesty the informant usually responds with the order given here, but for convenience in developing the argument I shall discuss them in reverse order.

By way of greeting, a Mosotho male will often say, 'Please give me tobacco,' an innocent request in most circumstances. If the other is feeling ungenerous, however, a suitable retort is 'Which? I've got only one.' This is baffling to the outsider until he appreciates the dual reference of *kwae* to tobacco and penis. A woman who greeted a man similarly, in a context where cross-sexual joking was at all inappropriate, may be considered grossly forward, because a woman should not initiate a sexual advance. Nevertheless I have seen women behave explicitly when drunk in male company, by taking a pinch of snuff and shoving it up their nostrils in deliberate suggestion of the sex act. One of my neighbours told me that the request 'Make me smoke' may be used between consenting adults to conceal a sexual arrangement from children. '*Kwae* is a thing smoked in the night by women'; '*kwae* of below there [the genital region] is smoked only by women.' While '*kwae* is for a woman what the breast is for a man' vividly expresses the complementarity of the sexes. *Kwae* is not alone in carrying the double referent. The word *koma*, diminutive *komana*, means snuff container, usually a small round tin nowadays but traditionally an animal horn. *Koma* also refers to penis.

When asked to explain the reference of *kwae* to the male sex organ, people will first point out that the use of the proper word (*ntotwane*) is taboo, so another name is necessary. And there are respect alternatives for many words. As an explanation, however, this evades the issue, which is why the word for tobacco *is* applied, not why the word for penis is *not* applied. The most common positive response, as informants grope for self-enlightenment, is to describe the behaviour of an elderly woman in terms that I have quoted in the first paragraph of this essay, where she comments on the 'fierce' quality of a male child's sexual parts by analogy with the effects of inhaling snuff, and thereby is said positively to enhance his potential procreative vigour. 'She shows the child that *kwae* [his penis] is very important *moithimolo* which opens up the nerves of his head.' *Moithimolo* is a medicine for curing the head which is inhaled through the nose; the word itself is from the root -*thimola*, (to) sneeze. In this way an old woman matures a child by 'smoking' him. The association between sex and smoking, then, is often made at an informal conversational level and is implicit, as an expression and instrument of morality, in the grandmother's game. In the following section I argue that one marriage custom shows that the association is also made at a formal level.

Marriage in Lesotho traditionally requires elaborate negotiations between the families of the boy and girl. Bridewealth payments are reckoned in cattle, although under modern conditions they are paid predominantly in cash, and may be spread over many years. Elopement is a common procedure nowadays, either in default of bridewealth payments or as a recourse to speed up negotiations. But whether a girl is 'properly' married or she elopes, one custom is still strictly adhered to. When the girl first arrives at her husband's home his people should slaughter a sheep for her. This animal[1] is called *kwae* and it is said, 'They give her *kwae*.' Prior to this the girl cannot eat any food of her husband's household nor take part in any of its domestic activities.

[1] Sekese (1970: 7) records this animal as a goat, likewise Ellenberger and Macgregor (1969: 276) who appear to be quoting him. Laydevant (1952: 67) suggests the offering is a goat and a sheep while the standard dictionary (Mabille and Dieterlen 1961) defines *kwae* in this context as 'goat'. Ashton (1952: 74) says sheep. My informants invariably quoted sheep as 'customary', and the three animals of *kwae* I have seen killed were all sheep. The discrepancy may reflect differences in clan custom but I think a change of custom over time more probable: owing to the increased scarcity value of mohair, a sheep is used nowadays instead of a goat.

I have observed this ceremony on two occasions. On the first, the boy had simply eloped one night with a girl from a village three miles away; her mother arrived the following day in furious disapproval of the match but she had to accept it as a *fait accompli*, for the girl insisted on staying. On the second, involving two neighbouring families in the village, an initial payment of six cattle was amicably transferred about a week before the girl was taken by her betrothed to his home. Events in both cases were very similar. A sheep was slaughtered the morning after the girl's arrival, and she sat the whole day behind the door of the hut in an attitude of demure shyness, eyes cast down and not speaking to anyone. In the evening adolescent boys and girls of the village took some of the meat of the slaughtered sheep and tried in vain to force each other to eat, a scene of hilarity and confusion in which all their faces were smeared and in which the new daughter-in-law maintained her posture of studied humility. Informants differed as to whether she herself could eat the meat. Against one opinion that in the old days she would have done so, two articulate neighbours argued, independently, that the girl refuses the meat of the animal called *kwae* precisely because she is now entitled to the *kwae* of her husband, she will be satisfied with that. This interpretation was also offered me by several other people, and it remains the only positive explanation I heard of why the sheep slaughtered on this occasion is called *kwae*.[1] In the past, according to some writers, the couple did not immediately engage in sexual relations, but waited a few days until the bride signified she was ready by placing a pot of water in her husband's hut (Laydevant 1952: 67; Ellenberger and Macgregor 1969: 277); but in my own experience, from statements on the matter both explicit and implicit, people assume that whether or not the couple have been covertly sleeping together beforehand, they will start doing so 'officially' as soon as *kwae* has been slaughtered. Ashton observes similarly, 'Nowadays, the couple usually sleep together immediately after the *kwae* rite' (1952: 75).

There is no doubt as to the general significance of *kwae* in this context. Informants were unanimous that 'giving her *kwae*' signifies acceptance of the new wife into her husband's family. The girl is now able to eat any food of the husband's household, can use its domestic utensils and will assume appropriate duties such as cooking and drawing water. Above all she assumes the status of married woman,

[1] Fr. Larour of Roma Mission hospital told me that he had heard the animal is called *kwae* by analogy with a medicine given to fowls, also called *kwae*, to prevent them wandering from the homestead.

manifest in the formal initiation of sex relations and in her donning the long skirt and head cloth typical of that status. The transition to full womanhood is a protracted process, however, and is fully achieved only by the formal presentation to her, often on the birth of a first child, of some sheep's intestine, which, like eggs, is taboo to an unmarried girl.

The transfer of ten head of cattle effectively establishes filiation of the children to the husband's family. In acknowledgement of these cattle the father of the woman should slaughter an ox and the sheep of 'agreement' for the man's father, and a feast is held at the former's home. It is also customary for him to slaughter the sheep of *kwae* reciprocally for his son-in-law when the latter arrives formally at his father-in-law's home. Perhaps this is to mark the persistence of amicable relations between the husband and wife, of which one aspect is the fulfilment of their sexual obligations. But the point I wish to make here is only that this sheep of *kwae*, slaughtered for the husband, is clearly distinguished in concept and practice from both the ox and the sheep of 'agreement' slaughtered for his father. On the two occasions when I have seen all three animals killed, the husband arrived after his father's representatives had departed, and the killing of *kwae* was conditional upon his independent arrival. Some people insisted that the husband's party and his father's party should not meet at all, although they are travelling from and to the same places. This seems to underline the point that the killing of *kwae* has little to do with the relationship of affinity between the two families; it has quite specifically to do with sex relations between the husband and wife.

I hope to have established, then, a kind of metaphorical identification between sex and smoking. *Kwae* is used as an idiom for the expression of sex relations between men and women: at an informal level, in the sense of the verbal games and gestures which are part of the vocabulary of everyday interaction; and at a formal level, in the sense that the killing of *kwae* is the official receipt of the bride by her husband's people, which marks the legitimacy of sex relations between the couple independently of the protracted series of bridewealth payments which will ultimately establish the paternal filiation of any children they may produce.

I now turn to the 'primary' meaning of *kwae* – tobacco. Nowadays *kwae* is used to refer to all kinds of tobacco, as smoked in a pipe and cigarettes as well as snuff. Before the introduction of 'European' methods of smoking, however, it referred to *Nicotiana rustica*, the

leaves of which were dried, ground and inhaled like snuff, or were
baked in small cakes when still green. Informants say that on any
occasion on which the shades (*badimo*) were honoured this *kwae* was
prepared and distributed to the people attending. It was expected that
even people who were not used to it would accept a pinch and give a few
token sneezes. Interpretation of this is variable. One comment made
it clear that this was explicitly to invoke the shades: 'You pray to the
shades by smoking through the nose'; another: the people '. . . are
given this tobacco of the shades, they smoke it . . . it is the prayer they
make together, they pray to the shades through that'. More generally
however the presentation of tobacco at a 'feast of *badimo*' is merely a
communal gesture to 'make the shades happy' in the same way that
the meat or beer or other food that the owner of the feast has cooked
for the shades makes them happy. In justification people explain that
their 'grandfathers and grandmothers' were very partial to tobacco.
The technique of inhaling snuff through the nose and the result –
violent sneezing[1] – approximate most closely to a 'proper Sesotho'
style of smoking and can therefore be assumed best to please the
shades. 'Smoking and sneezing . . . it is the same thing in the work of
the shades.' It is simply for this reason that snuff, which substitutes for
the traditional tobacco and is bought from the stores, is often described as 'tobacco of the shades'.

Many Basotho, of course, smoke simply for pleasure. The symbolic
significance is contextual. Thus informants readily admit that some
people just smoke because they enjoy it, while others are made to
smoke through being sick. It is the latter category that interests me
here, for the sickness they experience is often cured by the shades in a
mystical idiom – dreams. As I have indicated, the stimulating effects of
pipe- and cigarette-smoking are recognised but the shades only
prescribe snuff – 'tobacco of the shades'. In the field I could not help
being impressed by the frequency of the response, 'It was the shades
who told me to smoke . . .'; almost invariably the informant had been
sick, and was cured by inhaling snuff on medical advice direct from
the shades. Basotho also smoke *matekwane* (*Cannabis sativa*),[2] but
although its effects are well known this too is specifically distinguished

[1] It may be objected that habitual inhalers of snuff need not sneeze. But Basotho
commonly mix with their snuff the ground roots of certain plants, which are known to
strengthen it and cause sneezing in themselves. Examples are *motabo* (various species
of the genus *Senecio*) and *leshokgwana* (*Pachycarpus rigidus*).

[2] The seeds of cannabis are used, *inter alia*, in a recipe for weaning a child. I have
heard it referred to as *koma ya Barwa*, 'Bushmen's tobacco'. The word *kwae* may also
be of San origin.

from 'tobacco of the shades' and has no significance in the contexts I discuss below.

A common answer to the question 'Why do you smoke?', particularly from those who inhale snuff, is simply 'My head . . .' Amplifying, people explain that snuff clears one's head, so that one's wits work well. A neighbour elaborated on this point: 'Men are used to smoking through the mouth, because there is confusion . . . now when a man smokes he puts his family affairs in order, he will know where he is going.' Whereas 'a woman habitually smokes through the nose, so that she can put her mind to grinding . . .' or other domestic task without distraction. The implication that inhaling through the nose is a sex-linked habit is clearly supported by a statistical survey of smoking techniques in the village. Taking snuff by mouth is said to be a much less efficient stimulant than through the nose, so that it is primarily women who use it to relieve illness, as is clear from the following examples taken at random from my field notes.

Often snuff is indispensable for steadying the nerves. One of my best informants, accompanying me to hospital with her daughter-in-law, who had been stabbed with a knife, was very upset at the incident, and between gasps of emotion kept demanding snuff to calm herself down. Another woman claimed that since childhood any loud noise, such as a radio or gramophone at full volume, induced heart palpitations which could only be relieved by taking snuff, on the advice of her grandmother who had been alive at the time. The pattern is more common, however, in which such advice is given by one's senior kin after death, in other words they reveal their instructions in dreams. A neighbour of mine had been suddenly attacked by a sickness which defeated the doctors, who told her not to smoke under any circumstances. One night, however, her father's mother came to her in a dream and told her to take snuff. Thenceforth she was cured. Another woman started suffering severe pains in her head in 1963; two years later she dreamed of her father's father's mother and her husband's father's mother, who told her to take snuff so that she would recover. She did so, and now inhales snuff continuously; she claimed that, if she stopped at any time, the following morning she could be prostrate from the pain in her head.

Inhaling snuff provides effective relief from such tensions through inducing sneezing which clears the head, hence its widespread use in many parts of the world. What concerns me here, more particularly, is the Sotho cultural idiom in which symptoms of this sort may be relieved by the application of kwae on the advice of the shades; while more serious or persistent symptoms are readily attributed to mystical affliction *by* the shades – typically, a person is 'gripped' by *moya wa badimo*, spirit of the shades. The word *moya* is current in Sotho and other southern African Bantu languages to mean air, wind, breath, spirit. It has been adopted in Christian terminology to refer to Holy Spirit—Sotho *moya ohalalelang* – but traditionally it applies to the mystical influence of the shades. Affliction by *moya* is manifest in a variety of ways: fainting fits, bad dreams, prostration, abrupt and noisy belching, accompanied by spontaneous shuddering of the head and often of the whole body. The symptoms may occur sporadically; but often they are persistent, and the sufferer either will consult a doctor to discover the reason for the affliction through the divining-bones or will receive a set of instructions in dreams directly from the shades. They appear simply as *badimo bah'eso*, 'the shades of our family', but when pressed by the anthropologist the afflicted person will usually be able to identify one or several individuals responsible, parent(s) or grandparent(s) on the paternal or maternal side.[1] In either case – through divination or dream-revelation – it is established that the person is suffering from *moya*, and must undertake a prolonged curing ritual to initiate him into the company of *bakoma*.[2] I discuss this ritual more fully below. Meanwhile the important point is that there are symptoms of affliction which, if slight, may be relieved by *kwae* and, if persistent, require an elaborate public ritual of accommodation.

Basotho doctors may practise only as herbalists; more often they claim knowledge of herbs and divination, partly through instruction from another doctor, partly through revelation from the shades. Some doctors are also *bakoma*, in other words they have passed through the ritual referred to above to cure mystical affliction. I have not met a male *mokoma* who does not also claim to be a doctor; on the other

[1] Sotho shades are less discriminating than Nguni shades who only appear to their patrilineal descendants. Another difference between Nguni and Sotho shades is relevant in the context of a specific association with sexual activity. I have never heard Basotho refer to a shade in the singular except in the well-known injunction *modimo omotjha rapela wa kgale'* – inadequately rendered as 'New god pray to the Old' – which draws attention to the intercessionary role of the recently dead and, possibly, of elderly people while still alive. Otherwise the plural *badimo* is invariably used in ordinary speech, by contrast with the word for God, *Modimo*, which belongs to the second noun-class, cf. Setiloane (1973: 6–7). For a wider discussion of the signifiance of the roots for 'elder-hood' and of noun-classes in Bantu languages for understanding relations between the living and the dead, see Kopytoff (1971) and Brain (1973).

[2] Also known as *mathuela*. This ritual is not indigenous to Sotho culture but intrusive from Nguni. For full descriptions see Hunter (1936: 321–35) and Ashton (1943: 28–32) for Mpondo and Sotho respectively.

hand, the vast majority of *bakoma* are women, and only a few of these become doctors. Apart from chieftainship, the profession of medicine is the only sphere of traditional male prestige which remains viable today, and is certainly the most lucrative activity in rural Lesotho. Its boundaries are well guarded, and it requires exceptional divination skills for women to break the unwritten union rules for protection of male privilege and be recognised as doctors. Doctors in Lesotho are classified not by technique but by reputation. Thus, while the capacity to divine by revelation from the shades is a claim potentially made by all *bakoma*, they must pass the informal and frequently severe test of public opinion,[1] and registration and permission to practise are controlled by an official (all-male) body in Maseru. In practice, then, those who go through I. M. Lewis's (1971) 'primary' phase of possession – affliction – are mainly women; those who proceed to the 'secondary' phase – in which the experience of the *bokoma* ritual is exploited to cure those likewise afflicted – are almost all men. This sexual divergence has implications which will be developed later.

Effective divination requires communion with the shades. One very common method of achieving this communion is through *kwae*. Almost all male doctors use the bones for divination; many either inhale snuff immediately before throwing the bones or sprinkle a few pinches on the ground for the shades, to 'open up their heads'. Female diviners rarely use the bones – of those I have consulted, one uses eggs, one uses a candle with pinches of snuff, and a third uses snuff alone. This last seemed to me the only convincing performer in a public divining-session arranged by the chief to discover the whereabouts of a boy lost from initiation school. Her quiet confidence contrasted with the brashly competitive assertions of the men. She was not given the job of finding the boy, which reflects the tight male hold on the

---

[1] *Bakoma* are, in general, not very prestigious. Some are clearly regarded as frauds. One classification of doctors is the following, with the academic labels given me, ironically, by a sophisticated teacher:

– *nkgokgo kgerenkgwa* (Ph.D.): specialist in *mehlabelo*, black and red protective medicines kept in a horn and essential, for example, in initiation; formerly employed as a sort of Public Health authority; otherwise the term is simply applied to an expert doctor.

– *ngaka tjhitja* (M.A.): 'hornless' doctor, one who uses herbs and roots (*ditlhare*) and may divine but learns all his skills through apprenticeship to another doctor.

– *bakoma:* some become doctors (B.A.), many do not; specialists in divination who claim their knowledge through revelation from the shades rather than by instruction from another.

– *ngakana-ke-a-hetla* ('A' levels): uses herbs and roots only; a bit of a charlatan.

But these categories are by no means rigid. Some doctors claim knowledge of *mehlabelo* and *ditlhare* as well as having passed through *bokoma*.

profession. But what I am concerned with here is not the actual techniques of divination, nor its use in social situations, but the way in which it is regarded as a form of communication between the diviner and his shades, communication which is expressly and repetitively established by the use of *kwae* in dream-prescribed ways.

Let me sum up the ethnographic evidence presented so far. In my experience the word *kwae* has a triple referent for most Basotho:

(1) tobacco, and *kwae ya badimo*, 'tobacco of the shades', refers to snuff in particular;

(2) the sheep slaughtered to mark the acceptance of a daughter-in law into her husband's family and, by implication, the formal start of sex relations between the couple;

(3) the *hlonepho* (respect) word for the male sex organ (since the proper word *ntotwane* is taboo, *kwae* is that most commonly used in ordinary speech).

The idiom of 'smoking' – inhaling snuff in particular – is used in the following contexts, in addition to the simple object of smoking for its own sake:

(1) as a colloquialism for referring to the sexual act;

(2) *hohodisa ngwana*, as a 'game' in which an elderly woman matures a young boy towards virile manhood by 'smoking' him;

(3) at a 'feast of *badimo*', where smoking represents a communal invocation of the shades' blessing;

(4) to relieve nervous and other tensions, to dispel 'confusion in the head' and to generate mental clarity;

(5) as an aid in the technique of divination, to help establish communion with the shades.

Analysis

In order to grasp the substantive links between the three meanings of *kwae* in the several contexts I have outlined, it is necessary to explore what Victor Turner has called the 'positional' approach (Turner 1967: 50 and *passim*) – the relation of one symbol to other symbols used in the same ritual complex – an approach which is implicitly characteristic of analyses in the 'structuralist' style. In addition to the material based on exegesis and observation which I have presented above, the question arises: what else is used as an idiom of communication with the shades? In answering this it will be useful to develop a distinction between a 'feast of *badimo*' and a 'feast of *bakoma*'. Since both are expressions of communion between living and dead, the distinction may at first appear paradoxical. But it is clearly made by Basotho in terms of the aims of this communion, for the focus of the former ritual is departed kin, the focus of the latter ritual is an afflicted individual. At an abstract level, what Basotho refer to as a 'feast of *badimo*' involves controlled communication with the dead initiated by the living; while a 'feast of *bakoma*' involves uncontrolled communication with the living initiated by the dead. I argue that in both rituals the symbolism of *kwae* has its instrumental analogues, and some detailed though selective discussion of the *bokoma* treatment will help to establish the point.

An offering of *kwae* is a traditional element in a 'feast of *badimo*', as a prayer to invoke their sympathetic interest in family affairs. The ritual occasions relating to the shades are several: they include the feast simply for 'giving food to the shades'; the feast of 'accompanying' the dead or of concluding the mourning period; the 'cleansing' of a widow or orphan from death pollution; and 'holding a person by the hands' – a ritual to rid an individual of misfortune or illness caused by the anger of the shades. Laydevant (1952) would extend the list considerably.

But it is not easy to define without ambiguity what is and what is not a concern of the shades, for there may be little or no formal recognition of them, in word or action, by the participants. Nevertheless, on occasions when animals are slaughtered, the simplest practical criterion for the observer to adopt is whether or not the gall-bladder of the animal is placed behind the household pots on the raised shelf at the back of the hut. This action is an explicit setting aside of the gall for the shades, and it is often interpreted as a prayer in response to which the shades give peace and good luck. On other occasions the gall-bladder is simply thrown away and it may safely be inferred that the shades are not explicitly involved. The term 'prayer' is used loosely. There need be no formal invocation, and the word may be applied simply to physical actions such as the communal inhalation of snuff, or placing the gall-bladder behind the pots; even to the men's dance which invariably accompanies a gathering where much beer is available. This dance often reaches a level of excitement unparalleled in mundane activity, and may include an element of sexual confrontation between the dancing men and the watching, ululating women. It also involves the stylised recitation of 'praises' of senior chiefs and other prominent figures of the past. These praises are in themselves an invocation of the shades. Thus the significance of the men's dance may be interpreted in diverse ways by the actors themselves, from the profane – 'we are just drunk/happy' – to the sacred – 'it is a prayer'.

This example shows that any classification must allow for latitude
and idiosyncracy in the interpretations of informants. It is enough
here, however, to stress that the single occasion which is invariably
and unequivocally defined by Basotho as a 'feast of *badimo*' is a
spontaneous feast given to the shades to request luck in the future or
to give thanks for luck in the past. Slaughter of an animal is not
essential – one's obligations may be minimally performed with an
ordinary meal – but the shades, like their living descendants, are
particularly fond of meat and will respond the more readily if it is
available. The customary requirements common to a 'proper Sesotho'
method of propitiating the shades are, then, a cow or sheep, sorghum
beer and the distribution of *kwae*. A cow and a sheep are equivalent
for ritual efficacy, although not of course in economic value. The use
of a sheep is justified simply on 'customary' grounds, with perhaps a
little exegesis to the effect that a sheep is silent, therefore any trouble
will likewise be silent and go away, or (of the feast for concluding the
mourning period) 'we have been crying, now when the sheep is
slaughtered it is silent, and so we leave off crying too'.[1] An animal
slaughtered for the shades is seen as instrumental in obtaining their
goodwill, but there are no flesh offerings, it is merely understood that
'we are making them happy' by cooking food for them. As someone
put it, 'I have no way of talking to the shades except by giving them
food.' The presentation of *kwae* on these occasions should be understood in the same light.

The *bokoma* ritual in which a person is cured of mystical affliction
is a very different matter. A goat *must* be used. *Bakoma* initiates
cannot eat mutton, for it is said to 'choke' the head, whereas a goat
is their 'torch', it 'opens up' knowledge, it is 'white' in the sense that
the shades require, for 'the things of the shades are glittering white'.
'There is no whiteness like that of a goat', while a sheep is the epitome
of murk. The symbolic difference between them is the more striking
since sheep and goats are lumped together as 'small stock' for bridewealth and everyday economic purposes. It is the principal index
of the indigenous distinction between a 'feast of *badimo*' and a 'feast
of *bakoma*' – in the former sheep and *kwae* are appropriate, in the
latter goat and the frothy *sethoto* medicine are appropriate. The
substantive symbolic relation between *kwae* and *sethoto* I discuss in
more detail below. Meanwhile there are other correlates of the

[1] By contrast, the Matabele (a label used by Basotho for people of Nguni origin)
prefer a goat in offerings to the shades precisely because it does cry out when slaughtered,
cf. Hunter (1936: 249), Wilson (1969: 127).

distinction which I would summarise as follows: on the one hand (feast of *badimo*) men, the owners of family affairs (never women, for the shades 'fit' their patrilineal context), choose an occasion on which to supplicate their senior kin, the shades, by the offering of 'food' (cow, sheep, beer, tobacco) in expectation of reciprocal goodwill; on the other hand (feast of *bakoma*) the shades manifest themselves by unpredictable mystical affliction of women, rarely of men,[1] generating 'confusion' or 'madness' which can be 'tamed' only by the prescribed manipulation of a goat and *sethoto* medicine to 'open up' the afflicted person.

Although I have emphasised the apparently capricious and unpredictable nature of mystical affliction, the ritual to 'tame' the offending *mòya* is a standard cultural response. A doctor is appointed to administer the instructions of the sufferer's shades, the most important of which is 'churning (medicine) for' the afflicted person. In addition a white goat is slaughtered; the patient is told to wear white beads – 'whiteness' is often stressed as necessary for effective communion with the shades; and there are prolonged sessions of 'singing for' the patient by other *bakoma* who have already passed through the ritual. Other details may vary according to the dream-prescriptions of the shades, but the essential elements are the goat and the frothy mixture (*sethoto*) which is used in the 'churning'.

The afflicted person is usually instructed in a dream to go and dig certain medicines, which are mixed together with water to make a solution called *sethoto*. When vigorously stirred, this produces an effervescent froth. Either the patient is made to drink this froth or his body is smeared with it, or both; and this is said to enable him to divine lost objects. Indeed his 'vision' will be tested by other *bakoma*, who hide a bowl, money, or, in one case I recorded a white chicken (but any miscellaneous object will do), and instruct the patient to reveal its whereabouts. It is the *sethoto* which gives him this 'vision' –

[1] The argument here is consistent with Lewis's (1971) distinction between central (morality) and marginal (possession) cults. The statistical preponderance of women in the *bokoma* ritual has been noted by Ashton (1943: 32) and in the Nguni equivalent *ukuthwasa* ritual by Hunter (1936: 320), cf. also Lewis (1971: 125–6). These are examples of his 'primary' phase of possession: he argues that this applies typically to subordinate or marginal categories of people of which women are the most obvious and widespread example in the literature. In my view, however, the association of possession with the female conceptual role, in the Sotho context at least, presents a problem of explanation more complex than Lewis's functionalist model allows for. It also has a contagious aspect which must be viewed in the historical perspective of the *Difaqane* and its aftermath, cf. the general argument relating to the incidence of possession put forward by Beattie and Middleton (1969). I hope to explore these issues elsewhere.

essentially a capacity to receive clearly and interpret messages from the shades. There is a variety of recipes for *sethoto*: most involve the mixing of 'white' medicines, the symbolism of which is associated with the shades, and 'red' medicines, for seeing over a great distance.[1] A common mixture is the red *mabone* (*Galium capense, Mesembry-anthemum* spp.) with the white *hlokwana-la-tsela*.[2] The latter is generally known as a medicine for 'luck' and, more pertinent to my present theme, is also used to induce vomiting of thick and slimy saliva, or the discharge of clogging matter. Its use in *sethoto* is said to cause belching and in this way to clear the chest, just as *kwae* induces sneezing and clears the head. The details of another recipe were given me by a sophisticated doctor who habitually divines with *sethoto*. Two principal ingredients are mixed together: *maloleka* (*Myrica aethiopica*), which is also known as 'big tobacco of the shades'; and *pohotshehla*, which is 'white' and is said to produce violent sneezing.[3] The mixture is churned into the required froth and infused up the nose, and it expels the 'confusion' in the head.

In both these examples there is an evident parallel between snuff and *sethoto*. Sometimes, indeed, they may be used together. One young mother who had been troubled by her shades was called by the doctor in charge to spend a night's vigil in his hut while two *bakoma* danced for her in a rondavel next door. Before her he had placed a bowl of red *sethoto* and a bowl of white *sethoto*, surrounded by four candles, and then he sprinkled pinches of snuff on the floor in a circle round the bowls. Normally a friendly informant, the doctor was obviously discomfited by my presence and questioning at that time, and explained that the woman should be left alone in silent communion with the *sethoto*, for 'it speaks to her so that she might hear well what the shades have to say'. The following day they would return to the patient's home and slaughter a white goat, and she would be smeared with the *sethoto*. Informants were unanimous that it is *sethoto* which really helps a person to divine well: '*sethoto* removes misfortune from you, it directs good luck . . . it induces your medita-tions so that they work well . . .'. But *sethoto* is also used to tame the throes of inspiration. One elderly doctor I knew, after a long and tiring

[1] Black, white and red symbolism are all-important in Sotho medicine and initiation.

[2] In general I have followed Jacot Guillarmod's invaluable reference work (1971) for plant identifications. She identifies *hlokwana-la-tsela* as *Polygala* spp., whereas Tau (1972: 16) identifies it as *Dianthus scaber*. This is probably due to local differences in the Sotho names of plants, cf. Tau (1972: 14).

[3] Both *pohotshehla* and *leshokgwana* are identified as *Pachycarpus rigidus* and clearly have similar effects, cf. Ashton (1943: 17, 21).

divination seance, stirred up the effervescent froth, knelt and sucked it, spat three times around the bowl and then smeared the top of his head with white daubs of *sethoto* in the form of a cross, which I observed later left a red residue. He did this, he explained to me, to suppress *moya*, which was strong in him, which he had invoked to help him to divine. And he emphasised that it was the mixture that was important, not the red or white medicines on their own. In some sense, then, *sethoto* both initiates and controls the quality of illumination which enables the doctor to divine. It is clearly regarded as a very effective means of communion with the shades. *Kwae* is accepted as inferior to *sethoto* in this respect, but it has analogous effects.

Let me sum up the argument at this point. 'When the shades begin to trouble you, you become ill without knowing what is eating you. . . .' '*Moya* . . . is sickness, an affliction, a gift of the shades, knowledge of medicines.' It is 'madness'. The purpose of the curing ritual is not to exorcise the afflicting spirit, for in other contexts the shades are important moral agents, but to domesticate it, to come to terms with affliction in a way that enables the patient to participate in future rituals of the same sort. The shades manifest their closeness through a dangerous 'madness' which, through the ritual, is transferred into clarity of communion with them. The shades are held at arm's length, as it were, but in a special relationship: close but not too close. In the *bokoma* context the agent of transformation is above all *sethoto*. But in two contexts of lesser stress *kwae* is typically used: in the more ordinary context of sporadic or incipient affliction (the examples I have recorded are all of women) where the *bokoma* ritual is not necessary, inhaling *kwae* on instruction from the shades relieves tension or pain in the head or the heart; and in the more advanced context of divination – Lewis's (1971) 'secondary' phase of possession in which the experience of affliction is turned to practical advantage in curing those similarly afflicted – many doctors (of whom the large majority are men) use *kwae* to help them commune with the shades, through inhaling it or sprinkling it on the ground.

Sethoto, then, is the agent of transformation which turns 'madness' to 'vision' and establishes the special relationship with the shades that is characteristic of *bakoma*; *kwae* is the catalyst which may repetitively relieve mundane affliction, in the case of individuals who are not sufficiently ill to require *bokoma* treatment, or, in the case of practising diviners, may 'switch on' their capacity to see clearly. The metaphorical idiom is the same: both *sethoto* and *kwae* 'open up the nerves' to promote mental receptivity, and as regards one method at least of the application of *sethoto* – the ingestion of the potent substance through the nose to induce sneezing – the physical analogy is complete. Sneezing itself is a symbolic expression of the influence of the shades. A neighbour will immediately respond with the same exclamation as used in the grandmother's game: 'Thithia! Mosiya [or whatever the clan] . . .' followed by the appropriate clan praises, themselves being an invocation of ancestors.[1]

The striking point of interest here is the respective associations of the sex roles. Men are responsible for administering relations with the shades in the moral aspect – looking after the well-being of their surviving kin. *Kwae* is one important symbolic instrument for doing so. It is used both in the public sphere by family heads to make the shades happy and in the private sphere by ritual specialists to diagnose the reason for misfortune or illness. On the other hand, women are afflicted by the shades in the amoral aspect and experience illness, not as retribution for immoral behaviour but capriciously and unpredictably. The illness is handled as a private matter, through the prescription of *kwae*, or in a public ritual of accommodation which employs two significant analogues of *kwae* – goat and *sethoto* medicine. At a more abstract level, men manipulate *kwae* to initiate controlled communion with the shades, while the shades prescribe *kwae* or its potent analogue *sethoto* to relieve affliction, which is defined as uncontrolled communion initiated by the shades.

In the first part of the essay I discussed the sexual connotation of *kwae* and its colloquial usages, from which I derive some kind of metaphorical identification between sex and smoking. I argued further that the primary significance of killing the sheep called *kwae* is the legitimising of sex relations between the newly married couple. This is partly speculative, for exegesis on the point was not easily forthcoming, but it seems to me the most likely explanation of an otherwise curious coincidence. If the argument is acceptable, an instrumental analogue seems to follow. Just as, literally, the giving of her husband's *kwae* (penis) activates the bride's reproductive system, so, symbolically, the giving of her father-in-law's *kwae* (sheep) marks her acceptance as a daughter-in-law and the transfer of her procreative *potential* to her husband's family. In Victor Turner's phraseology (1967: 54) *kwae* has a 'grossly physiological' referent at one end of a polarity of meanings and an 'ideological' referent – fertility – at the other. The giving of *kwae* has a public significance for the families

[1] Compare the Nyakyusa '*Bakwemele*' (Wilson: personal communication) and the English 'Bless you!' which would appear to have similar significance.

and the neighbourhood, at the normative level; it has a private significance for the man and the woman, at the orectic level. The dual significance is indicated in Column A of the following diagram:

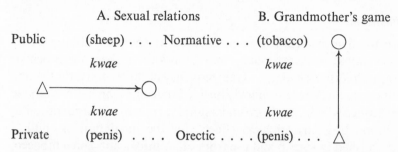

A. Sexual relations   B. Grandmother's game

Public   (sheep) . . . Normative . . . (tobacco)

kwae   *kwae*

kwae   *kwae*

Private   (penis) . . . . Orectic . . . . (penis) . . .

Here 'smoking' applies to sexual activity between adult men and women. What of the grandmother's game, in which an elderly woman 'smokes' a young child by touching his penis, holding her finger to her nose and sneezing? This gesture is inappropriate between members of the same sex (the physical analogy is impossible) and inappropriate by a woman on an adult man (lack of respect). Its performance is bounded by simple rules of 'grammar': sexual relations are legitimate between coeval adults, where the game cannot be applied out of respect; the game is legitimate between an elderly woman and a young boy, where sexual relations are impossible. The idiom of 'smoking' between male and female is appropriate, then, in only two contexts:

(1) actual sexual relations between adult men and women;

(2) a game in which a grandmother matures a young child by 'smoking' him like snuff.

What is the connection? At the level of social structure the idiom is an expression of intimacy in cross-sexual relations, which in turn is one aspect of the more general anthropological principle of familiarity between members of the same and of alternate generations, by contrast with distance/respect between members of proximate generations. At the level of symbolic statement sexual activity and the inhalation of snuff are precisely analogous: both 'open up knowledge'. Exegetical justification of this is readily apparent in the grandmother's game, in which the two ideas are nicely combined. By smoking the child, she is preparing him for manhood; the knowledge referred to is above all that of adults, carnal knowledge. 'This thing [penis] is called *kwae* because when the child can use it he already knows manhood, he knows the secret of adults.' While the emphasis in exegesis of the game is its 'ideological' significance in making the child grow, this is obviously lost on the boy himself, who is often scarcely a toddler – access, after all, depends on his not wearing trousers! The meaning of the gesture for him is confined to the simply 'orectic' sensation of having his penis fondled (see B in diagram above).

Conclusion

In the field my curiosity was aroused by three apparently trivial observations: conversational punning on *kwae* (tobacco and penis); the grandmother's game; and the frequency of the response that taking snuff clears one's wits. I quickly decided that smoking has a symbolic significance which cannot be understood merely by a consideration of its stimulating physiological effects, for the inhalation of snuff is distinguished in speech and use from other intoxicants (pipe tobacco, cigarettes, cannabis). There seemed to be two reasons for this: firstly its metaphorical association with sexual activity; secondly its identification with the traditional smoking habits of senior kin, above all of the shades. Accordingly it seemed worthwhile to explore each context in which I found *kwae* had some symbolic significance, and to record carefully exegetical statements relating to this. 'Smoking tobacco' is an idiom used to 'say something' about sexual relations between men and women. The metaphor is simple: procreative vigour is expressed in a woman's infusing a man's generative potency, just as a woman inhales snuff. Likewise the idiom of smoking 'says something' about relations between the living and the dead: broadly speaking, men give *kwae* to the shades to invoke their goodwill on the public behalf and to divine on behalf of a client, women receive *kwae* from the shades for relief and illumination. In the latter context a 'positional' investigation revealed the striking analogical relation of *kwae* with both goat and *sethoto* medicine: they all 'open up knowledge'.[1]

On the one hand, therefore, there is a 'horizontal' model in which 'smoking', the giving of *kwae* by men to women, represents sexual activity; on the other hand, a 'vertical' model in which *kwae* is given by men and received by women, independently, as expressions of communion between the living and the dead. The exegetical key to a synthesis of these two simple models lies in the grandmother's game itself. Not only is the senior generation responsible through sexual activity for producing the junior generation; its responsibility to educate and to promote the fertility of the junior generation in turn is explicitly evident in the grandmother's action of maturing a male child. By 'smoking' him she is making him aware of his potential procreative

[1] Having worked this out for myself, I was gratified to hear one doctor make precisely this observation: they are all important in the same way.

vigour. In this sense she is exposing the child to a fundamental truth about his identity as a Mosotho and as a member of a network of reciprocal kinship ties; his growth to maturity implies an awareness of his responsibility to procreate and thereby to perpetuate the system of interdependence between kin of which the shades are the ultimate moral arbiters. One old man gave me the cryptic response, '*Kwae* . . . is life.' From this point of view it no longer seems extravagant to regard *kwae* as a specific symbol of the highly abstract idea of generative power, a symbol with polyvalent properties which act as a catalyst in the linked processes of physical and mental regeneration.

Peter Carstens

SOME IMPLICATIONS OF CHANGE IN KHOIKHOI SUPERNATURAL BELIEFS[1]

In this brief essay I want to analyse the basic features of Khoikhoi[2] beliefs in the supernatural and to emphasise some of the changes that have occurred as a result of colonial domination and Christian missionary endeavour. I want to show also how the division of labour and social and economic inequality are reflected in certain specific beliefs. The methods of explanation used are to a large degree derived from 'Witch Beliefs and Social Structure' (Wilson 1951b).

The extent of Khoikhoi ethnography and history is considerable but there have been few attempts to look critically at the data on the traditional religious and magical systems since Schapera published his *Khoisan Peoples* in 1930. Some work has been carried out in recent years among the descendants of the Khoikhoi and I hope I shall be able to illustrate here some of the crucial links between the present and the past. The methodological pitfalls of moving from an unspecified period called 'traditional' to another termed 'contemporary' are fully recognised but unavoidable in an essay of this length. Elsewhere (Carstens 1966 and 1969) I have attempted to distinguish various intermediary historical periods and to analyse the processes of change in general. Here I shall merely mention that the chief factors effecting change were: the usurpation of land by foreigners, the conversion of the Khoikhoi to Christianity, intermarriage with European colonists, conflict with San[3] hunter-gatherers and European farmers and

[1] I would like to thank my colleagues, Tom McFeat and Maureen Stark, for their comments on various aspects of this paper. Their criticisms helped me to clarify important issues in the final draft.

[2] I have used the term Khoikhoi rather than 'Hottentot' since the latter has become an abusive term in contemporary South Africa. Moreover, these people (Khoin) used to refer to themselves collectively as Khoikhoin when *not* distinguishing between tribes, e.g. Namaqua, Hessequa, Outeniqua, etc.

[3] The term San appears to have been used by the Khoikhoi to refer to all Bushmen hunter-gatherers. The meaning of the word is not clear to me. (Compare Hahn 1881: 3; Stow 1905: 245, 248, 275; and Schapera 1930: 31.)

administrators, the creation of Reserves, economic competition with the Bantu-speaking peoples and general economic exploitation by Europeans.

THE SUPERNATURAL IN TRADITIONAL SOCIETY[1]

Religion: Tsui //Goab and //Gaunab

It is surprising that anthropologists in general have continued to accept the view that the Khoikhoi worshipped the moon, *Gounja*. For if we list the evidence on which this assumption is based, and reinterpret it, the old conclusion is not very convincing. The literature, for example, seems to furnish us with six oblique reasons why the Khoikhoi were regarded as moon-worshippers: First, that at both new and full moon they indulged in dancing, singing, and merrymaking. Second, that at the new moon some threw balls of clay into river water. Third, that the Cape Khoikhoi looked on the moon as their visible God, which they called *Gounja*, and at new and full moon danced throughout the night in its honour singing, 'Be welcome, give us plenty of honey, give grass to our cattle, that we may get plenty of milk.' Fourth, that the religion of the Nama consisted 'principally in worshipping and praising the moon'. Fifth, that in certain myths the moon is associated with the origin of death. And finally, that an eclipse of the moon was a bad omen which brought sickness and death. (Kolb 1731; Dapper *et al.* 1933; Hahn 1881; Schapera 1930; Jopp 1960.)

Both the literature and the oral tradition, however, provide additional data and show that there is some confusion regarding the so-called divinity of the moon and association of the moon with the worship of *Tsui //Goab*, a personified God. Hence the alternative interpretation offered here is that sacrifices were performed to the deity during certain phases of the moon. Moreover, it is not only the moon that is associated in this manner with the deity. For example, it has been noted 'that a religious dance was held at the first rising of the Pleiades after sunset, when prayers are offered to *Tsui //Goab* for rain'. Further, there do not appear to have been any sacrifices offered *to* the moon itself nor are there reports of priests officiating at any moon-worshipping ceremony.

Gysbert Hemmy (1767) spoke of an 'invisible deity [called] *Gounja Tekquoa*'. (See also Kolb 1931.) And it does not seem unreasonable to

---

[1] For ethnographic detail of the traditional period I have relied heavily on the work of Professor I. Schapera and the late Mrs. A. W. Hoernlé, the mother of social anthropology in South Africa. Dr. H. Vedder's work must also be regarded as a scholarly contribution to Khoikhoi studies in general.

suggest that *Tekquoa* is a corruption of *Tsui //Goab*. If correct, this evidence would favour the proposition that there has been a false association between *Gounja* and *Tsui //Goab*, analogous perhaps to a Martian's observation that Jews and Christians worship the moon at Passover and at Easter.

Tsui //Goab was, it will be argued, the High or Celestial God of the Khoikhoi. He was a creator since he is believed to have made the rocks and stones from which the first Khoikhoi came; he was omnipresent, extremely wise, and said also to have once been a notable warrior of great physical strength, as well as a powerful magician. Moreover, although he died several times, he was reborn. He sent rain and caused the crops to grow and flourish. In fact *Tsui //Goab* was so similar to the God of the Old Testament that one is tempted to argue that the early accounts of this remarkably versatile God were a blend of 'traditional' and missionary beliefs, but there seems reasonable evidence to demonstrate that these beliefs were independently derived.

Tsui //Goab was worshipped and propitiated, and many of the rituals involved were not without the element of sacrifice so general in all religion. The great annual rainmaking ceremonies[1] of the Nama at which the chief of a tribe fulfilled his role of officiating priest were essentially sacrificial rituals of the communion variety. On these occasions sacrificial animals were ritually slaughtered and the members of the tribe invoked *Tsui //Goab* asking for rain and plenty; they also praised him as follows according to Hahn:

> Thou, O *Tsui //Goab*!
> Father of our Fathers,
> Our Father!
> Let stream the thunder cloud,
> Let our flocks live,
> Let us also live, please;
> I am so very weak,
> From thirst,
> From hunger!
> Let me eat field fruits.

The Hymn of the Thunder, which Hahn also records, reflects another aspect of the relationship between the Khoikhoi and their God – their collective guilt, and the fear that he might cause misfortune:

[1] For a detailed account of the rainmaking ceremonies see Hoernlé (1922) and Schapera (1930: 378ff).

> Son of the Thundercloud!
> Thou brave loud-speaking *!Guru* [thunder]!
> Talk, softly, please,
> For I have no guilt;
> Let me alone, [Forgive me?]
> For I have become quite weak. . . .

The celestial supernatural actor which I have just described as the High God of the Khoikhoi was not without his rival in the mythology. For in opposition to *Tsui //Goab* was another male figure, *//Gaunab*, the personified spirit of evil – the Devil. Comparing the two characters missionary George Schmidt, although a poor observer of ritual, reports in 1744 that *Tsui //Goab* was a 'supreme Lord over all' and that *//Gaunab* was the equivalent of the Christian devil.

Schapera's analysis of the early literature regarding the nature of *//Gaunab* and of Khoikhoi attitudes towards *//Gaunab* is quite detailed. In the first place he shows that not only war, but all evil also was believed to come from *//Gaunab*. Further it is made clear that evil caused by *//Gaunab* included certain types of sickness, death from various causes, and sorcery. Evil spirits, those people said to have lived wickedly, moreover, were known as *//Gaunan* (common plural); and *Sares* (feminine), the whirlwind believed to bring sickness and death, was also occasionally known as *//Gaunab*. Here we could raise the question whether the extension of the term *//Gaunab* to a number of things evil in nature is not analogous to the 'moon-god' fallacy already discussed. Both the literature and the oral tradition do, however, suggest that Khoikhoi belief in the devil involved a complex set of phenomena reflected linguistically by the common plural form *//Gaunan* (literally, male and female devils).

The myths surrounding *Tsui //Goab* and *//Gaunab* indicate not simply a conflict between two supernatural beings, one good the other bad. Symbolically and at the supernatural level they may represent the conflict between good and evil, but in reality they represent a continuum between 'good' life and 'bad' death.

If we pause for a moment and ask what the division of labour was between *Tsui //Goab* and *//Gaunab* in traditional Khoikhoi society, it is clear that their respective actions are not always discrete. For if we perceive our two actors in the context of the simple cognitive model of who causes *good fortune* and *bad fortune*, and who effects *protection* against enemies and evil forces, the conclusion drawn earlier must be modified. It is too elementary to speak of the conflict between good and evil; and at the cognitive level the continuum between good life and bad death cannot be analysed. Rather we must recognise the confusion in the area of the causes of bad fortune because no Khoikhoi individual or group was ever sure who was responsible, //*Gaunab* or *Tsui* //*Goab*. The former certainly had the stronger association with evil, misfortune, and plain bad luck, but *Tsui*//*Goab* was hard to please and was not always successfully appeased by sacrifice. There were, moreover, only two fully-fledged sacrifices performed to him annually – the rainmaking and first-fruits ceremonies. For the rest of the year 'the two old enemies dished out punishments and misfortune from time to time as though they were friends', an old Nama once told me. In other words the people were constantly at loggerheads with these supernatural characters – nothing unfortunate was ever adequately explained at the religious level. Collective good fortune and successful social protection on the other hand were of a different order, and a sign that *Tsui*//*Goab* was as active on earth as he was in his celestial abode.

Table 1 below provides a simplified model of the collective activities of the two supernatural beings as they would have been perceived by any one tribe, clan or larger kinship group. To specify the reference group is essential in applying the principles involved because what was good fortune for one clan might have been bad fortune for another, as in the case of the outcome of an interclan dispute over the right to use a waterhole.

TABLE 1

Supernatural character	Sex	Good fortune	Bad fortune	Protection	Sphere of operation
Tsui //*Goab*	M	yes	yes	yes	collective
//*Gaunab*	M	no	yes	no	collective

Heitsi Eibib: the popular ancestral hero[1]

Up to this stage our analysis of Khoikhoi supernatural has been concerned with matters religious and therefore collective in Durkheim's sense. We move now to another category of actor, *Heitsi Eibib*, whose abode is terrestrial rather than celestial, although he is sociologically different from the celestial dyad by virtue of his dealing with individuals rather than groups. Should we argue from some

---

[1] Both my summary of *Heitsi Eibib* and my understanding of his place in Khoikhoi mythology have been greatly influenced by Hahn (1881) and Schapera (1930). My final interpretation was arrived at by working back through the sources to Kolb (1731: 103).

evolutionary perspective it could be hypothesised that *Heitsi Eibib*'s supernatural existence emerged with the growth of private property and the institutionalisation of inequality between people.

Heitsi Eibib was a sort of common ancestral hero to the Khoikhoi in general. He had the power to prophesy and he was a famous magician whose ability surpassed all others. He may in fact be regarded as the hero of the good magical tradition, an independent figure whose function it was to bring good luck to individuals.

According to the mythology *Heitsi Eibib* had once been a member of society. Yet he was no ordinary man, for he died many times – being successfully resurrected after each death except the last. The mythology, moreover, contains many examples of his anti-social history including the committing of incest. In this connection it must also be pointed out that his rebirth syndrome was unique and 'improper' among the Khoikhoi. Unlike the Bantu-speaking peoples, the Khoikhoi possessed no ancestor cult. In fact, the antithesis of this was true: the logic is open to wide speculation yet it is repeatedly made clear that the shades were dreaded for fear that they would rise from the grave and do harm. Not all deceased, however, were believed to be harmful: only those who became evil spirits because they had died suddenly or in great agony, or raving madly, or had resisted the moment of death, were believed to cause misfortune or disturb their descendants. Nowadays, the remaining Khoikhoi express these ideas in much the same form, asserting that the mortuary ideal is for every deceased person to remain peacefully in the grave and never bother anyone again. Thus they take extreme measures by most standards to carry out death rites with meticulous care, even though the financial costs are often high.

Earlier I pointed to the mythical relation between //*Gaunab* (Devil) and death and evil spirits who were sometimes referred to as //*Gaunan* rather than /*hei* /*nun* (ghosts). But this connection was far more real than mere myth since the fear of evil spirits (often called black ghosts) has persisted in many areas up to the present time, and their relation to the //*Gaunan* of older times is openly acknowledged.

The dead were occasionally prayed to among the Khoikhoi under circumstances involving misfortune attributed to 'bad' or mischievous ghosts who disturbed people. But the concept of ancestors as spiritual actors, resembling the shades of the Bantu-speaking peoples, was a theological and ritual absurdity to the Khoikhoi.

Returning now to *Heitsi Eibib*: it is tempting to regard him as an heroic mediator between the people and their High God, particularly as *Heitsi Eibib*'s graves [*sic*] may be seen all over territory that was occupied in former times by Khoikhoi people. But as I have indicated *Heitsi Eibib* was solely concerned with individual good fortune or good luck. His 'graves' consist of large piles of stones and these may be interpreted as monuments to *individual* good luck, reminders, as it were, that success and even protection were afforded by this real hero who was not a personified native deity. He is somewhat casually acknowledged by offerings of sticks or stones tossed on the grave, and sometimes honey or honey beer is left for him at night. When he is addressed in kinship terms he is referred to as 'grandfather' (a term of familiarity) not as 'father', which is used in prayers to *Tsui //Goab* (God).

Magic and sorcery

At this juncture it seems appropriate to turn our attention to the practice of magic and sorcery among the Khoikhoi. These people also believed in the almost universal principle that certain substances contain properties that can create, cure, and prevent particular physical and psychological diseases, as well as prevent and effect general misfortune.

In traditional society a magician, *!gai aob* (literally, magical medicine man), was also a diviner. Some certainly practised sorcery but a clear distinction between sorcerers and good magicians and diviners does not appear to have been made. Medicines used included such substances as local flora, the flesh and bones of small animals, human body dirt, jackal kidney fat, and sheeptail fat. All appear to have been derived from the local environment and in general from the smaller varieties of plants and animals. The details of the ingredients of substances used have been well documented by Schultze (1907) and Schapera (1930). In both the curing and prevention of disease elaborate 'scientific' formulae were worked out to ensure that the antidote was neither too weak nor too strong. The rationale behind this principle was that should the counter-medicine be too weak the other would harm or kill the victim, while if the preparation was too strong the patient could be driven insane.

Taking all the factors into consideration, we must point out that earlier assumptions that sorcerers were believed to work in league with //*Gaunab* (Devil) and evil spirits may be quite erroneous for the traditional period. Those who drew this conclusion may have been confused by the fact that sorcerers were believed to become evil spirits (//*Gaunan* or /*hei/nun*) after death. We must emphasise also that very little prestige seems to have been afforded to any medicine man. They did not become chiefs, headmen, or leaders of any other group: at the most they were respected (or feared) because of their assumed ability to manipulate the material and social welfare of individuals.

Division of labour and inequality among supernatural characters

The mythology of the traditional Khoikhoi is extremely rich in characters of many varieties. All cannot be discussed but I would like to add one other to the selection from traditional Khoikhoi society here, although discussion of it is included under the section dealing mainly with contemporary times. This character, the /nas,[1] a sort of African female Brer Rabbit, is barely mentioned in early writings but is very much a traditional animal. Knowledge of the /nas was derived almost entirely during my own field work (Carstens 1961 and 1966).

In Table 2 I have attempted to summarise the spheres of supernatural activity as I interpret them to have been among the Khoikhoi, and notably the Naman tribes.

TABLE 2

Supernatural character	Sex	Good fortune	Bad fortune	Protection	Sphere of influence
Tsui //Goab	M	yes	yes	yes	collective
//Gaunab	M	no	yes	no	collective
Heitsi Eibib	M	yes	no	yes	individual
/hei /nun	M or F	no	yes	no	individual?
Sares	F	no	yes	no	individual
!gai aob	M	yes	yes	yes	individual
/nas	F	no	yes	yes	individual

The political and economic systems of the Khoikhoi have been well analysed by Schapera (1930 and 1956). The people are shown as having been divided into political communities or tribes, each of which consisted of a federation of clans, one of which at least was senior to the others. In addition to this clan hierarchy was a 'class' of family servants, and a third category, of newcomers to a tribe, was also recognised. In the main, however, there was little other differentiation between people although a small number of individuals (not only

[1] Elsewhere I have used the spelling /has (1966: 182) for one community. The older form used in other communities was /nas. It is possible that both forms were derived from the *Nama* word !õas, a hare. (See also Schapera 1930: 369–70.)

chiefs) were acknowledged as owning private property, particularly in the form of livestock. Differences in rank were also recognised but these tended mainly to reflect political and military positions acquired by succession. These offices were only weakly reinforced by ritual duties and religious power. The status of women was relatively high in the economic field for not only did they have access to some private property but they also controlled the milking of livestock and the milk and its products. Politically women held office very infrequently and are not reported to have been members of the Popular Assembly.

As is reflected in Table 2, women were not well represented among the supernatural characters. However, research based on the oral tradition reveals that female /hei /nun (ghosts) were troublesome and greatly feared; and only women were believed to have the power of controlling the /nas: all /nas were female themselves. Sares, the whirl-wind, is feminine.

These few comments regarding women and the supernatural suggest, as I will argue later, that women and female characters tended to appear in the supernatural sphere when their position in a corresponding area of society was threatened.

THE CONTEMPORARY PERIOD

My discussion for this period will centre mainly on the descendants of the indigenous Khoikhoi who are nowadays classified as coloured by the South African Government largely because of their intermarriage and cohabitation with early Cape Dutch frontiersmen. I shall in effect be discussing those people who live in five Coloured Reserves in the magisterial district of Namaqualand. All the inhabitants call themselves Christians nowadays and demonstrate their recognition of the Almighty through lively participation in church matters, both sacred and secular. In addition to these Christian beliefs there are a host of other supernatural beliefs of the non-Christian variety, similar in many ways to those we have discussed for the 'traditional' period.

All these beliefs (Christian and non-Christian) of the contemporary period may be classified as follows:

(a) *religious beliefs*, all of which are geared to Christian teaching;

(b) *magical beliefs*;

(c) those supernatural beliefs associated with *rites of passage* (both (b) and (c) are largely derived from the Khoikhoi tradition);

(d) beliefs relating to the supernatural powers of certain *animals and monsters*, the origins of which are not always clear, but one animal, at least, is derived from Khoikhoi tradition.

It is not possible to discuss all of them but I shall attempt to demon-strate my main thesis by concentrating on some aspects of religion and the supernatural powers of certain animals and monsters, before linking the contemporary period with that of the past.

Religion

In three communities, which I shall refer to as category I, God is seen as the creator of the universe and the giver of life, plenty, and happiness to man. God's benevolence, however, is conditional on the good behaviour of all members of the community, and it is generally accepted that God usually punishes people collectively. Thus the innocent and the virtuous are both punished for the sins of the wrong-doers. Actually, it is said that God does not himself punish but that his wrath is manifested by his allowing misfortune to occur. For example, a drought is explained as follows by a conservative member of the community. 'God is very dissatisfied with the behaviour of the new elite (they swear, booze, fornicate, and ingratiate themselves with white government officials), but we all have to suffer with them through this terrible drought God has allowed to happen.' The new elite naturally has its own ideas regarding the cause of collective misfortune.

Heaven in these three communities, although in theory located in an upward direction at 90 degrees to the surface of the earth, is popu-larly believed to be considerably closer, and located on the terrestial plane in one of the local graveyards.

In another community (category II) the conception of God and the idea of heaven resemble the pattern in category I, with the exception that the idea of collective punishment is not present: God is said to punish individuals and groups separately according to their particular sins, and it is God who does the punishing.

In the fifth community (category III), although it is the most iso-lated and closest to the Khoikhoi tradition, Christian beliefs tend to be the most orthodox in terms of Calvinist theology with one excep-tion: although heaven is believed to be located in the sky, the whole biblical drama from Genesis to Revelation is believed also to have taken place in heaven.

There are undoubtedly many interrelated factors to be taken into consideration to explain these variations, but three important ones stand out clearly: differences in the structure of church governments; differences in systems of social stratification and the diversity of social cleavages; and the nature and intensity of interaction with the outside world.

All three of the communities in category I are characterised by a relatively high degree of stratification, and a great number of factions and cleavages. They are and have been dominated by mission institutions (only one in each community) whose systems of church government are based on the Calvinist pattern. Moreover, the missionary in each of these communities is a man of considerable power, and from about 1820 to 1913 he held the joint offices of minister and president of what resembled a little republic, and director of education. The office of minister has for nearly 150 years involved presiding over the church council, which is the major decision-making body in church affairs.

The interpretation of the beliefs in God for category I offered here is that they are related to the system of church authority as synthesised with systems of stratification and a variety of social cleavages. Just as God is believed to be the God of each community, so also are the missionary and his council regarded as the go-betweens between community and God: God's qualities, moreover, coincide remarkably with those of his mediators. Although people from all social strata and all cleavages are represented on the church council, they are united in their diversity through the leadership of the missionary. Together they represent the solidarity of the society: individually they characterise the components of the structure of which they are a part. As a superordinate group they embody the essence of the Almighty. Just as the church council is a function of the community, so also is the power of God limited. God cannot meddle too much with the *status quo* and therefore should not take sides in factional disputes. The wicked and the virtuous must suffer together.

Regarding the location of heaven – on earth – although the answer is surely not as simple as this, I suggest that its assumed position is probably related to the centripetal orientation of the majority in the community due to the imposed Reserve system, which imposes *inter alia* restrictions on the horizons of emotional expression.

In community category II, as we noted earlier, the belief in God is basically similar to that in category I with the exception that God is believed to discriminate between classes, factions, and cleavages when meting out punishment. This variation appears to be related to a difference in the structure of church government. Community category II has for the past 150 years fallen under the tutelage of the Methodist Church, which is characterised even at the local level by a federal administrative structure. Thus community category II for the purpose of church administration is subdivided into a number of semi-autonomous units. Here it is argued that one of the manifestations of this system has been its reflection in the idea of God and the nature of God's power.

Finally, in this regard there is the paradox of community category III, where the beliefs in God, Jesus, and devil conform more to orthodox Calvinist principles than in any other community, in spite of the fact that it is the most isolated and closest to the Khoikhoi tradition. At first this is puzzling, but when one takes cognisance of the additional belief that the Bible narrates the story of the 'goings on' in heaven, one gains an important clue, namely that the Christian religion to them is not a local commodity but one imported from without for special occasions. It is not surprising, therefore, to discover that the missionaries of category III have seldom lived in the community and that local church government was introduced as late as 1960. It is as though the Christian religion here has always been identified entirely with the white man's authority and power and the local residents have never been deeply involved from the inside through participation in the secular activities of the church. On Sundays they play 'church–church' as a special treat – when the missionary visits to rehearse with them part of the drama of heaven.

Animals and monsters

Further examples of the apparent connection between belief systems and social structure are found in those related to animals and monsters. In communities in categories I and II there is a lively belief in the /nas, described as a long red-eared spring-hare with supernatural powers, generally controlled by an old woman. Many people are believed to have this power of controlling the hare and in recent years some of them have been men. Nowadays, moreover, the commercial value of this South African Brer Rabbit has been exploited, and practitioners charge a fee for 'sending' it on behalf of others (Carstens 1966:184).

/nas is believed to exercise its supernatural powers only when sent, the purposes being fourfold:

(1) to warn people who have offended its sender to mend their ways;

(2) to frighten irresponsible people and if necessary to punish them physically;

(3) to spy on people absent from home – to see that they are not fornicating or drinking; and

(4) to protect people travelling on long journeys.

Whereas the belief in the /nas is also present in category III community, significantly fewer people here become involved in its activities. Moreover, only a few women (and no men) are believed to send the /nas. This community, however, manifests the traditional Khoikhoi pattern in this regard.

Another belief concerns a snake of an unusually large variety. In the category I community it is described as a mythical monster who lives in the category III community. In the category II community the snake is legendary, belonging, it is said, to the community's past. The members of the category III community, however, really believe in the snake (the Big Snake), which is said to be 'so large that when its head is resting on the north bank of the Orange river, its tail is still on the south bank'. It is described in minute detail and is said *inter alia* to have an attractive light-brown body with a head resembling that of a beautiful man. It has bright eyes and long black eyelashes. On its forehead is a large precious stone, which shines like a torch at night while it feeds in the hills. The Big Snake is hated by all males, towards whom it is equally unfavourably disposed, and it is said to become angry at the sight or smell (especially the latter) of a male. Moreover, the snake when angry is believed to give off a smell which is lethal to all males, and it spews a deadly venom. On the other hand, women are believed to fall in love with the Big Snake, which is also said to have fallen in love with certain women, some of whom are alleged to have had sexual intercourse with it and conceived children.

A final belief of the animal-monster variety concerns the *tokoloshe* (derived from *uthikoloshe*), described as either a little baboon or a small hairy black man who wears a large hat. *Tokoloshe* is essentially malicious and is reputed to have both frightened and bitten people. One man's mother reported that her son had turned quite black after being frightened by it. *Tokoloshe* is said to operate only in certain mine-compound hostels. The belief was found to exist in two communities only, both of which belong to category I.

The problem of interpreting these variations is clearly as complex as that of interpreting the traditional religious beliefs, but the examination of structural differences between the communities does throw some possible light on the processes involved. Here it is suggested that an examination of the relative statuses of men and women, and the nature of each community's interaction with the outside world in both space and time, will prove rewarding.

It is not difficult to see that one of the functions of the /nas is its role as an instrument of social control. More specifically, however, its function is to compensate low-status adults for their lack of power, and to reinforce the authority of those placed in situations where they cannot effectively control their spouses. Thus we find that in communities of both categories I and II, where women have relatively low status locally and where male migratory labour is common, the supernatural powers of the /nas help women and men to compensate for the inability to control important personal social situations. In category III on the other hand, only two women and no men out of a total population of 600 persons were said to have the /nas (in one community in category I the incidence of /nas activity in terms of senders was ten times greater). This we may attribute, I think, to the comparatively higher status of women in category III and the fact that migratory labour has only recently begun to influence domestic and other social relationships.

In order to attempt some explanation of the lively belief in the pro-female and anti-male serpent occurring in category III, the phenomena of the local relations between the sexes and the nature of the contact with the outside world will again be utilised. In category III, as we have said, there is an egalitarian tendency in male–female relations; yet this situation does not give rise to overt rivalries or jealousies between the sexes at either the marital or the premarital level. There are, moreover, no battles of love here, and the losers merely accept their lot.

Whatever the origin of the belief in the Big Snake is, the very tentative hypothesis offered here regarding its function is that it provides an emotional outlet for male jealousy and aggression towards other males who are their sexual (or otherwise) competitors. The snake is a man, a beautiful man, he falls in love with and seduces women, who both love and admire him. Men hate the snake, 'it makes them furious and gives them an empty, jealous feeling'. The snake, moreover, is antagonistic to all men. From the woman's point of view it could be argued that the snake symbolises the wealthy lover, strong and virile, who tolerates no rival, especially in property and economic and other relations.

But what of the snake's light color, his long eyelashes, his attractiveness, and his jewelled forehead? What of his great strength and size, and his constant foraging at night in the hills? May we not look beyond the boundaries of the community and interpret the daily accounts given of the snake also in terms of white encroachment, especially the suntanned white prospectors and mining magnates who hover round the territory waiting for the government to violate the Reserve boundaries still further in the event of a new discovery of diamonds, gold, or other valuable minerals?

Whatever else the snake symbolises, he is a powerful, wealthy outsider; and as an outsider, he is a great threat to local men, a threat

which is expressed through women. His absence in the other communities (in addition to the male–female status factor) is most probably
related to the greater interaction with the outside world through
church, local government, schools, migratory labour, etc., than occurs
in category III.

Categories I and II, however, have their own external threat – the
arrival of the Bantu-speaking peoples as labour competitors in the
mines. In terms of the current mythology or belief system, these Bantu-
speaking peoples are symbolised by the image of *uthikoloshe* with new
pronunciation (*tokoloshe*) and out of his old context as familiar to
Nguni witches.

If there appears to be a contradiction in my basic propositions
regarding the Big Snake it needs to be noted that migratory labour is a
relatively recent activity in category III. Thus when we speak of outsiders the term refers in part also to those migrant workers who are
identified by local men and women with the 'powerful people', those
believed to have easy access to money. From the point of view of the
community, the institution of migratory labour has reinforced the fear
and apprehension of outsiders, including its own people who venture
into the world beyond the boundaries of the Reserve. The manifesta-
tion of this attitude towards the migrant labourers as outsiders is
overtly expressed in the gestures of joking behaviour, for example, the
elaborate violent handshake inflicted on returning migrants. The handshake, although a form of greeting, is calculated to throw a man off
balance to the ground, where he nurses a painful elbow while the
bystanders laugh aggressively. The performance resembles a brief rite
of passage and reintegrates the man into the community.

To understand the tension between insiders and outsiders fully in
category III community therefore, we must recognise that local people
have not institutionalised their perceptions of the two kinds of outsiders. In the other communities the great influence of the church,
local government, and schools on people's lives tends to regularise
behaviour and perception in new terms based on the philosophy of
the wider society as dictated by the ruling class. The people in category
III community are still resisting domination, and migrant workers
there constitute what Turner (1967) might regard as a 'betwixt and
between' group.

CHANGING BELIEF SYSTEMS & SOCIAL STRUCTURE

From many very significant points of view these two periods have
provided us with incomparable data and situations. Over the years

there have been vast changes in the size, density, and quality of population; the whole ecological framework of the people has been modified as a direct result of the creation of Reserves; the impact of migratory labour has been enormous; and the whole system of an imposed administrative structure together with the establishment of Christian churches has in itself created a sedentary population out of semi-nomadic pastoralists.

Yet in spite of these radical changes and the perpetrators of coercive change, a cultural tradition (including some of the language) has survived, providing a continuity with the past. Much of this cultural tradition is embodied in myth, legend, and belief – the supernatural. It is this continuity with the past that is articulated by the people themselves. Perhaps this is what Geertz (1966:4) was really indicating when he wrote that a religion as a cultural system in the broadest sense is: 'a system of symbols which acts to establish powerful, pervasive, and long-lasting moods and motivations in men by formulating conceptions of a general order of existence and clothing these conceptions with such an aura of factuality that the moods and motivations seem uniquely realistic'.

What I am urging is that the importance of trying to compare the present with the past be fully recognised even when the data are hazy and almost inadequate. There is a whole area, which I shall call 'information through symbolism', that provides clues to the codes of culture and behaviour through time as well as at a particular period of time. Moreover, it was only by studying this information that I was able to gain insights into the meaning of these belief systems as perceived by the people themselves. If they had not discussed these perceptions, there would have been no way of evaluating changes in either belief or action.

Perhaps the most significant change in the area of supernatural systems was a cosmological one involving Christian teaching and practice with particular reference to the idea of God. The shift in perception was not, however, radical for the Khoikhoi, whose theology was so close to Calvinism and to the dogma taught by missionaries of the Reformed Churches. The change was merely the incorporation of a simple idea, that of an *omnipotent* God who was able to provide explanations of the unknown in a more comprehensive way than a God such as *Tsui //Goab* who was also a creator and a powerful High God but only *omnipresent* not *omnipotent*. It should perhaps be noted at this juncture how knowledge of apparently minor shifts in perception can sometimes provide symbolic information about major social and economic change.

I have shown earlier that there was a much greater degree of division of labour in pre-missionary times between supernatural characters. *Tsui //Goab* seems to have been outside of the magical and other related traditions although he did have a sparring partner in *//Gaunab*. With the advent of Christian missionaries and other culture agents many of the non-religious traditions remained (and some new ones appear to have been added, for example, the Big Snake) but their efficacy became conditional on a God who is said nowadays to allow even sorcery to be performed effectively, even if it is not his work. God merely lets things happen if he feels like it. Through his omnipotency he can also prevent misfortune, just as he can cause it if he wishes.

Another significant change in belief has been the virtual disappearance of *Heitsi Eibib* from the magico-religious system. The only connotation the two words have nowadays are in reference to a precocious child, i.e. a child who knows too much for his age. *Heitsi Eibib* has been variously translated but it is clearly derived from *Heisi*, to tell or to know, and *Eibe*, early, beforehand, previously (cf. Schapera, 1930: 383).

I have already suggested that old *Heitsi Eibib*, the hero of the magical tradition, emerged *inter alia* with the growth of private property in early times. But why does the belief in this popular ancestral hero disappear so suddenly to be forgotten in three generations, especially as private property increases and more marked class and status divisions develop? The answer may be found in the tension generated by the process whereby subordinate beliefs are incorporated into religion in general, but where magic is still believed to operate in so many respects as an independent system. Thus one might wish to argue that there has been a change from the conflict between good and evil (good life and bad death) to a more subtle conflict between religion (corporateness) and magic (individualism). This generalisation does, however, need to be refined so that it takes into account the observation that nowadays individual misfortune can be attributed to God's punishment, or to sorcery, or to a parent's curse, or to the */nas*, or simply to bad luck. Let it be remembered, however, that it is God who is believed to have the final say.

If we wished to measure the relative frequency of the various causes of individual misfortune we would find it difficult to record the specific explanations of their origins. Collective misfortune like collective good fortune is, however, attributed mainly to God (Carstens 1966: 171–89). Upon rethinking the contemporary material from

Little and Great Namaqualand I am of the opinion that the cleavage between works attributed to God and those attributed to other supernatural characters and devices has widened with the growth of greater individualism especially in areas where personal esteem furthers economic and political advancement. Max Weber might have included this process within the framework of the Protestant ethic. Superficially this would be an appropriate position, but it does not explain the intricacies of subordinate beliefs (for example, magic). However, if we follow Weber's thesis we might argue that the Protestant ethic stimulates and fosters the efficacy of good magic to further individual ends for those who aspire to elite status. From the other angle it could be stated that the individualism inherent in the Protestant ethic is reinforced by magic and magic-like practices. In the contemporary society, moreover, the number of magicians as recognised specialists has decreased, but there are a greater number of laymen using medicines than in early times. From an analytical point of view this trend demonstrates very clearly the need to make clear-cut distinctions between religion and magic as well as between other supernatural systems. For if we think in terms of who is said to have caused good or bad fortune we have no difficulty in understanding that the division of labour, the system of stratification, and social life in general are reflected also in rituals, beliefs, and other aspects of symbolic systems. And we may conclude that the study of symbolic forms in general steer anthropologists to the kernel of human societies as they have been and as they are at the present time. Symbolic forms also throw light on the manner in which people have reacted to conquest and other external forces. As anthropologists continue to focus their studies on the less privileged peoples of the world, the systematic study of information derived from symbols will provide new insights into social relationships, very different from those cherished by the ruling classes. We will surely agree also with the scholar who delivered the Frazer Lecture (Wilson 1959b: 27) in 1959 that, 'it is peculiarly incumbent upon those of us who claim to be African by birth and sympathy to seek to interpret the old ideas and symbols in terms of the new Africa'. However, this sentiment must not be construed as constituting the end of a struggle. In essence it is but the beginning of a process of action tied to the practical needs of those who signalled the crises of domination in the first place.[1]

[1] Bertrand de Jouvenel's influence on this notion should be clear, but I do not expect him to agree with my formulation.

PART 2: THE RESTLESS CHRISTIANS

Bengt Sundkler

THE CHURCHES' HINTERLAND

J. S. Moffat, an observant son of Robert Moffat, remarked in about 1888 upon a change that was 'already touching the country' of southern Africa. In a letter (12.9.1888) to J. Wardlow Thompson of the London Missionary Society, he called this 'the northward movement of the white race'.[1] It is this perspective, the trend and movement north as a theme in the history of southern Africa that we are emphasising in these pages, limiting the account to the aspect closest to the hearts of Robert and John Moffat, the missionary outreach north.

This was the period when in the United States historians and economists began to study a similar trend in their own country, the westward movement. In 1893 F. Jackson Turner formulated what was to become one of the most striking and durable, albeit controversial interpretations of American history, the frontier thesis. Addressing the American Historical Association, Turner spoke on 'The Significance of the Frontier in American History' and set in motion research and debate about the receding west with its open spaces and apparently unlimited opportunities.

J. S. Moffat was in an excellent position to follow the northward movement of the missionary thrust. He was himself part of the great Scottish Moffat–Livingstone tradition that had established what there

[1] The following archives were consulted: London Missionary Society ('Africa Outgoing' 22, 23, 24. Matabeleland I 1836–96, folders 2 and 4; Matabeleland II 1860–99) at S.O.A.S. The Methodist Missionary Society (M.M.S.) (Mashonaland letters 1891–1899. Rhodesia 1899–1904. Isaac Shimmin: Journal of the Mashonaland Mission, 1891. Isaac Shimmin: The County, 1892). U.S.P.G. (Africa and Australasia 1891, 1893. G. W. H. Knight-Bruce: Journals of the Mashonaland Mission, 1892). All the foregoing are in London. Church of Sweden Mission, Uppsala (letters from A. R. Kempe and A. Liljestrand to Mission Director. A. Liljestrand: Report on the Explorations of the Matabele Expedition, July–Nov. 1902. In Swedish). It was not possible to consult the following theses: N. M. B. Bhebe, 'Christian Missions in Matabeleland 1859–1923' (Ph.D. thesis, London, 1972), E. Mashingaidze, 'Christian Missions in Mashonaland 1890–1930' (Ph.D. thesis, York University, 1973).

was of a 'Missionaries' Road' north through Kuruman towards Matabeleland and central Africa. Further, his father had established remarkably good personal contacts with Mzilikazi, a relationship which was to facilitate the opportunities of his London Missionary Society for the northern expansion of its work. Moffat also knew that Bishop Gray of Cape Town had a special interest in this northern horizon of the church. Gray had been one of the first, in 1858, to propose a 'Universities Mission to Central Africa' (Groves 1954: 189). It was however Cecil Rhodes and the formation of his Chartered Company that struck the hour of opportunity in the north and catalysed the new set of forces.

It was for some such event that the missions seemed to have been waiting. About 1890 there was suddenly new activity on the part of South African missions eager to share in the evangelistic opportunity. A considerable number of missions entered Rhodesia in the following decade. Theirs was an exercise in missionary strategy (Van der Merwe 1952, 1953).

The London Missionary Society was already present. In 1859 Robert Moffat had received land from Mzilikazi in the valley of Inyati and this became the name of the first Matabele station of the Society. In 1870 Lobengula followed his father's generous example and granted the L.M.S. land south-east of Bulawayo. Here the Hope Fountain mission was established. From 1875 C. D. Helm resided there, close to the king and his court. The missions occupied large tracts of land, Inyati covering some 8,000 acres and Hope Fountain over 6,000. By its prestigious connections with the Moffats and their 'legacy of heroism' (Goodall 1954: 241) and with Lobengula, the L.M.S. seemed to be in a better position than the others to avail itself of the new opportunity farther north. This, however, was deceptive.

The Matabele Mission was a frustrating experience for the energetic English missionaries. After thirty-five years with four missionaries at work the statistical result in 1895 was one unordained African teacher and one baptised convert, with some 100 hesitant inquirers (Goodall 1959: 243). Lobengula's influence had produced a sullen and effective resistance to the new message. This was a warning which the missionaries did not take amiss. Some of them had been biding their time to go north, where the Shona seemed to promise a greater response.

The directors of the L.M.S. in London were disappointed and the Foreign Secretary of the Society, W. Thompson, wrote to Helm (21.3.1889):

'It is quite impossible for the Society to undertake any further work in Matabeleland in its present condition. In fact we are seriously considering where we can most conveniently curtail our operations. Were it not for the importance of holding our positions in Matabeleland in view of the political changes which are going on, I think there would not be wanting those who would strongly urge that we should retire from that field of labour.'

So much was this discussed among the L.M.S. missionaries that J. S. Moffat in a letter to Thompson underlined the importance of a missionary's presence at the court. He noted, 'Mr Helm is fully alive to the importance of more time being spent "*enkosini*",' (with the King at court) and continued (12.9.1888): 'It ought to be an absolute rule that each one of the missionaries spend three months in each year with the chief, in actual residence on the spot, not flitting to and fro like a bird which leaves no trace or footsteps. I am certain that this will tell within an appreciable time.'

There were already several gentle and meek birds hopping about, but more important were the predators. 'Gold and the gospel are fighting for the mastery and I fear gold will win', was David Carnegie's forecast from Hope Fountain when he wrote to his society in January 1889.

The first English missionary to arrive on the scene was the young Bishop of Bloemfontein, G. W. H. Knight-Bruce, who made a preparatory tour of Rhodesia in the second half of 1888. Soon afterwards, Rhodes's emissary C. D. Rudd visited Lobengula and, as is well known, 'I Lobengula, King of Matabeleland, Mashonaland and certain adjoining territories' eventually signed the Concession. C. D. Helm, the senior L.M.S. missionary at the court, acted as interpreter and was asked to sign as a 'witness' (Fripp and Hiller 1949: 220).

It was a difficult decision to make and a great responsibility for the missionary on the spot. It was rather easier for the mission administration in London to know what the missionary should have done in an unwonted situation of this kind. Thompson felt that, however valuable it was for his mission to be represented at the court, in the long run the missionary's assistance might do harm even in the subordinate role of interpreter. Thompson was the 'statesman' (Goodall 1954: 553) with a tradition of Liberalism and Independentism. He was by nature inclined to give the individual missionary his personal freedom although he emphasised the responsibility which membership in a District Committee laid upon the man in the field.

He wrote to Helm (13.6.1889): 'Your explanation shows that you were led into the whole business quite innocently. I am only sorry that before undertaking to act the part of interpreter in such an important matter, it did not occur to you to have a consultation with your brethren.'

To D. Carnegie, the missionary at Hope Fountain, he wrote (3.1.1889): 'I do not see how Mr. Helm could avoid acting the part which he was required to act on the occasion, yet I wish it were possible for our Missionaries to be entirely free from any connection with the bargains between the natives and the white men.'

Yet Thompson was prepared 'to discern a Divine hand' in the political dealings. Helm himself followed the subsequent opening up of Mashonaland to white influence over the following months and seemed to overcome any doubt that he might have felt in regard to the wisdom of his linguistic intervention: 'I should be very sorry to have had anything to do with the introduction of a force of white men into Mashonaland. But now that circumstances have brought it about I rejoice greatly. . . . I firmly believe that it will be better for the Matabele themselves and immeasurably so for the Mashona' (11.8. 1890). He was supported in his attitude by his colleague Elliot, 'We on the spot hail the Charter with joy as a God-sent deliverer' (19.2. 1890).

Missionaries of other denominations now joined the northward march. As has been noted, Bishop Knight-Bruce led the way with his first tour in 1888. He had come well prepared for the advance. He had been Bishop of Bloemfontein since 1886 and had decided to make the tour and to visit Lobengula to explore the possibility of an Anglican mission among the Shona. He sought the advice of other missions, chiefly the L.M.S. with their long experience. Early in 1887 he wrote to Thompson in London, explaining some of his plans. He was anxious to avoid competition with an established mission and emphasised that he was going to work not among the Matabele but among the Shona.

Thompson sent a generous reply. He appreciated having been informed of the Bishop's intentions and told him that his own L.M.S. missionaries 'have long looked wistfully' towards Mashonaland. But the L.M.S. was not in a position to take on new work farther north: 'We have neither the men nor the means to attempt at present any settlement in such a district. Consequently it seems to me to be our plain duty to wish you good speed and a satisfactory opening for mission work in the country' (23.6.1887).

When Bishop Knight-Bruce visited Lobengula he mentioned the

idea of contacting the Shona but wisely avoided asking the King's permission to go there as he did not want to risk an outright refusal. He established excellent contacts with the L.M.S. missionaries: 'Nothing can be nicer than the intense cordiality of the London missionaries about my journey' (Fripp and Hiller 1949: 91).

Knight-Bruce and the missionaries had high hopes for the new land which they were conquering in the name of the Lord, and the bishop wrote enthusiastically to the secretary of the Society for the Propagation of the Gospel (14.1.1891): 'Events seem to [lead to] our being the influence in Mashonaland corresponding to that which Dr. Moffat's and Dr. Livingstone's successors are in Bechuanaland and Matabeleland.'

The L.M.S. missionaries felt that their opportunity had now arrived. They had waited for a long time with little apparent result among the Matabele. For them too the Shona in the north seemed far more promising. There had to come a change: 'The idea of "as you were" is well nigh intolerable as anticipatory of the future,' wrote Elliot (21.6.1890). He had started learning Shona and soon had a vocabulary of 1,300–1,400 words in preparation for 'an exploratory trip to the North'.

Carnegie agreed with Elliot. He had heard that the Shona were intelligent and industrious and hoped to form the nucleus of an industrial institute, 'a future Lovedale, say'. This projected enterprise in the north would not exclude advance in the south. On the contrary the plan meant, he felt, 'that the down-trodden Mashona would become the instruments by which the Matabele are to be brought to Christ' (14.2.1890).

The suggestions and proposals directed to the mission headquarters in London failed to move Thompson, the Foreign Secretary. He had a wide view of the world missionary endeavour and knew competition between missionary societies for what it was – a disgrace. On behalf of his Society he had given an undertaking to Bishop Knight-Bruce not to enter Shona country and he insisted on the principle of 'comity', a new concept in missionary strategy that had been introduced, largely on Thompson's initiative, at the Centenary Missionary Conference in London in 1888. Comity meant 'mutual division of missionary territory in spheres of occupation together with non-interference in one another's affairs' (Beaver 1970). Thompson felt that his fine principle must be followed in the case of Mashonaland. He told the missionaries on the spot what had been decided on their behalf between the bishop and himself as Congregational Missions Secretary:

'This left the field free to the Bishop and he certainly has the first right to occupy it. It is therefore quite clear that our duty is to stay where we are' (10.7.1890).

Thompson made an effort to moderate this blunt declaration by a conciliatory word to encourage his missionaries, emphasising Carnegie's point that a new day would also dawn for the Matabele. He tried to console Elliot by remarking, 'No one can object to your attempting to reach the Mashona who are actually in Matabeleland, especially the Northern part of it' (24.7.1890). It was, however, a crushing blow. Elliot had the habit of referring to himself and his colleagues as 'we on the spot' and he now wrote on behalf of his colleagues and himself (15.8.1890):

'I have been more bitterly disappointed over this matter than over almost anything else in all my life. . . . That the hope that has done so much to sustain us during the weary, miserable years should be dashed to the ground is almost heart-breaking. I still hope for the chance of getting to work among the Mashona. Fiat voluntas tua, Domine.'

The Anglicans and Methodists now set out to work in their new field, and both were provided with ample farms by Rhodes's representative Dr. Jameson (Knight-Bruce to Tucker, 14.1.1891). Knight-Bruce's view was comprehensive; the whole of Mashonaland was, in principle, his responsibility. Isaac Shimmin, the Methodist, did not agree: 'I am afraid he is rather inclined to look with suspicion upon other churches as intruders in his diocese,' he wrote in his journal (25.11.1891). The Bishop's inclusive view put him at some advantage in his approaches to the chiefs. In what appears to be a reference to the Methodists his report for 1893 stated: 'The representative of one of the most energetic of Missionary Societies after travelling through the country for some time came back saying that all the great chiefs in the country were in the hands of the English church.' He felt this was an exaggeration, but was nevertheless glad to note, 'We have an almost unbroken chain of places visited among the chiefs for 200 miles to the North through Fort Salisbury and to the South of Umtali for 70 miles' (yearly report, November 1893, to S.P.G.).

It was this view that led Knight-Bruce to participate in the Matabele War in 1893. He did so with a grand gesture; he was the Bishop, after all, and were not all those who fought, black as well as white, actual or potential members of his flock? He asserted, 'I went as the Bishop of the country in which the war took place, and not as the chaplain to any force. Both the combatants, the Matabele and the British

South Africa Company's troops, were my people, and the fighting was all in my diocese' (Knight-Bruce 1970: 220f).

Against the Anglican claims the Methodists felt that they had to defend their rights and that they could not afford to be as complaisant as were their L.M.S. brethren in the south. Shimmin considered the Bishop's activities somewhat overbearing and insisted that his reaction was shared by others: 'Mr. Watkins will be able to tell you', he wrote to Hartley at the London headquarters, 'about the Bishop. I think his Lordship's exclusiveness of spirit is very absurd, especially in a country where all churches can have plenty of elbow room' (13.4. 1892).

The Methodists from South Africa felt that they had now become pioneers again, and one may observe their fascination with the northern horizon in their writing from this time. Isaac Shimmin was elated at having crossed the Limpopo: 'We felt devoutly thankful that we had been permitted to cross the barrier that had so long stopped our progress Northward. I reflected that I was the first Wesleyan Minister to set foot upon this new Land' (Journal, 14.7.1891).

Soon he was coming closer to an even mightier river and felt the thrill of having reached farther north than any of his colleagues:

I could not help feeling rather proud of the task. Here I was nearer to the centre of Africa than any other Wesleyan minister had ever been before – within miles of the great river Zambesi – the first to carry the gospel into those wild regions, hundreds of miles of unoccupied country behind me and in front an open door to millions of heathen. But I have no doubt regarding the future. The people called Methodists believe in Forward Movements – here there is a mighty stride onward in the foreign field. Since last June our Church has moved forward nearly seven hundred miles beyond Good Hope, our most northerly Mission Station in the Transvaal. . . . And surely the fact that our flag is now waving within a few days' journey of the river Zambesi is sufficient to intensify the enthusiasm of every earnest worker in the Kingdom of Christ.

The flag took him to flights of imagination and expression that had a touch of his contemporary Joseph Conrad writing about the Congo. Shimmin wrote: 'Our flag and we must never desert it, rather will we fight up to it and beyond it, until we cross the Zambesi and join hands with the other great churches in penetrating the darkest parts of the heart of this great Continent' (Report, April 1892). His mind's eye saw Methodist influence stretching far north: 'My hope is to have eventually a chain of stations from Marico in the South to the Zambesi in the North.'

He wrote to Hartley, his Mission Secretary in London, anxious to enlist his name in support of his enthusiastic drive northward:

'Tomorrow I start for the North in order to select a Mission Farm as near as I can to the Zambesi. . . . We shall call it Hartleytown, unless you make some serious objection. It would give great pleasure to many of your friends to have your name associated with the farthest advancement post' (Journal, 25.11.1891).

Both Anglicans and Methodists insisted on bringing in African staff from South Africa. In the light of his missionary experience in South Africa Shimmin felt it desirable to take 'several African evangelists' with him on his first journey to the north: 'I hold the view very strongly that the best way to reach the natives is by the natives themselves. . . . I was sorry that my advice was not taken. We could find immediately work for a dozen at least, at important native centres' (Journal of the Mashonaland Mission, 29.11.1891). Very soon, however, he was able to report that his Methodist establishment included two missionaries (Shimmin himself and the Rev. Eva) and eight African evangelists ('The Mashonaland Mission', n.d., received 19.12.1892).

In the same way, Knight-Bruce had insisted on taking African catechists with him for the journey north. The Bishop's party in 1891 included five such catechists, among whom were two Zulu and the remarkable Bernard Mizeki, a Capetonian of Shangaan/Chopi birth and descent (Farrant 1966). By March 1891 Knight-Bruce was planning a Catechist College, but ill health and the climate took their toll upon his youthful energies and he who had travelled so far so swiftly was of necessity invalided to England by 1894.

The Bishop's chaplain, Douglas Pelly, was also aware of the need for African co-workers in the task of evangelism. His first linguistic efforts suggested that he was probably right in so thinking. In a letter to his parents in England he gave an unconscious illustration of the difficulties encountered, an idea of how it all began (how we all began): 'I am trying to get them to say a prayer which I have taught them and I think they will do so and appreciate what they say. It is, "*Inkoss, Makoola Inkoss, foona moshli m'beelo; nika meena moshli m'beely. Meena feeli, tata meena parolo.*" Quite literally it means, "Oh Chief, Great Chief, I wish for a good heart, give me a good heart. When I am dead, take me up above" (17.7.1892. Printed in Mashonaland Paper III, January 1893). The young missionary must have felt that he was indeed far north in the wilds of Africa, for he adds the reflection, 'In a way, perhaps, beginning with so small a knowledge of the language may be good, as it limits one to *very* rudimentary and simple ideas.'

Beach has shown very convincingly the decisive role of African evangelists in pre-1890 missionary endeavours among the Southern Sotho (Beach 1973). His observations are a timely reminder of a dimension in African church history often much too easily overlooked. In this connection there is a great need for a diachronic study of African clergy in certain churches from South Africa with early missionary outreach to Rhodesia and Zambia. A general observation which I have made requires testing on a wider scale: that the second and third generations in the families of those first South African catechists who settled in Rhodesia provide a significant number of pastors and church presidents (or bishops) in Rhodesia and Zambia. This observation would appear to apply to African independent churches too, and Daneel's important research on Shona Zionists (Daneel 1972) indicates the need for an historical study of the origin of such churches in Transvaal organisations like the Zion Christian Church.

From a number of South African missions that penetrated Rhodesia before the turn of the century three have been selected here to illustrate their view of the northern horizon. In the years immediately after 1900, the situation changed. Conditions now seemed to indicate Matabeleland rather than Mashonaland as being receptive to new missions. An example of the new arrivals is the Church of Sweden Mission, which had been active in Natal since 1878.

Among Lutheran organisations, the Church of Sweden Mission was a comparative latecomer. Decades earlier, Norwegian and German missions had begun their work according to strategically well-planned patterns, and the latecomers to Natal and Zululand had to fit in as best they could. A feeling of being squeezed made this particular mission look northward towards the open spaces. This perspective was, of course, only relative, for while the Swedish Lutherans eyed Rhodesia, some missionaries in Mashonaland were already beginning to feel crowded. Alfred Sharp, a Methodist, wrote to London (28.9.1900): 'The condition of the country does not offer much hope for any very wide extension. I sometimes think that Rhodesia is played out.'

During the Anglo–Boer War the Swedes discussed plans for an extension to Rhodesia and in the latter part of 1902 a Swedish 'Matabele expedition' explored prospects in Matabeleland. The commission suggested the Belingwe and Selukwe districts as being suitable for their work. Once again the frontier idea was basic to their considerations. Rhodesia seemed to open up new and virgin conditions:

[In Rhodesia] we shall always have the essential advantage of being the first in the field, thus a very different proposition from entering an area where perhaps decades earlier older missions have established themselves, others having to squeeze in between. In the suggested districts, our Mission will be freed from the rather delicate task of negotiations with other missions. That would apply to Mashonaland where at least five mission societies have built their stations. It should be pointed out that as soon as the railway crosses the Zambesi, which is imminent, the road lies open to Rhodesia north of the Zambesi for such missions as would otherwise have to squeeze themselves in between those working in Southern Rhodesia. The proposed field affords the only opportunity for a field where the frontiers will not be felt as too narrow. (Liljestrand: Report, July–November 1902)

The Commission's proposal was accepted and the Swedes came to Rhodesia. Among them was a young poetess, Ida Granqvist, who had come to Natal in 1908 and in an emergency helped for a short while in the new field in Rhodesia. Such was the strength of *Zeitgeist* – then as always – that the Swedish lady was as inspired by Rhodes's vision of a hinterland as any compatriot of Rhodes. As a poetess, her response was to write poems about Rhodes, his hinterland and her own missionary task. Her volume of Swedish poems, *Runes*, published in 1916, is a paean to the Victorian heroes of Empire, with sixty-two poems on David Livingstone, twenty-two on Charles Gordon and thirteen on Cecil Rhodes. The last poem in the book shows the young missionary posing at Rhodes's statue in Cape Town in 1915. Some of her credulous verse is here translated as a poetic definition of the missionaries' northern horizon and as a reminder of an age that is no longer.

At the Rhodes Statue in Cape Town, 1915

Here I came, and seven years have passed,
  Arrived an alien from a foreign strand.
I asked: is this my goal at last,
  But knew: '*There* is your hinterland.'

Cecil Rhodes, your voice led me along
  The road made known by your own hand.
Until my end I shall hear this song,
  Again and again: '*There* is your hinterland.'

V. W. Turner

DEATH AND THE DEAD IN THE
PILGRIMAGE PROCESS

It is appropriate to begin with three brief quotations directly connecting pilgrimage with death and salvation, three themes of this study. The first is from Leslie Farmer (1944: 79) on the Christian pilgrimage to Jerusalem: 'It was a common custom to bring one's shroud to be cut to the size of the Stone of Unction' (in the Church of the Holy Sepulchre). The second is from Sir Richard Burton (1964, vol. 2: 183, n. 2): 'Those who die on a pilgrimage become martyrs . . . the ghost departs to instant beatitude.' And the last is from Romain Roussel (1954: 240–1): 'The pilgrim [to Mecca] knows that he will present himself at the Last Judgement covered with his *ihram* pilgrim's garb [two simple white pieces of cloth]. That is why many of those who fulfil the *haj* wish to be buried in the dress they wore at Mecca.'

But it is only death on the way to or at the shrine that makes a pilgrimage a true rite of passage, as we shall see, though pilgrimages do share many features with initiation rites.

Pilgrimages in the salvation religions, like initiation rites in tribal religions, are full of symbols and metaphors for death, and are also directly concerned with the dead. The dead may include the founder of a religion, his kin, disciples or companions, saints and martyrs of the faith, and the souls of the ordinary faithful. This is partly because both pilgrims and initiands are undergoing a separation from a relatively fixed state of life and social status and are passing into a liminal or threshold phase and condition for which none of the rules and few of the experiences of their previous existence had prepared them. In this sense, they are 'dying' from what was and passing into an equivocal domain occupied by those who are (in various ways) 'dead' to quotidian existence in social systems. To use terminology favoured by Radcliffe-Brown (1957: 22), initiand and pilgrim cease to be members of a perduring *system* of social relations (family, lineage, village, neighbourhood, town, state) and become members of a transient *class* of initiands and pilgrims, moving *per agros*, through the fields or lands.

This entails that the actors in ritual and pilgrimage processes leave a domain where relations are complex, for one where they are simple. Their relations with others are, at any rate at first, no longer those of interconnectedness but of similarity: no longer do they occupy social positions in a hierarchical or segmentary structure of localised status-roles; now they are assigned to a class of anonymous novices or plainly and uniformly garbed pilgrims, all torn or self-torn from their familiar systemic environment. Again, while a system has *characteristic form*, and is governed by rules of social and cultural construction, a class of liminal initiands or pilgrims is *without form*, is a homogenised mass of like components – at least initially. While homesteaders are *co-ordinated by interdependence*, pilgrims and initiands are co-ordinated by *similarity*, by likeness of lot rather than interdependence of social position. And whereas members of an established social system play roles and occupy statuses that are functionally consistent, there may be no functional relationship among novices or pilgrims. Again, a stabilised social system has a structure, but novices and pilgrims confront one another at first as a mere aggregate, without organic unity.

In these respects, 'system' may be symbolically equated with 'life', in ritual, and 'extrusion from system' – as a phase of a ritual or pilgrimage process – as 'death', since all that makes for interconnectedness, integration, co-ordination, form, structure, and functional consistency – all that constitutes the order of daily life in the lives of the actors – is annulled or abrogated. Metaphorically, the novice or pilgrim experiences 'the pains of dissolution'. This is one reason why symbols of death, dying, and katabolism proliferate in tribal initiation rites. For example, Monica Wilson writes (1957: 205) on what I would call the 'liminal' (threshold) phase of the rituals of birth, puberty and marriage, death, abnormal birth and misfortune among the Nyakyusa:

'There can be no doubt that the induction [into the ritual situation] and seclusion represent death. Strewing leaves – or laying a litter – which is an essential act in every induction, is a sign of misfortune and death; and at the induction of a bride her "mothers" sing: "Go, go and never return," and "We wail a dirge". The mourners, the nubile girls, the mother of a new born child, and the parents of twins are all "filthy" and one with the dead; Kasitile [Wilson's best informant] said of mourners: "We have died, we *are* the corpse".'

In my book, *The Forest of Symbols* (1967), I give many further examples, drawn from tribal societies, of symbols and metaphors for death in initiation rites: 'The initiand may be buried, forced to lie motionless in the posture and direction of customary burial, may be stained black, or may be forced to live for a while in the company of masked and monstrous mummers representing, *inter alia*, the dead.'

Again, among the Ndembu of Zambia, in several types of ritual an officiant known as the 'hyena' (*chimbu*), characteristically a snatcher both of carrion and of the young of other species, 'snatches' the novices from their mothers to be circumcised in the *Mukanda* circumcision rites, while the bloodsoaked site of the operation is called *ifwilu*, 'the place of death or dying'. Circumcision is partly a metaphor for killing, since it 'kills' the novice's childhood state. Such instances could be greatly multiplied from ethnographic literature. Symbols and metaphors (and other tropes) for structural erasure, rendering the initiands faceless, 'dark', and 'invisible', and anonymous, through disguise, body painting and use of a generic term of address instead of a personal name ('novice', 'neophyte', 'initiand') also abound.

But the detachment of an initiand or novice from the system in which he has been embedded may also have a religiously positive aspect. It may be interpreted as rebirth and growth. From this perspective the abandoned system may be 'death', and the new liminal state the germ of 'life' or spiritual development. Thus, while from one point of view, the shift from complex, interconnected relations to simple relations of likeness may be regarded not so much as a negative dissolution of an ordering, articulating structure, the decay of a complex living organism, but rather as a positive release from the distancing between individuals which their membership of social positions in a system involves.

Structural distance may, then, be an apt symbol for death, the dissolution of distance, rebirth into authentic social life. They may see the move *away* as an opportunity for a direct, immediate confrontation of others as total human beings, no longer as segments or facets of a structured system. Thus among many West Central Bantu peoples, the circumcised novices become fast friends during a long period of seclusion together, even though before the operation they lived in different villages and even chiefdoms, structured units normally in continuous low-key conflict with one another. Moreover, even the most harmoniously articulated structures in any culture produce some degree of 'alienation', for the fullness of an individual's being overflows the totality of his roles and statuses. Structure, too, whether of small-scale or large-scale social systems, is provocative of competition and conflict. Social and political systems contain offices, high, medial, and low; chains of command; bureaucratic ladders. There are systems of promotion, rules and criteria for status elevation and degradation, laws concerning the protection, disposal, transference, and inheritance of property, and succession to high office. There are social controls over sexuality and reproductive capacity, rules governing marriage and prohibitions on incest and adultery. In this many-levelled, ordered and sanctioned field, individuals find it hard not to envy their neighbour's good fortune, covet his ox, ass, or lands, strive with him for office, compete with him on the promotion ladder, seek to commit adultery with his wife, become greedy or miserly, or fall into despair at their own lack of success.

But when they are lifted by initiation ritual or voluntarily elect to go on pilgrimage, they may see the metaphoric death mentioned earlier as a death from the negative, alienating aspects of system and structure, as an opportunity to take stock of the lives from which they are now temporarily detached, or, alternatively, regain an innocence felt by them to have been lost. They may feel that a death from self, or in traditional Christian terms from the World, the Flesh, and the Devil, may be simultaneously a birth or rebirth of an identity splintered and crushed by social structure. Ordinary, mundane life may be reinterpreted as the Terrene City; its abandonment as a first glimpse of the Heavenly City. The move into liminality is here, therefore, a death–birth or a birth–death. This is explicitly formulated by Monica Wilson in a continuation of the passage already quoted. Furthermore, as you will see, this quotation raises the problem of the second term in my title; what is the role of the dead in initiatory liminality? Later we shall examine this role in pilgrimage liminality: now we see it in tribal initiation, of which Wilson writes (1957: 205):

'The period of seclusion implies a *sojourn with the shades* [my italics], and our hypothesis is that it represents *both* death and gestation. The hut appears as a symbol of the womb in the pregnancy and "gasping cough" [a Nyakyusa category of illness] rituals, and the doorway which "belongs to the shades" is a symbol for the vagina.'

Wilson interprets certain symbolic actions, as when mourners or the girl novice in puberty rites run in and out of the doorway, to represent rebirth. I have noticed 'gateway' symbols not only in African rituals but also as an outstanding feature of the precincts of Catholic pilgrimage shrines, as at Lourdes, Remedios in Mexico City, and Chalma in Mexico State.

Thus we have metaphorical death in tribal rituals, parallel perhaps with 'mystical death' in the salvation religions of complex societies; and metaphorical rebirth, homologous to 'spiritual regeneration'. Or perhaps we might speak of ritual liminality as an exteriorised mystical way, and the mystic's path as interiorised ritual liminality. We also have the involvement during liminality of the dead; in the Nyakyusa case, of the ancestral shades. The dead also partake of the ambiguous quality of liminality, the state of betwixt-and-between-ness, for they are associated with both positive and negative processes and objects, with life and death: 'We have spoken', writes Wilson (1957: 207), 'of the Nyakyusa disgust for filth (*ubunyali*), which is associated with a corpse, menstruation, childbirth, intercourse, faeces, and all these are identified in some fashion with the shades. Faeces "go below to the land of the shades".' There is about all this the image of 'dust to dust'. But there is an opposite quality attached to the shades. Wilson writes (p. 205): 'All through the rituals the connection of the shades with potency and fertility is emphasized . . . they are present in intercourse and ejected as semen; they control conception; they control fertility in the fields. "The shade and semen are brothers," said one informant. And another said: "When they shake the millet and pumpkin-seeds [after ritual connection] the seed is semen . . . and it is the shade" ' (quotations from various informants of the Wilsons).

The shades therefore represent both the decay of the body and the spirit of fertility, reminding one of the Biblical seed that must first die before it can yield much fruit. This metaphor has of course to be seen in the context of a religion of personal salvation, and not, as in the Nyakyusa case, of a religion of community maintenance, where localised community has facets of system, class and *communitas*. In the Christian case the death metaphor applies both to the 'death' of the individual *from* the local structured community, and to the death of that 'organic' group for the individual. Nevertheless, both in Nyakyusa pagan and Christian modes of liminality there are notions that initiands and pilgrims are simultaneously undergoing the death of social structure and regeneration in *communitas*, social anti-structure. First they must cease to be members of a system and become members of a class, then they must be reborn in that modality of social interrelatedness I have called, for want of a better term in English, existential *communitas* – which might be paraphrased as true fellowship, or *agape*, or spontaneous, altruistic love – if one also concedes that there is a well-defined cognitive or 'intellectual' (in Blake's sense) component in the relationship. For it is not a merging of consciousnesses, nor an emotional melding, but rather a mutual recognition of 'definite, determinate identities' (to cite Blake again), each with its wiry, unique, indefeasible outline. All are one because each is one. In this process of death and regeneration – at both social and individual levels – different types of religions assign a mediating function to the human dead: those who have already undergone the passage from visible and tangible to invisible and intangible states of being.

This function is on the one hand concerned with maintaining the social structure of the system in its characteristic form, with all its moral and jural rules, by acting as a punitive sanction against any major transgression of the basic legal, ethical, and commonsense principles determining the shape or profile of that system. On the other hand, the dead are concerned with two extra-structural, perhaps anti-structural modalities: biological (or 'natural'), and spiritual. In the first modality, as in the Nyakyusa case, and quite typical of many parts of Africa, and elsewhere as we shall see, the dead are thought to mediate between the invisible, ideal world of paradigms and arche-types and the sensorily perceptible world of sex and economics, begetting and food production, distribution, and consumption. If the dead are honoured, known, and recognised, they will differentially, and in terms of structural differences, bestow blessings. Meyer Fortes's work on *pietas* is most pertinent here. But the dead, as we have seen in Wilson's work, are also regarded as *powers*, as themselves being the 'force that through the green fuse thrusts the shoot' and through the loins and wombs of human beings thrusts progeny. In the Ndembu *Chihamba* ritual, a spirit or arch-ancestor is 'planted' in symbolic form, including the seeds and roots of food plants, in order that people and crops will multiply. And in salvation religions the dead are also regarded as possessing a mediating role in the drama of salvation, the freeing or binding of the immortal human soul, that invisible formative principle, which is believed to survive death, but to undergo punishment or reward for its consciously willed acts during life.

The dead have *influence over* the living and are reciprocally *influenced by* their thoughts, words, and deeds. The dead can spiritually fructify the living, in Catholic theological thought at least; and it is not only in the folk dimension but also in theological terms that they are regarded as having an influence on the physical fertility, and certainly on the health, of the living. I quote from the *Knock Shrine Annual* for 1968, which records news of all group pilgrimages to the famous Irish shrine and publishes letters expressing gratitude to its mediating saints for favours believed to have been received through their mediation with God. One letter runs (p. 119): 'I wish to acknowledge my thanks to Our Lady of Knock, St. Joseph and St. John for the gift of two little girls and also recovery from heart trouble, and for many other favours and graces over the years. A client of Our Lady.' This is typical of many hundreds of letters published by journals connected with pilgrimage shrines.

I am not competent to discuss the relationship between the living and the dead in such salvation religions (to use Weber's term) as Hinduism, Islam, Buddhism, Judaism, Taoism, and Jainism, to mention only a few of those which profess to offer permanent or temporary surcease or release from the 'human condition' of what one might term *structural* morality and its behavioural consequences, either of 'uptight' virtue or the slavery of sin. But I have in the past few years gone, both as participant observer and observing participant (the anthropologist's perennial human dilemma, which he resolves one way or the other to his creative loss), on a number of pilgrimage journeys to Catholic shrines such as Guadalupe, Ocotlan, Remedios, Chalma, Izamal, Tizimin, Acambaro, Amecameca, and others in Mexico; Knock, Croagh Patrick, Lough Dearg, Limerick, and Cork in Ireland; Walsingham, Glastonbury, Canterbury, and Aylesford in England, the Catacombs, Santa Maria Maggiore, St. Peter's, Santa Maria Ara Coeli, and other Roman churches of the pilgrimage path within Rome, in Italy; Lourdes in France; and other pilgrimage centres, in the Old and New Worlds. These travels in space led to travels in time, and I have been avidly reading historical records of Christian pilgrimage through the ages in many places.

What put me on to this recent research? Partly, of course, personal needs, some of them probably unconscious, which I am therefore the last person to understand. But there was also a theoretical or disciplinary component in the decision to study pilgrimages. I have always regarded anthropology as a process of *reculer pour mieux sauter*, which may be paraphrased as 'going to a far place to understand a familiar place better', which incidentally, might also serve as a part-definition of the pilgrimage process. One might also see pilgrimage partly as a rehearsal of the pilgrim's own death, as a process of death-readiness. Sooner or later, we anthropologists have to come home having experienced a partial death of our home-born stereotypes and domestic values – a point outlined by Lévi-Strauss in his *Tristes Tropiques* (1955). 'Home' for me is the tradition of Western European culture, and since I have always defined ritual as 'quintessential culture', if I were to come home I felt I should look at the domestic forms of the ritual process.

What I was looking for was, in fact, the characteristic cultural modality of liminality in the salvation religions, specifically in Christianity, and established in the formative period of that religion. In other words, *what* was to Christian salvific belief and practice the homologue of the liminality of major initiations in tribal religions? I was looking for a homology that was substantial rather than merely formal. Superficially, the Christian sacramental system, plus funerary, purificatory and some other rituals, might seem to supply liminal phases equivalent to those in tribal *rites de passage*. But in terms of differences in scale and complexity between the societies having these religions, it seemed to me that pilgrimage was to complex salvation religion what the protracted seclusion periods of initiation rites were to tribal and archaic religions.

Christian pilgrimage, as an object of study, may have escaped Western intellectuals because it is too 'familiar' to us, too close for comfort, whether we are scientists or theologians. I would distinguish pilgrimage from initiation as a locus of liminality by saying that it is, like many features of life in large-scale, complex societies, rooted in optation, in voluntariness, while initiation is founded in obligation, in duty. Initiations fit best in societies with ascribed status, pilgrimages in those where status may not only be achieved, but also rejected. In tribal societies men and women *have* to go through rites of passage transferring them from one state and status to another; in post-tribal societies of varying complexity and degree of development of the social division of labour, people can *choose* to go on pilgrimage. This is true even when, as in medieval Islam and Temple Judaism, pilgrimage was held to be of obligation, for a variety of mitigating circumstances and escape clauses were spelt out which made pilgrimage a matter of optation rather than of duty. Christian pilgrimage remained in principle a matter for the individual conscience, though it became in the waning of the Middle Ages almost a matter of obligation under the church's penitential system for those who had committed serious civil crimes as well as religious sins. In Catholic theology it was, and remains, an eminently 'good work', of counsel, not precept – thus differing from the obligatory 'recourse to the sacraments' – which may *aid* the individual's salvation by securing for him many 'graces' but cannot, after the manner of an initiation, *guarantee* it.

This is the crucial difference between the two liminalities. Initiation is an irreversible, one-way process, transforming the state and status of the initiand. Pilgrimage is part of a lifelong drama of salvation or damnation, hinging on individual choice, which itself involves acceptance or rejection by an individual of 'graces', or freely volunteered gifts, from God. Irrespective of one's intention, one is *changed* by initiation, *ex opere operato*. Moreover, initiation's primary referent is to the total social system. Individuals have meaning in this frame only insofar as it is necessary for the structured group to redefine them cognitively from time to time as members of a class other than that which they belonged to before, and more than this, to alter them substantially to perform the duties and enjoy the rights of that class by means of symbolic action. Initiation rituals are, as Fernandez would put it, 'sets of enacted correspondences', metaphorical actions which, by virtue of the novices' involvement in them, teach them, even non-verbally, how to comport themselves when they are inducted into their new station in life. They are to be returned, furthermore to the same structural system, even if it be at a higher level or position in that system.

Life and death are often thought of, in these societies, to be what the poet Rilke called the 'great circulation'. Rilke, like all poets, was nostalgic for societies where nature and culture were more directly conjoined in metaphor and metonymy than in our literate, industrial society – where, as Eliot writes, 'the shadow' (or scientific objectification, making possible both the use and misuse of nature by culture on a large scale, as well as 'original sin') falls between them. Organic processes and the seasonal round provide root-metaphors for cultural processes which are perceived, therefore, as cyclical, and proceed through the life and death of vegetation, the fertility and latency of animals, which mark the annual round. Thus, although initiations are irreversible, in their total sequence they convey the ageing individual to the beginning again, to be reborn after the funeral (which is an initiation) as an infant from one of his own totemic clan descendants perhaps. In initiations, too, the *fiat* of the whole community, expressed through its representative elders, is crucial for inaugurating symbolic action.

Initiations, too, fairly regularly exhibit the *rite de passage* form discovered by Van Gennep with its three phases: (1) separation; (2) margin or limen; and (3) reaggregation or reincorporation, conceived of as an irreversible sequence, like the human lives they service and mediate. But pilgrimages, though liminal (or perhaps better, *liminoid*, since the liminoid resembles but does not coincide with the liminal), are in principle quite different from initiations – though, as salvation religions become routinised, their pilgrimages tend to revert or regress to initiatory devices. In Christian terms pilgrimage becomes the sacrament of penance writ large, though not ever acquiring a completely sacramental character. But the very fact of its not being sacramental, not therefore being *necessary* for salvation, not being a matter of ecclesiastical precepts, makes pilgrimage already a major expression of the 'modern' spirit, the spirit expressed in the primacy, say, of contract over status, in Sir Henry Maine's terms, of ethics over magic, of personal responsibility over corporate affiliation.

Pilgrimage is to a voluntaristic, what initiation is to an obligatory system. The fact that people opt to go on pilgrimage rather than *have to* be initiated, that they make a vow to a patron saint to be his client by making a pilgrimage to his shrine, to my mind, accounts for its paradigmatic charm for such literary figures as Chaucer, Dante (with his immortal *pellegrini* of *Il Purgatorio*, the transitional book of *The Divine Comedy*), and Bunyan. The plain truth is that pilgrimage does not ensure a major change in religious state – and seldom in secular status – though it may make one a better person, fortified by the graces merited by the hardships and self-sacrifice of the journey. Folk-belief, in Christianity and Islam, does of course insist that if one dies at the holy places, Mecca, Jerusalem or Compostella, one goes straight to Heaven or Paradise, but this very belief lends support to the view that in salvation religions, of the Semitic type at least, it is one's stance that is all-important for one's personal salvation. Death sums up and epitomises the quality of an individual life. But even the best pilgrims may backslide. This is precisely because the will, the *voluntas*, of the individual is the fulcrum of the whole matter. Shift it a bit and past achievement falls to the ground. The role of the social in pilgrimage differs markedly from society's role in initiation. In pilgrimage the pilgrim divests himself by personal choice of his structural incumbencies; in initiation social pressures enforce symbolic, transformative action upon the individual. In neither case is communitas ensured; the pilgrim may leave the familiar system and become a member of a class of pilgrims. But he need not necessarily enter a communitas of pilgrims, neither in the easygoing Chaucerian fellowship of the road nor in the eucharistic communion at the shrine itself, mentioned by pilgrims such as Holy Paula or the Abbot Daniel, whose narratives are included in the volumes of *Palestine Pilgrims Text Society*.

In initiation the actor may enter the class of novices without helping to generate a communitas of novices. But the dying from *system* into *class* may, in each case, facilitate the communitas experience, the subjective sense of antistructure which has had so many important objective results in the history of religion.

Another difference is that initiation is often localised in a protected place – though its ordeals may be dangerous – whereas pilgrimage is often hazardous. Pilgrims, on the other hand, are exposed to a wide range of geographical, climatic and social conditions, sometimes traversing several national frontiers. Though at the end they perform formal rituals, on the way they are vulnerable to historical accident. This implication with history is, again, modern. I have recently been studying pilgrimage systems – that is, processes focused on specific shrines – in their historical dimension, both from the perspective of their internal dynamics, their *entelechy*, and from that of the currents of thought, movements of political power, and shifts in popular opinion, supporting or assailing them. Pilgrimages, though rooted in atemporal paradigms, experience temporality in ways rather foreign to the protected milieux of initiation rituals. All this is consistent with the emphasis on free-will, personal experience, casting one's bread on the waters, the capacity to retract from commitment, etc., characteristic of salvation religions arising in and helping to shape social relations in international communities, which are ethnically plural, multilingual and multicultural.

It may also be worth mentioning that the limen of pilgrimage is, characteristically, *motion*, the movement of travel, while that of initiation is *stasis*, the seclusion of novices in a fixed, sacred space. The former liminalises time, the latter space; time is here connected with voluntariness, space with obligation.

One could ramify differences here but I must return to the central themes of death and the dead. In the liminality of initiations, the dead often appear as near or remote ancestors, connected by putative ties of consanguinity or affinity with the living, part of a communion of kin beginning with the founding ancestors, and hopefully, with due performance of ritual, continuing to the end of the world. The dead, as ancestral spirits, punish and sometimes reward the living. Kin are punished for quarrelling or for having failed to remember the ancestors in their hearts or with offerings and sacrifices. Specific ancestors usually punish specific kin or groups of kin. Most misfortune, sickness and reproductive trouble, in Central African society, for example, is attributed to the morally punitive action of the 'shades'. Once recognised, named and propitiated, however, they become benevolent guardians of their living kin, usually their lineal kin.

The dead are at once the jural and moral continuators of the society formed by their jural descendants, and by the procreative biology, the increase and multiplication, which ensures the continuance of the human matter on which that structural form is imprinted. When initiands become their companions in liminal seclusion, they, too, become moral and fertile. When I came to investigate Catholic Christian pilgrimage processes, sensitised as I was to the role of the dead in African initiation and other *passage* ritual, I soon became aware that these, too, were pervaded by ideas about how precisely the living and the dead were interconnected, but that the nature of these interconnections was consistent with the *voluntaristic* nature of the religion and indeed, the total culture, in which they were embedded.

In a crucial way, the Catholic faith itself hinges upon the self-chosen, the voluntary, *death* of its founder for the sake both of those who would come after Him, His spiritual posterity, and also of the good pagan dead, neither in Heaven nor Hell, but in Limbo, who had preceded Him, and whom He released by His descent into the nether regions during the three days between His death and resurrection in the body. This *via crucis*, death, and resurrection paradigm became the inspiration of the early martyrs, whose 'imitation of Christ' led to their death for the faith and future faithful at the hands of the pagan political authorities. Hence the well-known expression, 'the blood of the martyrs is the seed of the church', where blood equals spiritual semen.

Scholars generally hold that after the Holy Places of the Holy Land, the tombs of the martyrs, scattered throughout the Roman Empire, but particularly numerous in Rome itself, became the first pilgrimage centres. They exemplified the supreme act of Christian free-will, the choice of death for the salvific faith rather than life under the auspices of state religion. It was also believed by the masses that these places of redemptive self-sacrifice – since their martyrdom was thought to be a projection into history of Christ's redeeming self-sacrifice – were places where heaven and earth came close, even intercommunicated through the media of prayers, miracles and apparitions. Here there might be 'gaps in the curtain'. The notion of miracle, 'an effect wrought in nature independently of natural powers and laws', the extreme expression of the rare, unprecedented and idiosyncratic in experience, is counterposed to that of order and law, supreme symbols as well as agencies of social structure. It exemplifies for the faithful the *volitional* character of faith as against the 'necessary cause and effect' character of both natural and state law. Miracles might happen at martyrs' graves, because martyrs gave up their lives for the belief that God Himself alone is above and beyond Nature, and is the direct and immediate cause of salvation, defined as the 'freeing of the soul from the bonds of sin and its consequences and the attainment of the everlasting vision of God in heaven'. Miracles occur fitfully, not systematically or regularly, precisely because they are supreme acts in the drama of free-will and grace, *creative* acts in the moral order.

From these beliefs and other sources, the development of the pilgrimage process became closely linked with the doctrine of the 'communion of saints'. This postulates that under certain conditions the dead and the living can freely help one another to attain heaven, that is, the beatific vision of God in the company of all the other saints and angels. Roman legalism has worked on the notion of the communion of saints and has come to define it as 'the unity under and in Christ of the faithful on earth (the Church Militant), the souls in Purgatory (the Church Suffering), and the blessed in Heaven (the Church Triumphant)'. In principle, all these people living and dead are in the Church in the first place through optation, for even if it was the parents' will that their child should be baptised, it is as the result of his own will that the child ultimately attains salvation. God plies the soul with graces, the devil plies it with temptations, the flesh is weak, and the world is full of occasions for sin.

The drama goes on until the General Judgement. But the different components of the Church can help one another. Prayer is the mode in which communion or fellowship is most active. The living pray to God and the saints on behalf of the suffering, and to God in honour of the saints. The saints intercede with God for the suffering and the living. The suffering, the souls in Purgatory, pray to God and the saints for others. It is thought to be particularly efficacious if the living seek the intercession of the saints with God on behalf of the souls in Purgatory. Here the system comes closest to tribal animism, for, in practice, people pray most often for and to their own dead kinsfolk.

My own Catholic background and field research among Catholic countryfolk in Europe and Middle America have made me familiar with the doctrine of the *Benditas Animas* (in Mexico) or Holy Souls (in Ireland), the members of the Church in Purgatory. Purgatory, in Catholic thought, is the place and state in which souls suffer for a while on account of their sins and are purged after death, before they go to Heaven. Dante's Mount of Purgatory is, of course, the supreme literary expression of the doctrine. Most souls, it is thought, go to Purgatory, if on the whole they have shown themselves to be reasonably moral, decent people, Walt Whitman's 'Divine average'. These souls are there, either because they have committed unrepented venial sins or, having in the sacrament of penance confessed their grave sins, and been forgiven, are still required to pay a 'debt of temporal punishment'. They are purged by the pain of intense longing for God, whose beatific vision is delayed, and by some pain of sense, popularly believed to be by material fire. In this liminal period between earth and heaven, it is of faith that the souls in purgatory can be helped towards heaven or eased of pain by the prayers and sacrifices of the living, and especially by the sacrament of the eucharist – thus, virtually every mass is, even today, offered on behalf of a named relative of some parishioner. And, although there has been no ecclesiastical decision on the matter, it is widely believed throughout the entire Catholic Church that one should pray not only *for* but also *to* the souls in Purgatory that they will intercede for the living with God. In popular belief, the Holy Souls do not have immediate access to God – that is part of their purgative suffering – as the saints in heaven do, but their prayers for the living, made while in Purgatory, in a sense accumulate and, when the Holy Soul finally becomes a Saint (and no man knows the hour of this), such prayers are considered to have surplus efficacy for having so long been pent up. Therefore, so argues the Catholic peasant in many lands, it is a good bet to pray both for and to the Holy Soul, for if you pray *for* him, he will be grateful to you for speeding up his release from Purgatory, while if you pray *to* him he will carry to Heaven a great heap of your requests for God's immediate attention.

The Holy Souls resemble the Nyakyusa shades in several respects. One is that they are polluted and polluting, since they are not yet cleansed of adhering sins, but are at the same time sacred and capable, if remembered and propitiated by sacrifices, of bringing such benefits to the living as fertility of people, animals, and crops, and to fend off or remedy afflictions, such as illness, accident, injury, famine, drought, blight, plague, or reproductive disorders. There may well be some delay here, but the outcome is virtually certain. Neither Holy Souls nor shades are Saints, for these two categories are liminally in between the *moyen sensuel* of the living and the ideal sphere of the perfectly moral dead. They need help as well as bestow it. In practice, too, both Holy Souls and shades are one's kinsfolk, though in the tribal case kinship, particularly lineal kinship, may often be the very frame of institutionalised social life, while in the Catholic case the fact that kin are prayed for and to is the result of residential continuities in feudal, post-feudal and industrial–rural concrete circumstances rather than of societal axiomatic rule. But in both types of religion a normative communitas is postulated among the living and the dead. The dead need the sacrifices and prayers of the living, the living need the fructifying powers of the dead, either as mediators with Divinity for the living, or as a direct emission from the benevolent dead themselves.

Now pilgrimage may be regarded as an accelerator of normal liturgical practice. It is popularly felt that the merits acquired by the saint or martyr lent power to masses said on the altar of a church dedicated to him. Also, popes and bishops grant indulgences to those receiving communion there. When the pilgrim reaches his goal, the target-shrine, he is expected very speedily to perform two rituals of the sacramental liturgical set. These are penance and the eucharist, 'confession' and 'mass', as they are usually spoken of. The fact of having made a pilgrimage oneself is itself an amplifier of these two sacraments, in the pilgrim's eyes. These sacraments differ from the others – baptism, confirmation, marriage, ordination, and extreme unction – in not being life-crisis rituals, *rites de passage* properly speaking, but rather what anthropologists might call 'contingent' rituals, being concerned with the day-to-day maintenance of concrete individuals and groups in a state of moral, spiritual, and hence (in terms of medical theory which regards body and informing soul as a dynamic continuum) *physical* health. Thus when a pilgrim asks for a mass to be said for his dead relatives in Purgatory, this mass is thought to be the more effective on account of the time, energy and patience expended on the pilgrim's journey to the shrine, and of his other sacrifices, exposure to danger and bad weather, loss of comfort, and his overcoming of temptations on the way. There is a general theory among pilgrims, however vague, that one's personal sacrifice can be the source of graces and blessings for others. These personal losses may be transmuted, like base metal, through the pilgrim's sacrifice, into the gold of graces and blessings, released from God's treasury, in which are also stored the merits of the faithful in all the ages, for the benefit of those whom the pilgrim specifically names as beneficiaries. It is in this specificity of benefaction that purgatorial notions most remind us of animistic religions.

It is almost a truism that universal Catholic ideas about the fate of the dead in Purgatory have received most reinforcement from pre-Christian religious beliefs in the western fringes of Europe, in the surviving haunts of the Celtic peoples, Ireland, the western highlands of Scotland (Barra, South Uist), Wales, Armorican Brittany, Galicia in Spain. As William A. Christian, Jr., has recently written in an excellent account of Spanish folk-Catholicism in the Nansa valley of northern Spain (1972: 94): 'Devotion for and worry about the dead is characteristic of the entire Atlantic fringe from Galicia, through Brittany, Ireland, and England.' Similarly Georgiana Goddard King (1920, vol. 3: 235–49) and Walter Starkie (1965) have stressed connections in purgatorial beliefs between Galicia and Ireland, and Starkie has quoted from old traditions how spirits of the dead, temporarily released from Purgatory, have begged mortals, in the twilight, to pray for them that they might complete the pilgrimage to St. James's shrine at Compostella and so have their sufferings remitted. If pilgrims are companions of the dead, it is the dead of the Church Suffering, and if pilgrims are equivalent to the dead, it is to the dead in Purgatory.

My own most vivid encounter with the continuity between Celtic animism and Catholic pilgrimage beliefs about the Holy Souls has been in the west of Ireland – though Mexico, too, has its Christian cult of the dead uniting Galician and Asturian beliefs of this type to pre-Columbian Aztecan traditions, for example, in the 'Day of the Dead' in Morelos, where, on 1 November, all household members make offerings in the house and cemetery (*pantheon*) not only for the direct ascendants of the family but for all household residents, including women married into it.

My wife and I spent some months in the summer of 1972 going on and studying pilgrimages in the west of Ireland. The most important contemporary pilgrim shrine in Ireland is that of Knock in County Mayo, where, it is credibly estimated, at least 700,000 people each year visit the shrine during the pilgrimage season, a substantial proportion of the total Catholic population of Ireland, north and south. This pilgrimage is of the type I have called elsewhere 'apparitional'. The type has become established in the post-Napoleonic, industrial era of Europe, and includes such major shrines as La Salette, Lourdes, Pontmain, Pellevoisin, Fatima, Beaurang and Banneux. The Latin countries of France, Portugal, and Belgium (though here Flemish speakers have also been involved) have been the main sites of apparitions of the Virgin Mary, usually to children, alone or in groups. In most cases a message has been given by the Virgin; at La Salette in France and Fatima in Portugal especially, the message has been minatory and apocalyptic, prophesying disasters for men on earth and Hell for them after death, if they do not mend their ways. But Knock, though apparitional, contains no threatening *anima* figure portending disaster for over-technocratic and rationalistic man. The Knock apparition was peaceful and silent. Moreover, it was seen, not by children alone, but by at least fifteen people ranging in age from 75 to 6. Nor was it the Virgin alone that was seen. A number of people saw a group of supernaturals, or so they believed and testified to with convincing mutual consistency before a commission of three senior priests convoked by the Archbishop of Tuam, under whose aegis the affair came, less than two months after the apparition occurred.

On the rainy night of 21 August 1879, during one of Ireland's afflictions by potato famine and in the political context of Michael Davitt's and Parnell's struggles for land reform, Margaret, Mary and Dominick Beirne, Mary McLoughlin, Catherine Murray, and eventually, at least a dozen more villagers of the small hamlet of Knock, consisting of about a dozen or more cottages, claimed that they saw 'a sight such as was never before seen' near the gable of the village church, itself one of the first fruits of the Catholic Emancipation of 1829. What did they see? Let Michael Walsh take up the tale (1967: 6–7):

They saw three figures standing at the gable wall of the church, about eighteen inches or two feet above the ground. The central figure was recognized as that of Our Lady. She was wearing a large white cloak fastened at the neck and on her head was a brilliant crown. . . . She was raised slightly above the other figures. . . . On her right was a figure recognized as that of St. Joseph. On her left was a figure considered by Mary Beirne [the chief informant] to be St. John the Evangelist . . . on the grounds that he resembled a statue of St. John which she had seen in the church at [the coastal Mayo town of] Lecanvy. He was dressed like a bishop . . . held an open book in his left hand . . . and appeared to be preaching. On his left was an altar, full-sized, and on it was a lamb . . . facing the figures. Just behind it was a cross. . . . The figures were 'full and round as if they had a body and life . . . but they spoke no words and no words were addressed to them'.

One of the informants, Patrick Hill, 13 years old, testified that he saw 'wings fluttering' (see pp. 7–8) around the Lamb. It is to this statement that those who relate the apparition to the Holy Souls often refer. Some regard the wings as signs of angels, others as indications of the presence of the Holy Souls. The apparition began about seven o'clock in the evening and lasted several hours before fading away.

Despite anticlerical criticisms of varying kinds, for example that the apparitions had been produced by a concealed Jesuit with one of the primitive magic lanterns of that period, or that they were really a heap of holy statues ordered by the parish priest Archdeacon Cavanagh, or that Mary McLoughlin, the priest's housekeeper, a well-known alcoholic, had stirred up the lively fancy of the villagers (none of which hypotheses actually stood up to the test of evidence), the news of the apparitions spread, soon crowds collected at the gable, and miraculous cures were reported. The Archbishop's Commission's report, though not positive, was not negative either, attesting to the honesty of the fifteen witnesses, and a full-blown pilgrimage began which, with ups and downs over the decades, has finally succeeded in obtaining a papal coronation for the image of the Virgin of Knock, who is now known as the Queen of Ireland.

I first became aware of the intimate connection of Knock with the doctrine of Purgatory when my wife went on pilgrimage on 20 August 1972, to Knock from Castlebar, Mayo's County seat, thirty kilometres or so away. This was the Sunday nearest to the day of the apparition, a day on which many who were normally at work in the week could attend. She went with Bridgy Lydon, a pious old lady, who spent much of her time travelling, a true palmer, from shrine to shrine. At the Knock Shrine Society Office, Bridgy, an old-age pensioner, gave a 'widow's mite' of £5, more than a week's pension, for masses for the 'Holy Souls'. Later we learnt that the people have the theory that the testimony about 'wings' or indistinct 'flames' seen by witnesses were not angels, or beings in Heaven, as some supposed, but were indeed souls in Purgatory. As can well be imagined, the theological imagination of several generations of Irish clergy and laity has exercised itself most eloquently upon the 'meaning' of the silent apparition. Most agree that the apparition itself was a reward to Ireland for keeping the faith through centuries of persecution, and was not a warning that divine retribution would follow loss of faith, as in some of the French and Portuguese apparitions, which manifested themselves in periods of anti-religious and anti-clerical ascendancy. Many also agree that the Holy Souls believed to be present were those of the countless heroes and martyrs of the Irish struggle, since the Reformation also a Catholic struggle against English overlordship. They argue that since for many years Catholic priests were forbidden, under the Penal Laws, to administer the sacraments, including the Last Sacrament, many souls through no fault of their own must have died unshriven, so that they would have to spend much longer in Purgatory than they would otherwise have had to endure.

Clerical endorsement of the belief that the apparition was connected with the souls in Purgatory is not lacking. For example a Franciscan Capuchin priest, Fr. Hubert, wrote a pamphlet in 1962 for the *Knock Shrine Annual*, entitled 'The Knock Apparition and Purgatory', in which he comments on the fact that the apparition was seen just after the parish priest Fr. Cavanagh had offered his hundredth mass for the souls in Purgatory. He, therefore, suggests that Our Lady of Knock should 'very fitly be styled the helper of the Holy Souls and Mother of the Church Suffering' (p. 8). He then focuses on the composite figure of Lamb, Altar, and Cross seen in the apparition, illustrates it with a drawing showing wings hovering above the altar, and suggests that this apocalyptic vision was 'showing forth of the glorious vision for which the souls in purgatory are continually yearning and to which many of them have already attained through the sacrifice of the Mass which had just been offered the hundredth time for them in the church at Knock' (p. 7). From these and other signs, Fr. Hubert concludes that the apparition itself 'was due to the intervention of the holy souls' (p. 8). Ordinary pilgrims, the kind that swarm at the shrine every day, have deduced that the apparition was a response to the prayers of the countless Irish martyred dead, and that it was somehow connected with the Book of Revelation popularly supposed to have been written by St. John the Evangelist (one of the figures by the gable) during the persecution of the then-scattered Christian communities by the Roman Emperor Domitian, identified by some of the Irish clergy with the English. Fr. Michael Walsh has written (p. 57): 'It can reasonably be said that the immediate purpose of the apparition at Knock was to console the afflicted Irish community.'

The cover picture of the *Knock Shrine Annual* for 1967 makes the purgatorial component quite clear. It purports to represent the apparition. But unlike earlier portrayals of this event, it quite frankly places to the left of the altar – now given a central position – and balancing the group of Mary, Joseph and John to the right (i.e. looking towards the people from the gable), a shadowy crowd of suffering souls in Purgatory, regarded as both the initiators and the benefactors (through the prayers of the faithful) of the apparition. The wings over the altar have now become explicit, full-bodied angels, no longer regarded as suffering souls, now that these have been openly portrayed. In this way iconography follows popular thought.

Irish pilgrims go to Knock to seek help from the supernatural powers there with reference to much the same problems and afflictions which send Africans to the ancestral shrines. The *Knock Shrine Annual*, like many Catholic journals associated with pilgrim shrines, publishes letters from pilgrims expressing gratitude for favours received after fulfilling their vows to visit the shrine. They refer mainly to the cure of illness, the gift of children, success in examinations, recovery from operations, the cure of sick farm animals, and similar matters. Often there is reference to the intercession of the Holy Souls. At Knock, the pilgrims feel that the whole church is present in a communitas of prayer. The living pray to Joseph, Mary, Jesus, and John and the angels (the Church Triumphant), for the Holy Souls, the Church Suffering, and to the Saints and Holy Souls to intercede with God for them in their own troubles as members of the Church Militant. All this reinforces their faith that death is not extinction, and that the dead of all the ages are still in loving communion.

In the interstitial, interfacial realm of liminality, both in initiation rites and the pilgrimage process, the dead are conceived of as transformative agencies and as mediating between various domains normally classified as distinct. These include the sensory as against the world of ideas; birth and death, structure and communitas, person and God, culture and nature, visibility and invisibility, past and present, human and animal, and many more fundamental dyads. It is important to note that the symbolic or metaphorical death undergone by initiands or pilgrims puts them in the in-between state of life-in-death, like the seed with rotting husk but thrusting cotyledon in the ground. Illness is one of the signs of this liminal condition and it may be turned to fruitful account if it is made by ritual to lead to an opening up for the initiand of the communitas dimension outside of social structure. In tribal society communitas is associated with physical fertility, in Christian pilgrimage with spiritual fruitfulness. The seclusion camp and the pilgrim's road are also schools in which gnosis (liminal wisdom) is communicated to the individual in passage. Thus when we are outside structure, in initiation or pilgrimage, whether literal or metaphorical, we are, in a sense, in communion with the dead, either the saints, prophets, philosophers, poets, or impeccable heroes of our own most cherished traditions, or the hosts of ordinary people, the 'Holy Souls' who sinned, suffered, but loved enough to stay truly human, though now invisible to us.

In that we may fear 'destructuration' we may regard our dead as filthy and polluting, for they make themselves known in the liminal space that is betwixt-and-between all 'pure' classifications and unambiguous concepts. But if we regard them as part of a space-time communitas of mankind spanning the ages, may we not see them, on a wider scale than either the world of the Nyakyusa or that of traditional pilgrimage, as a fructifying force, a tradition of grace rather than of blood?

PART 3: INTERACTION WITH CHRISTIANITY

Eileen Jensen Krige

TRADITIONAL AND CHRISTIAN LOVEDU FAMILY STRUCTURES

Studies of the modern African family in its various aspects in South Africa have been directed largely to urban areas (Hellmann 1948; Levin 1947; Pauw 1963). The only rural study has been the pioneering work of Monica Wilson on kinship groups and social structure in the Keiskammahoek district of the eastern Cape (Wilson 1952). It is as a tribute to this aspect of Monica Wilson's contribution to social anthropology that an attempt is made here to examine contemporary rural Lovedu[1] domestic groups and family structures, both Christian and traditional, and to explore their bearing on some common assumptions in regard to the elementary family.

Keiskammahoek and the Lovedu Reserve differ considerably in a number of respects. Keiskammahoek was reserved for African occupation as early as 1853, some seventy to eighty years after the first clashes of black and white on the eastern frontier. Here, on the expulsion from the area of the Ngqika section of the Xhosa people after the war of 1850, the British government at the Cape settled small scattered groups of Mfengu (or Fingo, recent-comers to the Cape, uprooted from their homes in Natal by Shaka's Zulu armies), together with a few Xhosa, under their own local leaders, in a series of small 'locations' or 'villages', each politically independent of the other (Wilson 1952). A variety of systems of land tenure was introduced, which today ranges from the recognition of the traditional 'communal' system to freehold tenure. In contrast, the Lovedu of the north-eastern Transvaal, who lived in an unhealthy, fever-ridden area, came into contact with whites only towards the end of the 19th century. In 1881 the first missionary arrived and it was only *after* this that farms were surveyed and the Lovedu confined to a small Reserve. The Mission was given land of which the Lovedu had been dispossessed, but it allowed the people living in the area to remain there. In their location

[1] The letter v is used here for the bilabial fricative in the word Lovedu.

the Lovedu today (1975) still hold land which their forebears had occupied for centuries before them; and they cultivate their fields under their traditional system of land tenure. It was not until the period after World War Two, when malaria was stamped out, that full European exploitation of the far north-eastern Transvaal became possible. As one would expect in these circumstances, much of the traditional family system still operates among the Lovedu.

Yet the first missionary had introduced not only a change in the ideology of the converts but also, by his insistence on monogamy and the Western-type nuclear or elementary family, in their family structure. These changes were reinforced by his policy of cutting off converts from their pagan kin and settling them in orderly fashion on the mission station in a European-style settlement with cottages in 'streets', within call of the church bell. As time went on, similar small settlements round church and school were established within the Reserve itself and also in outlying areas on Crown Lands. Here beer-drinking, tribal songs, drumming, and anything associated with traditional rituals were prohibited, lest Christians be tempted to relapse into heathen ways. The Christians formed small communities separated from the other subjects of the queen, paying no taxes to her (because these took the form of beer), but rendering church dues to the Mission and bringing their disputes before elders of the church, with the missionary as final arbiter. The number of Christians has never been great. Today they form less than 10 per cent of the population. They still tend to congregate round church and school, though the pattern of 'streets' has all but disappeared; and it is still rare to find a Lovedu couple married by Christian rites living in a traditional kraal or village (*motse*, plural *metse*). In Keiskammahoek, on the other hand, Christians slightly outnumber pagans, there is no sharp distinction between them and they are often found living together in the same homestead (Wilson 1952: 129). Another difference is that there is only one Christian denomination among the Lovedu, as compared with many in Keiskammahoek. Zionist sects play little part among the Lovedu, for reasons which can not be considered here.

The missionary saw the elementary family of husband, wife and children as an essential part of Christian living. He insisted on the spatial separation of the newly married couple from the living-quarters of the groom's parents, and the need for the bridegroom to build a suitable new home for the bride before marriage, in contrast to the traditional practice of the initial incorporation of the new unit into the 'house' (*mosha*) of the husband's mother. This, and the emphasis on the economic responsibilities of the husband, had the effect of postponing Christian marriage until some personal saving on the part of the husband had made possible the accumulation of economic resources for the launching of the new family unit. Other major changes affecting family structure introduced by the missionary were the abolition of brideprice (since then observed in the breach and transformed in the process into something different in character), the abolition of woman-marriage, and of preferential marriage between a man and his mother's uterine brother's daughter (or with the daughter of whatever person had been married with the mother's brideprice) on the grounds that this was incest, 'like marrying your sister'.

Not to be confused with the Christian section of the population are those traditionalists who have received a school education without becoming confirmed in the Christian faith, as well as relapsed Christians who have reverted to polygyny. They hold jobs commensurate with their education, make full use of the amenities of Western culture, but live in a traditional family set-up, very often with their pagan relatives.

Traditional Lovedu family structure

As Christians form a small minority constantly in touch with, and affected by, the way of life and values of traditionalists, let us turn first to a brief examination of traditional family structure. Two features of traditional Lovedu marriage that are far-reaching in their consequences for family structure are the passing of brideprice and the system of polygyny. Associated with brideprice is, firstly, the right, enforceable by law, of every woman to the services for herself, as mother-in-law, of the daughter of any other woman who has been acquired with her brideprice; and, secondly, the system of cross-cousin marriage. For usually it is her uterine brother that uses his sister's brideprice for his own marriage, though sometimes a stranger may be allowed to use it on the promise of a daughter of the marriage. Should a woman have no son she could nevertheless 'marry' a daughter-in-law and appoint a genitor to raise children (Krige 1974). It is interesting to see how faithfully many a widowed daughter-in-law even today remains at the side of her deceased husband's mother.

Associated with polygyny, the second of the two factors mentioned above, is another fundamental aspect of Lovedu social structure: the unity and economic independence of the 'house' (*mosha*) established by the marriage of each wife, which gives the Lovedu an orientation that in certain circumstances might easily develop into a matrifocal bias. Not only is it a son's duty to look after his mother, but his position, rights and future are inextricably tied up with his mother – her status in his father's kraal or dwelling-group (*motse*), her links with her brothers, her ritual position in her father's family. Each unit of wife and children (*mosha*) is an incipient *motse*. Its development can be forestalled, in cases where there are serious quarrels between wives, by the husband's placement of one of the wives and her children in a separate *motse* of her own, which, however, remains under his control.

The *mosha* must not, however, be thought of in terms only of a woman and her children. Essential to it is the husband or father, shared with other 'houses'. He need not necessarily be the biological father. The children belong to their father's family group, the eldest son of his chief wife inheriting any position, for example that of headman of an area, which his father may have held. Children derive their status from both father and mother, that is from the particular *mosha* into which they are born. A man's rights to a wife in preferential marriage are derived from his mother or his father's mother (in which case he is inheriting his father's rights through *his* mother).

The *mosha* continues over time into more than one generation. In it the father is replaced by the eldest son of that house, the mother very often by her brother's daughter, who marries her son. There are special arrangements for its continuation if there is no male heir, more particularly in the case of the chief house, where there may be cattle or a position to be inherited. One of these arrangements is for a daughter to hold the position and raise a new heir to her brother.

The term *mosha* has a certain flexibility. While basically every wife can be said to have her own *mosha*, all married sons of a woman, with their wives and children, are thought of, and referred to, as belonging to the old mother's *mosha* while she is still alive and they are living in their father's *motse*.

We now consider the differences between a *mosha* and an elementary family of husband, wife and children. Though the husband/father is essential to the existence of a *mosha*, it is a unit very different from an elementary or nuclear family of husband, wife and children in Western society. The term elementary family is often rather loosely defined, largely in biological terms. Murdock, for example, says the nuclear family 'consists typically of a married man and woman with their offspring; it is familiar to the reader as the type of family recognised to the exclusion of all others by our own society'; it is 'always recognisable and always has its distinctive and vital functions – sexual, economic, reproductive and educational' (Murdock 1949: 1, 3). Essentially however, the elementary family in Western society is a jurally (and in most cases also economically) independent unit of husband, wife and children, usually forming a dwelling-unit, in which the father is responsible for, and has full control over, the children until they are of age. In contrast to this a Lovedu traditionalist remains subject to his father as head of the *motse* so long as he lives in his father's *motse*, which may be a lifetime. If he wishes to leave, he must obtain the consent of his father. Otherwise he forfeits all right to assistance and inheritance from his father and breaks the relationship. The husband/father in a *mosha*, then, is not necessarily jurally independent.

A Lovedu man's rights over his wife are shared with his mother, and furthermore – and this constitutes an important difference between a *mosha* and an elementary family – the mother has a right to his wife's services, and controls, especially during the early stages of marriage, his relationship with his wife and children. That is why mother and son are inseparable unless there is more than one son. A man's sister also has an interest in his marriage. She has a right, if he used her bridewealth, to the services of a daughter of this woman as a daughter-in-law. In any case, if she is the eldest daughter, she exercises ritual control as priestess of the family. A man cannot divorce a wife without the consent of his cattle-linked sister (Krige 1974). Each new *mosha* established by a marriage begins as part of the *mosha* of the husband's mother, becoming fully independent only after her death. The husband's mother is thus an integral part of the household of her son after his marriage. If she has several sons and one of them moves away from his uterine brothers before her death, which is rare, she will generally remain with the eldest son unless other considerations, for example cattle-links, dictate otherwise.

The *mosha* of a woman's eldest son's chief wife follows in the direct line of that of her own, holding an important position in relation to *mesha* of her other sons.

The developmental cycle of the Lovedu domestic group (*motse*)

But the developmental cycle of the Lovedu domestic group or dwelling-unit must not be conceived in terms of stereotyped phases in a single pattern or cycle. At every turn there are alternatives, depending on special circumstances and personal relationships, and on the stage of development of minor *mesha* ('houses') as well as of the chief *mosha*, which may be complex because we are dealing with a polygynous society. In the classic analysis of Fortes (in Goody, ed., 1958), the marriage of the eldest child is said to mark the beginning of the phase of dispersion of a family. For the Lovedu this is true as far as girls leaving on marriage are concerned. From the point of view of the males, the climax which inaugurates the fission of the *motse* into its constituent sections, each of which generally leaves to establish a new *motse* under the eldest son of the *mosha*, is the death of the father. Even then, fission may be long delayed, the half-brothers continuing to live together under the eldest son in the chief *mosha* for a long period, especially if he is older than they are.

Since the *mosha*, established by marriage and consisting of a shared husband, his wife and children, is so basic a unit among the Lovedu, let us begin our summary of the developmental cycle at the first marriage of a man. On marriage a Lovedu man (Ego) brings his wife into the *mosha* of his mother, where he remains for all or the greater part of his life under the over-all control of his father, sharing with his mother his rights over his wife. His wife will cook for his mother and assist her in cultivating her fields, using his mother's utensils and implements. Later, Ego will build a hut for his wife and acquire a field for her and himself from his father or mother or from his mother's family (in the last-named case merely on loan, as his son could not inherit such a field). Even if, on the marriage of his younger brother, Ego's wife is allowed to have her own hearth, she will always have to send a plate of food at each cooking to her mother-in-law.

Marriage brings with it duties and responsibilities in relation to Ego's wife's family, who will look to Ego for assistance when in trouble, for example if the wife's father is unable to pay a fine in a court case.

The birth of Ego's first child is an important event, but it is the marriage of his daughter which is the important landmark in the development of his family. For this brings in brideprice for the use of his son and provides Ego with a son-in-law, to whom he can turn for assistance at all times. His sons may now be nearing the stage when they leave to do migrant labour, if they have not already begun. So although, in a sense, the marriage of a daughter is the first step in the disintegration of the family, in another it is a step towards its further development economically. At this stage Ego has become less dependent on the economic assistance of his agnates and he would be able to stand on his own should anything happen, a quarrel or an accusation of witchcraft, which precipitates his leaving the *motse*, or if he and his father decided that, to obtain more land or more grazing for the cattle he might wish to accumulate, he should move to the more sparsely populated farms which were bought by the queen in the uninhabited Crown Lands to the north and north-east.

The marriage of Ego's eldest son is an important step in increasing the size and importance of Ego's first wife's *mosha*. It brings into his home domestic help for his wife, who is now beginning to grow older. It also links his son more closely to Ego's wife, who shares rights over the new bride with her son. All these developments generally take place while Ego and his sons are still in the *motse* of Ego's father, living in the *mosha* of Ego's mother. By this time Ego may also have acquired a second wife. Later on he may acquire a third wife, perhaps by inheritance from a brother who has died young.

The death of Ego's father, head of the *motse*, is a crisis with important consequences for all in the *motse*. What these will be depends on a number of factors. If, for example, Ego is the eldest son of the chief wife, he will step into his father's place as head and take over control. Any brother of his father living in the *motse* would decide to move out at this stage, rather than be under the control of a nephew. If, however, the heir is too young, a uterine brother of the deceased might be asked to act as head. There are various other alternatives in the case of an heir being under-age or non-existent, which we need not go into here. If a son does not belong to the chief house, there are other alternatives open to him on the death of his father:

(*a*) He and his half-brothers in the various houses of the deceased may remain under the leadership of the son of the chief house, especially if the latter is older than they are, and this may be very convenient if they are migrant labourers, absent at work most of the time. The distinctions marking the chief house become clearer at this stage. Only the chief house is responsible for the debts incurred by the deceased father; and the houses of his father in which the children are still young must be provided for and looked after by the heir in the chief house, who has stepped into his father's shoes. The economic independence of any house in which there is a married son is guarded by such son in this case.

(*b*) Any half-brother who is the eldest son in his house and who wishes to move away and be independent, may take with him his mother, if she is still alive, his brothers, their wives and children and any unmarried brothers and sisters in this house, and move out. But this does not necessarily take place immediately. The death of the head of a *motse* usually inaugurates a period of gradual segmentation, which may take a long time, depending on the age of deceased's wives and dependants. On segmentation each house moves as a whole.

Young widows without children, or with very young children, and any girl engaged to be married to the deceased, will be inherited by the heir, who will raise seed to his father. Other older widows will be inherited by a husband's brother, who, however, will have to visit the widow in the *motse* of the deceased so that all remain together. Such a seed-raiser has even, in one or two cases I have come across, left his own wives in his *motse* and moved into the *motse* of the deceased, where he had been chosen to act for an heir.

Sometimes there are fierce quarrels between widows. On such occasions a widow with young children may seek shelter in the home of her father. Her children belong to her husband's family, though she may take very young children with her. If a widow has a married son, her house is in a position to hive off and become independent. A small *motse* consisting of a widow, her married son (more often than not away doing migrant labour), his wife and young child, or children, is quite frequently found today.

Uterine brothers among the Lovedu remain together as a 'house' and do not separate until the younger brothers are married and have adult or married sons, or a married daughter, or perhaps more than one wife. Then the younger brother may move away to become independent. Today there is a strong tendency for uterine brothers to separate earlier than in the past.

Dispersion after the death of the head of the *motse* is not inevitable. In the capital today there are men with grandchildren who are still living in the *mosha* of their aged mothers. *Metse* are very rapidly becoming smaller, however. Though there are still *metse* with from 20 to 35 inhabitants, the average number of inmates in three districts in which a census was taken was 4, 9 and 12 respectively.

It would seem from our analysis that the elementary family is *not* normally a stage in the developmental cycle of the Lovedu domestic group and one would not expect to find it very frequently as an independent domestic group. How far is this conclusion borne out by the statistical facts, by the actual composition of domestic units as they are found to be at any moment in time?

Domestic groups in four areas

To get a picture of the realities of the situation, a census was taken and a study made of the composition of *metse* in four different districts, L, K, Ma, and M (see Table 1). M, a small subdistrict (population 196 in 16 *metse*) was wholly pagan. In district L, with a population of 569 and 60 *metse*, there were only two 'Christian' *metse* (one of a relapsed Christian with two wives and one Zionist one); the population of K was pagan, except for one Zionist *motse*; in Ma, a portion of a tribal farm in which a census was taken (population 354 in 35 *metse*), there were two Zionist *metse*. The virtual absence of Christians in these districts is not unrepresentative of the population as a whole. For comparative purposes, one of some half-dozen Christian settlements in the Reserve (which comprises 69 districts) is dealt with in Tables 2, 3 and 4.

The most striking aspect of the four areas in Table 1 is the predominance of *metse* composed of the traditional compound (polygynous) and extended families (87 per cent in M, 78 per cent in L, 61 per cent in K, 77 per cent in Ma) and the extremely low percentage (from 5 to 17 per cent) of *metse* composed of an elementary family of husband, wife and children. The main forms taken by extended families are indicated in Table 1. The most common form is that of husband, wife and children (or widow and children) plus one or more married sons with their wives and children. Often a divorced or widowed sister or daughter with children is found also in an extended family but in such case her presence in no way alters the classification of such family, already extended in type.

Elementary families constituting independent metse[1]

Let us look more closely now at the domestic groups classified in Table 1 as elementary families in the four areas.

Of six domestic units, or *metse*, that were classified as elementary in K area, two were, in fact, residual compound (polygynous) families (a compound family here being defined as composed of a husband, two or more wives and their children). They had been compound families and had become elementary in form only because of the death of one of two wives in both instances. In one case the deceased had been a barren woman; in the other she had been a woman whose orphan children had been sent in traditional Lovedu manner to be reared by the deceased mother's family. In a third case, one of two wives had deserted her husband, taking her children with her; in the

[1] The difference between a family and a domestic group or dwelling-unit should be borne in mind. A family does.not always and at all times constitute a domestic group, e.g. among the Ashanti, husband and wife after marriage often go on living among their own kin. In a study made by Fortes three-quarters of the wives in a traditionalist-orientated village and nearly half of those in a village strongly influenced by modern ideas had lived all their lives among their own kin (Fortes 1949: 54–84).

fourth, a man (who with his wife and children had sought asylum with his wife's mother's brother) had been chased out for assaulting his benefactor in a drunken frenzy and had thereupon built himself a new *motse* of his own. In each of the two remaining cases, one of two wives in a polygynous family had moved away with her children because of death attributed to witchcraft, leaving the other wife and children behind with the husband in the *motse*, now consisting of an elementary family. All had become elementary in form owing to untoward circumstances.

Of three elementary families in district L, one was of Shangana–Tsonga origin, whose family structure is not quite the same as that of the Lovedu, and two were newcomers to the area. There is some evidence that when people move from one area to live in another, or go to a tribal farm in search of larger fields and better grazing, their old mothers often choose to remain behind, as usually only one son is sufficiently adventurous to move out of the house and *motse* to which he is attached, in search of pastures new. Usually his family is at a fairly late stage of development, with perhaps a married daughter or full-grown sons.

In Ma there were six elementary families in independent *metse*: the head of one had recently moved away from his uterine brother next door, while of those remaining, four were newcomers to the area from European farms. The only *motse* composed of an elementary family in M was similarly of recent origin, having also moved away from his uterine brother's *motse* to establish his own. One situation in which a *motse* composed of an elementary family can come into existence fortuitously, which does not appear in the districts chosen at the time of the census, is one in which a *motse* composed of a widow and her married son with wife and children loses the old mother by death.

The elementary family of husband, wife and children is, then, quite clearly not an inevitable stage in the developmental cycle, nor is it commonly found. When it does occur, it has often come into being as a result of untoward circumstances such as a death or a witchcraft accusation. It is found, if it occurs at all, not in the early stages of married life but usually at a later stage when the sons are adult, capable of earning an income and ready for marriage themselves.

It would take us too far afield if we were to discuss fully the various aberrant forms of family that have been classified under the heading 'Other' in Table 1. Many are cases of widows living alone or with a sister, because their married sons have taken their wives and children to town with them. A few are cases of divorced women or women with illegitimate children.

It should, perhaps, be indicated that the traditional family structure has not been untouched by modern developments. A serious problem today is the high incidence of desertion of wives. Developing light industry in neighbouring areas and the proliferation of labour compounds, as well as the easy communication made possible by the Modjadji Bus Services, have enabled dissatisfied, neglected, or even merely adventurous wives to leave home to find work in canneries or on farms, or to make their way to labour compounds where they are readily met and accommodated as wives by men anxious for home comforts. In M area, the percentage of married women that had absconded was found to be 33 to 40 per cent. A few of these had returned after some years, asking to be taken back.

Christian domestic units

We have seen that it was the policy of the first missionary to establish a Western-type elementary family as a domestic group among his converts. We should expect, therefore, to find the elementary family of husband, wife and children predominantly established in this group.

It is a remarkable thing that, after over eighty years, KS (which differs from other small Christian settlements only in having a large proportion of well-qualified teachers − a factor which should, if anything, have swelled the number of domestic units composed of elementary families) had only 5 homesteads or domestic units composed of husband, wife and children out of a total of 28 (see Table 2). A further 10 were composed of elementary families with an accretion of one or more unmarried individuals, usually relatives. (In much of the literature, especially that dealing with modern Western families, such households are termed 'extended' family households; see Laslett 1972: 29). There was one case of a teacher living alone, while the remaining 12 households were extended families in the sense in which the term is used here, operating lineally over more than two generations. Clearly the elementary family composed of husband, wife and children only, is not the commonest form of domestic group even among Christian Lovedu. Yet, if households composed of an elementary family plus one or more related or unrelated accretions are counted as a form of elementary family, then just over half (54 per cent) of the total number of households in KS can be said to have been composed of elementary families. The domestic group composed

of an extended family comes a close second, forming 43 per cent of
the total number of domestic groups (Christian homesteads) in KS.

In the urban area of East London the situation is comparable.
Pauw (1963a: 145) reports: 'Fewer than one-third of the households
(in terms of population of the sample the proportion is about the
same) are based on the elementary or compound family of father,
mother and children. The proportion consisting of only this unit,
without any attached members, is less than a quarter [my emphasis].
It cannot be said, therefore, that the elementary family, usually
associated with Western patterns of living, is at present the predominant form of household unit among the urban Bantu.'[1]

These additional individual relatives, present in all categories of
household in East London and among Lovedu Christians in KS,
require closer examination. Though such additional individuals are
found also in our own Western domestic groups, this appears to be
infrequent enough to account for their having been assigned no
category in the tables of Firth, Hubert and Forge. Who are these
individuals attached to modern African households of various kinds?
In Table 4 are set out the main categories of such accessions to the
Christian family.

Quite the largest category was that of 8 children of relatives,
attached to families for the purpose of attending school. In addition
to these there were also 4 unrelated children as paying boarders in
the houses of one or two teachers, i.e. a total of 12. For the rest there
were orphans and abnormal or neglected children (i.e. people in need
of care) and also relatives employed as servants living in the family.
Some of the children attending school had parents who neglected
them and were being cared for by the family with whom they lived.
In spite of their individualism, the Christian element of the population
has a strong sense of responsibility towards the relatives of both
spouses. A Christian is not allowed to inherit his brother's wife, but
he is prepared nevertheless to take on full responsibility for children
of both deceased and living brothers. There appears to be little
difference between elementary and extended Christian families in
the frequency with which individual accessions to the family occur
among the Lovedu.

In Keiskammahoek 27 per cent of the sample of 90 homesteads had

[1] A compound family, as the term is used here by Pauw would, it seems, following
Wilson's definition (1952: 54), be a compound (elementary) family composed of a
husband, his second wife and children of one or both wives. Wilson distinguishes this
from the compound (polygynous) family established by polygynous marriage.

additional unmarried relatives – 20 per cent in elementary families, 7 per cent in extended (extracted from Wilson 1952: 52, 53). It is not stated to what extent they were people in need of care. Pauw mentions a similar phenomenon for East London (Pauw 1963*a*: 145) and enumerates categories of people similar to those found among the Lovedu – neglected children, the blind, the mentally ill, relatives who can find no other accommodation (p. 151).

In a society in which welfare services are absent or grossly inadequate it is the family that must shoulder responsibility for the needy. The traditional Lovedu extended family has such responsibilities written into its very nature – care of the aged, for example, is bound up with the relationship of a son and his parents, the right of a mother to the services and care of a daughter-in-law. Thus, as is illustrated in Table 2, the traditionalist area M, with 87 per cent of its *metse* consisting of extended or compound (polygynous) families, is characterised by the complete absence of *metse* composed of an elementary family with additional unmarried relatives.

The various factors operating to produce the domestic unit of an elementary family with accretions of individual relatives among Christian Lovedu in KS include then firstly the need for some body or group to provide for those requiring care in an area in which traditional family institutions and values have broken down; secondly the supreme importance attached to school education by Christians – two-thirds of the cases of individual accretions to the elementary family were directly associated with lack of adequate schooling facilities elsewhere; thirdly the appearance of a class of professional women, nurses and teachers, who require domestic help and use kinship relationships for securing it in the home.

The extended family among Lovedu Christians in KS

There is a relatively large proportion of extended families among Christians – 12 out of 28, or 43 per cent (see Table 2). This figure is shown in Table 2 to be greatly exceeded in M (a strongly traditionalist sub-district of a size comparable to KS) – 87 per cent, more than double the percentage in KS. (On the other hand compare this with Table 3, where the highest percentage of extended families among whites in certain parts of London and Durban is shown to be only 11 per cent.) Christian extended families in KS are slightly different from traditionalist ones in that families composed of brothers with their wives and children and their married sons and families are absent; but a married son often remains on in the parental family, a custom that is based on traditional values in regard to the relationship of parents and children, and that is supported also by the system of migrant labour and the long absences of husbands. Wilson reported for Keiskammahoek that 33 out of a sample of 90 homesteads, or 37 per cent, were three-generational extended families. Here land shortage and the difficulty in securing fields to cultivate were factors in keeping married men in their parental homes. This does not appear to operate among the Lovedu for a variety of reasons: it is possible to obtain a field in a district without living in it; the purchase of tribal farms has made it possible to obtain land by moving away; sons do not depend on parents only for land; and today people rely on wage-labour rather than agriculture for their food. The density of population in Volovedu is, if anything, higher than in the Ciskei – over 160 to the square kilometre.[1] It would appear that administrative interference in the traditional arrangements in regard to land tenure may well have engendered feelings of land-hunger and frustration in Keiskammahoek that are far less marked among the Lovedu, where the traditional arrangements have been allowed to remain and have proved to be more adaptable.

A new development, still only in its infancy among the Lovedu, is the three-generational family composed of husband, wife and children plus a daughter with an illegitimate child. According to Pauw the majority of the three-generation male-headed households in East London consisted of a married couple with husbandless daughters and their children, most of them unmarried mothers (Pauw 1963a: 152). In three-generation female-headed households in East London (which outnumber the male-headed ones) 'the family consisting of a woman with unmarried children and the children of unmarried daughters, is very distinctly the main representative of this type' (p. 153). There are very few households, Pauw says, where married sons of the head and their spouses, as in the traditional extended family, are members of the household (p. 151). He reports the existence in East London of 'a type of family which is mother-controlled and lacks a father altogether', or, as he puts it also, of 'a distinct type of fatherless family which has a tendency to develop into a three-generational span'. (He hesitates to identify it wholly with the matrifocal family of the West Indies.) What Pauw has described here is absent among the Lovedu.

Daughters with illegitimate children among Lovedu Christians

Although the presence of daughters with illegitimate children has

[1] 400 to the square mile.

not yet greatly affected family structure, the problem of illegitimacy among the Lovedu is beginning to be felt. It is associated in their area with school education and co-educational schools. Among traditionalists marriage is early, and it is rare for a girl who has not attended school to have a child before marriage. If this does happen, the girl generally marries some polygynist, and the child will belong automatically to, and even inherit from, the man who has married its mother. With the Christian schoolgirl the situation is different. Attendance at school delays marriage and it is quite common for a schoolgirl to be made pregnant by a fellow-scholar or by a teacher. Such a girl has little chance of marriage. The boy in question (or the teacher, who probably is already married) is not available or prepared for marriage, wishing to continue his education and, if possible, take up some profession or job elsewhere. The girl cannot, as a Christian, marry a polygynist, and Christian men, having taken over the Western attitude to illegitimacy, are unwilling to consider marrying a woman with children not their own. Underlying the whole situation is the fact that it is not usual among the Lovedu to consider marriage as a desirable consequence of, or as a means of setting right, the seduction of a virgin. For seduction there is a fine. Marriage, however, is something different, a difficult matter involving delicate negotiations and long-run relationships between families.

A Christian girl with an illegitimate child remains with her parents at first. It has happened in one or two cases where boy and girl were living in the same neighbourhood, with opportunities to continue their relationship, that marriage between them has eventually taken place. In a case known to us this was after the birth of a second illegitimate child *by the same father* (who had in the meantime completed his education). In another, in which the woman concerned was a young teacher, her father (a minister) arranged a marriage to cover up the 'scandal' and undertook to finance the education of the young man concerned at a teacher-training college. But such cases are extremely rare. Usually a girl with an illegitimate child, living in her parents' home, sooner or later gives birth to more illegitimate children, leaves home to seek work to support her children (who remain at home with their grandparents) and ends up by remaining in the urban centres, unmarried. This applies also to many schoolgirls whose families still live in a traditional manner.

Social and economic conditions of Christians and pagans compared

The high value placed on education by the Christian community among the Lovedu has brought benefits. There is a striking contrast in level of education, occupation and income between Christian and pagan, which can be brought out most clearly by comparing KS with M, the traditionally oriented sub-district similar in size to, and situated within half a mile of, KS. In M only a small proportion of men have attended school and they, with two exceptions, have reached no further than Standard 2 or 3. The women with one exception are completely illiterate. In contrast, every adult (male and female) in KS has been to school, the level of education varying from Standard 4 to one or two years of university education for the best-qualified employees of the Department of Education. Bound up with education is diversity of occupation. Whereas in M the greater proportion of men over 18 years of age are engaged in unskilled migrant labour (exceptions being a ticket-examiner on the tribal buses, a policeman, and two builders and carpenters), in KS there were teachers of various levels, including principals of the primary and high schools, an inspector of schools, a minister of religion, shop assistants in nearby European towns, clerks in the Departments of Health and of Bantu Administration and Development, bus drivers, and policemen.[1]

These differences between KS and M stem, not from lack of opportunities in the case of M (KS and M are close neighbours), but from the inability of the people of M, through their lack of education and their tradition-oriented values, to make use of the general demand today for more skilled labour both in urban areas and in the Lovedu Reserve itself. In KS, only 39 per cent of adult men were migrants away at labour centres, compared with 67 per cent in M.

How domestic units of Lovedu Christians compare with those of other groups, African and Western

We have already indicated certain similarities between KS, Keiskammahoek and East London: the relatively low percentage of domestic groups composed of an elementary family of husband, wife and children; the relatively high proportion of extended family domestic groups in KS and Keiskammahoek, on the one hand, and

[1] Eight heads of domestic groups in KS had been importations for educational purposes from outside the village itself. Of these only four came from beyond the borders of Volovedu (including the Mission station) and of these, three families had been resident in KS for twenty years or more. When the secondary school, which later became a high school, was established, it had to draw quite heavily on outsiders for staff, as is usually the case when the first new schools are established in an area. Some of these teachers now live in special accommodation provided near the high-school grounds; others are in charge of, and live in, the school hostels. The high school does not fall within KS, although it is close by.

of multi-generation families of a rather different type in East London on the other; also the presence of a type of domestic group composed of husband, wife and children, augmented by one or more unmarried relatives of various kinds. Daughters with illegitimate children were said to be common in Keiskammahoek, but there was no case in Wilson's sample of 90 homesteads in which the presence of a daughter with an illegitimate child in the home accounted for an extended family, though there were two cases of widowed daughters and children living in their parental homes and three cases in which an unmarried woman was the head of the family (Wilson 1952: 53). An arresting development in Keiskammahoek not found among Lovedu Christians was that departing migrants often left their women and children in the homes of relatives, taking them back on their return, which led to frequent changes in composition of domestic groups and a population constantly on the move (p. 119). Hobart Houghton (1952) complained of this ever-changing composition of domestic units, which rendered any census taken unusable within months. The development of three-generational, mother-controlled families lacking a father altogether in East London is thus unparalleled in Volovedu and seems to have been absent in Keiskammahoek.

The low percentage of domestic groups composed of elementary families *without* an attachment of individual relatives, the comparatively high proportion of groups composed of extended families, and other characteristics that have emerged from our study of the domestic units of Lovedu Christians and of the Keiskammahoek (rural) and East London (urban) areas, raise the question how the family structure in these African groups compares with that of whites in South Africa and elsewhere. Table 3 has been compiled to present such a comparison. For London, figures have been taken from Firth, Hubert and Forge (1969: 73); for Durban (South Africa) figures I am indebted to Professor W. J. Argyle of the Department of Social Anthropology, University of Natal, who is conducting a study of kinship in the suburb of Z; for Keiskammahoek I have extracted information from Wilson's table indicating the composition of a sample of 90 homesteads (Wilson 1952: 52–3); and for East London, South Africa, from Pauw (1963: 145, 147). The East London situation can hardly be fitted into the categories used by Firth *et al.* without distortion, because of the differences between the type of extended family found there and in the other areas. Nevertheless, East London has been included and the table presented for what it is worth. A further unsatisfactory feature of Table 3 is that we do not know in detail what kinds of cases were included under the heading 'composite family' in the different areas.

Table 3 highlights, however, the high percentages of domestic groups composed of extended families in the African groups, as compared with their virtual absence among whites, and the correspondingly low percentages of domestic groups composed of elementary families of husband, wife and children among Africans in relation to the marked predominance of the elementary family as the major domestic unit among the white groups. The domestic unit composed of an elementary family, augmented by one or more unmarried relatives, which is common in the three African groups, does not appear to be of any significance in the white groups, no doubt owing partly to the social services and better opportunities for advancement available to the latter. Childless families of husband and wife are uncommon in the African groups, less so in the white; and there are other interesting differences in the various groups that do not concern us here. The general picture then is, on the one hand, of the overwhelming predominance of the elementary family in the London study and to a lesser extent in Durban, South Africa, to the virtual exclusion of extended families, more especially in London, where the percentage is between 5 and 7; and, on the other hand, the high percentage of extended families in all the African groups (between 35 and 43, compared with 11 in Durban, the highest in the white group).

Conclusion: Is the elementary family universal?

Murdock, expressing an opinion fairly widely held among anthropologists, has referred to the nuclear or elementary family of husband, wife and children as 'this elemental social group' (Murdock 1949: 3) and has claimed that it is 'a universal social grouping'. He continues, 'Either as the sole prevailing form of the family, or as the basic unit from which more complex familial forms are compounded, it exists as a distinct and strongly functional group in every known society.' There appears here to be some confusion of the universal biological unit of father, mother and child with the family as a social unit. R. N. Adams (1960) has criticised Murdock's views, largely on the grounds of the existence of the matrifocal family in many areas of the world. And it is clear also from the discussion in the present paper and the evidence of the figures presented in the tables that among the Lovedu the Western-type, jurally independent elementary family of husband, wife and children is rare among traditionalists. It occurs, if at all, only at a fairly late stage in the developmental cycle of traditionalist Lovedu domestic groups, or may arise as a result of untoward events which have reduced some other form of domestic group to the form of husband, wife and children. Among Lovedu Christians the elementary family forms under 20 per cent of domestic groups unless we classify as elementary family groups those families which have been augmented by one or more individual relatives, when the proportion reaches 54 per cent, just over half the total. In East London the elementary family is not the predominant form, while in Keiskammahoek, where it is said to preponderate, the proportion of extended families is nevertheless high.

It has been argued in this paper also that a polygynous family does not, as Murdock and others would have it, consist simply of two or more elementary families linked by relationship to a common father. (Evans-Pritchard 1951: 127 also refers to the 'house' or 'hut' in a polygynous household as an elementary family.) When the Lovedu *mosha* is examined as an operating unit and not as a mathematical abstraction, it becomes clear that it is not a Western-type elementary family affiliated by plural marriage (i.e. by having one married parent in common) to other similar units. For the greater part of the existence of a *mosha* the husband's mother is an integral part of this unit, because she has rights to the services of her son's wife; and the husband (her son) shares rights over his wife with his mother. Even his cattle-linked sister has an interest in his wife, because she has a legal right to a daughter-in-law from this woman. A *mosha* may even be composed of a married woman, who has no son, her 'wife' or *noeji* (daughter-in-law) and children raised by a genitor (Krige 1974). It is our belief that a number of these characteristics of the Lovedu *mosha* apply also to other societies in southern Africa.

In the light of the above discussion the elementary or nuclear family does not by any means appear to be universal, 'a distinct and strongly functional group in every known society'.

Emerging clearly from this paper also is the need for far more rigorous methods in comparing family structure and in defining various types of domestic group than have been used up to now. There is a regrettable lack of uniformity even in the terminology employed. Before any generalisations can safely be made in regard to various types of domestic groups it is essential to consider very carefully the relationships, duties and responsibilities of members of the units that are being compared; the principles underlying the type of marriage on which such groups have been based; their jural aspects and their relationships to other groups and institutions in the society as a whole.

TABLE 1

Composition of Lovedu domestic groups (metse and kraals) in four areas

| Area and population | Elementary family type | | | Compound (polygynous) and extended families | | | | | | Other | Number of metse (kraals) |
	Husband, wife & children	Elem. plus one or more related individuals	Total elem. type	Compound — Husband and two or more wives & children	Extended — Brothers, their wives & children, plus married sons, wives & children et al.	Extended — Husband, wife & children plus married sons, their wives & children et al.	Extended — Widow & children plus sons, wives & children et al.	Extended — Husband, wife & children, plus widowed or divorced SS or D & children or/and D & illegitimate children	Total compound and extended		
M sub-district (pop. 196)	1	—	1	3	1	9	1	—	14	1 denuded extended family	16
Percentage	6%	—	6%	19%	6%	56%	6%	—	87%	7%	100%
L district (pop. 569)	3	—	3	9	2	11	25	—	47	10	60
Percentage	5%	—	5%	15%	3%	18%	42%	—	78%	17%	100%

Area or group and population										
K district (pop. 409)	6	2	8	4	12	14	—	34	13	55
Percentage	11%	4%	15%	7%	22%	25%	—	61%	24%	100%
Ma district section (pop. 354)	6	—	7	4	9	6	1	27	2	35
Percentage	17%	—	20%	11%	26%	19%	3%	77%	6%	100%

TABLE 2

Comparison of domestic groups in KS (Christian) settlement with those in M, a sub-district comparable in size

Area or group and population	Elementary family and variations thereof			Extended and compound (polygynous)				Other	Total number of units Christian homesteads or traditionalist metse (kraals)
	Husband, wife & children	Husband, wife & children plus one or more unmarried relations	Total elementary type	Extended	Extended plus one or more unmarried relations	Compound (polygynous) husband & two or more wives	Total extended or extended & compound		
KS (pop. 209)	5	10	15	4	8	—	12	1 individual living alone	28
Percentage	18%	36%	54%	14%	29%	—	43%	3%	100%
M (pop. 196)	1	—	1	11	—	3	14	1 denuded extended	16
Percentage	6%	—	6%	68%	—	19%	87%	7%	100%

TABLE 3

Comparison of domestic groups of Africans with those in parts of London and in a white group in Durban

Area, group and date of investigation	Married couple only	Elementary family (husband, wife & children)	Elementary plus one or more unmarried individuals (relatives)	Denuded elementary family (one parent lost)	Extended family	Composite kin unit	Siblings only	Two individuals (non-kin)	Individual alone	Total number of households	
WHITES **LONDON**[1] Highgate, 1851 Census: Categories I & II – gentry, local traders, minor professionals; Category III –	11%	39%	not indicated	13%	6%	14%	3%	not indicated	14%	408	100%
manual workers.	14%	46%	,,	16%	7%	6%	1%	,,	10%	421	100%
Greenbanks, 1961: middle class	22%	49%	,,	3%	5%	7%	1%	,,	13%	60	100%
DURBAN[2] 1973 Z suburb artisan and service workers	20%	39%	,,	8%	11%	13%	2%	3%	4%	233	100%

BLACKS										
N.TVL. LOVEDU Christian, 1968 (excluding independent churches; rural)	3%	15%	36%	—	43%	—	—	3%	28	100%
KEISKAMMAHOEK[3] predominantly Christian; rural	4%	16%	14%	4%	35%	1%	24%	2%	90	100%
EAST LONDON[4] 1963 90% Christian; urban	2%	21%	11%	20% (no father 16% no mother 4%)	36%[5]	6%	—	4%	109	100%

[1] Taken from Firth *et al.* 1969: 73, 74.
[2] Figures kindly supplied by Department of Social Anthropology, University of Natal.
[3] Extracted from Wilson 1952: 52, 53.
[4] Extracted from Pauw 1963: 145.
[5] The vast majority of Xhosa East London families are three-generational rather than extended in that they are composed of parent(s) and their unmarried *daughters* with their illegitimate children, rather than parents with married *sons* and their families.

KEY:
Elementary family: parents and their dependent child/children.
Denuded family: elementary family which has lost one parent by death, divorce, desertion, etc.
Extended family: kinship unit in which relations of the family type operate lineally over more than two generations, e.g. grandparents, parents and children.
Composite unit: any set of kin, e.g. siblings and their children, or aunt and niece, living in one household.

TABLE 4

Categories of individual augmenting Christian elementary and extended families in KS

Categories of additional individuals augmenting Christian families in KS	In conjunction with elementary family (number of cases)	In conjunction with extended family (number of cases)	Total
Orphan or abnormal child of relative	3	—	3
Child(ren) of relatives for schooling	3	5	8
Children of non-relatives for schooling	4	—	4
Relative employed as servant	—	2	2
Mother's brother's son	—	1	1
Total	10	8	18

B. A. Pauw

UNIVERSALISM AND PARTICULARISM IN THE BELIEFS OF XHOSA-SPEAKING CHRISTIANS

In this contribution the particularistic and universalistic elements in the beliefs of Xhosa-speaking Christians are examined in relation to the process of increase in socio-cultural scale. The following general information on Christianity among Xhosa-speaking people serves as background to this discussion.

Christianity among the Xhosa-speaking Nguni

To those acquainted with Monica Wilson's writings the Xhosa-speaking Cape Nguni need no introduction. Their present 'homelands' are the Transkei and Ciskei in south-eastern South Africa, and they predominate in the non-white population of towns and farms in the eastern Cape Province. They further account for the great majority of Bantu-speaking people in the industrial ports of Port Elizabeth and East London, and are well represented in Cape Town and on the Witwatersrand. In this article the name 'Xhosa' is used for all Xhosa-speaking peoples but it should be remembered that it may also be used in a more restricted sense of a cluster of chiefdoms of the Xhosa proper, distinct from chiefdoms of the Thembu, Mpondo, Mpondomise, Bhaca and others grouped together as Cape Nguni.

My own material presented here derives from fieldwork conducted in a rural community in the Transkei during 1960–1 and in Port Elizabeth during 1962–4. Although the Transkei community is part of Thembuland, Mfengu people predominate in the churches, and in Port Elizabeth the majority of Bantu-speaking people are Xhosa proper or Mfengu. A direct comparison of Christians in the Transkei community with those in Port Elizabeth is justified in view of the high degree of homogeneity in respect of indigenous traditional culture among the Cape Nguni. For detailed ethnographic and quantitative data substantiating generalisations presented below, the reader is referred to my book on belief and ritual among Xhosa-speaking Christians (1975).

In rural areas of the Ciskei and the Transkei there is a clear distinction in dress and manners between 'School people' and others called *abantu ababomvu* (Red people) or *amaqaba* (Those-who-smear). The latter names refer to the use of red ochre as a cosmetic, and indicate non-Christian Xhosa traditionalists, mostly illiterate. The School people are Christians or nominal Christians who send their children to school and are in general more westernised than the Red people.

Concerted missionary activity started among the Xhosa during the first quarter of the 19th century, and by the middle of the century several missionary societies had founded mission stations in different parts of the Ciskei and Transkei. Today the majority of Xhosa are Christians or nominal Christians, but Red people form a substantial minority in rural areas. Among Christians the Methodists have a distinct numerical lead, with Anglicans in a clear second position. Their churches and others like the Roman Catholic, Presbyterian-Dutch Reformed and Lutheran churches I refer to as *orthodox*. *Non-orthodox* churches among the Xhosa are mostly Pentecostalist or Sabbatarian–Baptist. Churches emphasising independence from whites in church affairs account for a significant minority of Xhosa, speaking Christians.

Increase in scale

Increase in scale has been the crucial concept in Monica Wilson's interpretation of the changes experienced by African peoples that have until fairly recently been non-literate. She has defined change in scale as primarily a change in social relations, 'a change in the number of people interacting and the closeness of their interaction' (Wilson 1971*b*: 7; cf. G. and M. Wilson 1945: 40), but has shown that these changes in social relations are related to changes in, *inter alia*, technology, economic activities, knowledge, morality and religious beliefs (Wilson 1971*b*: 12–25 and *passim*). Increase in scale therefore refers to a comprehensive process of change in social structure as well as culture in general.

It is hardly necessary to demonstrate the increase in scale experienced by Xhosa-speaking Nguni peoples since the time they lived in completely non-literate and relatively isolated tribal communities. Wilson (1971*b*) often refers to these peoples in discussing religious change and expansion in scale in Africa, and her essay on the growth of peasant communities in South Africa (Wilson 1971*a*: 49–103) demonstrates how the social relations of the Cape Nguni gradually extended through trade, churches, schools and political developments, and describes the resulting changes in the relative importance of social relations based on voluntary association as opposed to those based on kinship, as well as changes in patterns of ranking, stratification and leadership.

Here I wish to emphasise that increase in scale is a relative concept and that a people's system of social relations sometimes reveals features typical of large-scale society only to a limited extent, or may reveal such features in combination with others that are typical of small-scale society. Among rural Xhosa-speaking Christians there is, for example, greater economic specialisation (a feature of large-scale society) than among their forebears of the early 19th century, but it is still limited. For the great majority stock-raising and agriculture remain basic economic pursuits, although almost invariably supplemented by migratory labour for wages. Further, although there is considerable opportunity for voluntary association in churches and other groups, kinship, age and sex are still important in determining the individual's social position and role in rural communities. Moreover, while each individual may be involved in certain impersonal relations typical of large-scale society, a considerable part of his life is spent within a few neighbouring *iilali* (neighbourhood units) in which most people are personal acquaintances, often linked through kinship or marriage, and grouped according to patrilineal descent.

Features of small-scale society are more in evidence among the Red people, the non-Christian Xhosa traditionalists, than among the rural Christian School people, and least, but by no means lacking, among urbanised Xhosa. Among the latter, for example, lineage groups are not significant in their daily life, but kinship in general is often still important in people's social relations, and the value of kinship ties finds expression on certain ceremonial and ritual occasions. For urbanised Xhosa, as for Xhosa-speaking people in general, clan exogamy continues to impose a significant limitation on the choice of a spouse (Pauw 1963a: 166–70; cf. Wilson and Mafeje 1963: 74–90). Further, apart from kinship ties, personal face-to-face relations with neighbours and members of small musical groups, clubs, associations and churches often predominate in the individual's social activities (Pauw 1963a: 170–6; cf. Wilson and Mafeje 1963: 91, 99–100, 113–36).

'Small-scale' and 'large-scale' should therefore not be applied as taxonomic concepts in the classification of particular communities, peoples or cultures, since small-scale and large-scale features occur together within the same community or among the same people. Redfield, whose concepts of 'folk society' and 'civilisation' have much in common with those of 'small-scale' and 'large-scale society', warned that these terms he suggested should be used with the full recognition that 'In every isolated little community there is civilization; in every city there is the folk society' (Redfield 1960: 146).

Wilson (1971b: 90) has related increase in scale to the expansion of moral obligations, and Hammond-Tooke (1962: 242) has contrasted 'the application of a universalized code of moral rules to mankind in general ... found in Christian teaching' with the dictates of Bhaca morality, which have a limited application to kinsmen and tribesmen. Here we are not concerned with this shift from a particularistic ethic to a universalistic one (cf. e.g. Peacock and Kirsch, 1970: 63–4) but consider the way in which Christianity has contributed to a shift in the relation between particularistic and universalistic elements in the beliefs of Xhosa-speaking Christians as a concomitant of increase in scale.

Beliefs of orthodox Christians

Members of orthodox churches explicitly believe in God (uThixo in the Xhosa translation of the Bible) and pray to and preach about him in language that reflects acquaintance with the Bible and its terminology in connection with God. This includes references to Christ as the Son of God, who became man, and to the Holy Spirit. But the majority also believe that dead ancestors, as spirits, have powers exceeding those of the living, which they exercise to assist and protect their descendants and bring them good fortune, or to punish them with misfortune. Many also believe in witchcraft and sorcery as possible causes of misfortune.

In the traditional Xhosa religious system beliefs and rituals in connection with the ancestors and with witchcraft and sorcery predominate. In the ancestor cult the group sharing concern with a particular ritual is usually a patrilineage, and the dead with whom they are concerned are mainly their patrilineal ancestors. Certain beliefs and rituals concern clan ancestors, while a chief's ancestors are 'gods' for the whole chiefdom. Xhosa ancestor beliefs are therefore particularistic, not only in the sense that many of the beliefs involved are peculiar to a limited ethnographic 'province', but especially in the sense that each lineage, clan and chiefdom venerates its own ancestors as its own particular gods.

Present-day Christians and pagans alike regard the belief in a supreme being, uThixo, as part of the traditional Xhosa belief system, some maintaining that he was known by the name uQamatha in pre-Christian times. The belief that the ancestors mediate between him and their descendants is also regarded as part of Xhosa tradition. In her early work Monica Wilson (Hunter 1936: 269–70) held that belief in a supreme being is foreign to the Mpondo (a Xhosa-speaking people), showing that the contemporary name, *uThixo*, introduced by missionaries via the Zulu language, is of Khoikhoi origin. The name *Qamatha* is also derived from a Khoikhoi word. Other authors (e.g. Hammond-Tooke 1962: 237; Soga 1932: 149–50), however, accept a vague belief in a supreme creator-god as part of Xhosa tradition, and Wilson (1971*b*: 32) later seems to have accepted this view. All agree that he was hardly ever approached in ritual. Similar beliefs among different South African Bantu-speaking peoples support the conclusion that the indigenous tradition did include such a vague belief in a single god of all creation, in which the germs of universalism may be discerned.[1]

Xhosa-speaking Christians seldom speak of the ancestors openly, whereas one continually hears them referring to *uThixo*, whom they daily address in prayers in their homes and churches. Nevertheless the belief in the ancestors influences their interpretation of dreams, good fortune and misfortune, and occasionally finds expression in ritual. Whereas chiefdom and clan ancestors have lost much of their significance for Christians, lineage ancestors, but especially immediate patrilineal ancestors, remain important. While it is said that *uThixo* and the ancestors 'work together', many lack a clear idea of the nature of this co-operation, but some think of the ancestors as interceding with God on behalf of their living descendants.

For most Christians the relation between Christ and the ancestors is not clearly defined, but they are well aware that Christ has the same significance for believers among many different peoples, whereas their ancestors are obviously their own particular concern. They believe that their ancestors are especially interested in family and kinship affairs; they are 'the gods (*oothixo*) of inside the house'. Their ancestors intercede for their own kinsmen, whereas 'Jesus is the intercessor for all people'. A Xhosa author (Madala 1965: 45) has referred to Christ as *uMnyanya* (Ancestor Spirit) of all peoples. This kind of interpretation is not peculiar to Xhosa-speaking Christians; Möller (1972: 32) quotes an active urban Tswana Methodist as explaining that it is not fit to speak about matters in connection with *badimo* (ancestor spirits) in church, because these are intimate family matters; in church Christ

---

[1] This universalism was extremely vague compared to that of the Kalabari 'in whose traditional thought, *tamuno* [the supreme being] is a being concerned with all men and known to all men – whether they are Ibo, Efik or Europeans' (Horton 1970: 209).

takes the place of the ancestor spirits (*kwa kerekeng badimo ke Kreste*, literally, in church the ancestor spirits are Christ). Unlike the ancestors of Xhosa tradition (and other Bantu traditions), who are involved in relations with limited groups of kinsmen, Christ's significance is universal: he is an 'ancestor spirit' in the context of the church and relevant for all peoples.

The implication of the foregoing is that Christ is brought closer to the level of the dead ancestors than he is in Western Christian tradition, and is not considered to be on the same level as God the Father. Further, the Holy Spirit seems to have very little significance for many members of the orthodox churches. In conjunction with other information that cannot be presented here this indicates a tendency among orthodox Christians towards a unitarian conception of God: *uThixo* is primarily a Father-god, Christ is less prominent in their thoughts and is more like a unique ancestor spirit, while the Holy Spirit is completely relegated to the background.

I suggest that orthodox Christians identify *uThixo* of the Bible with *uQamatha* of Xhosa tradition, and that the unitarian tendency is the result of their reinterpreting belief in *uThixo* in terms of Xhosa tradition. Their daily concern with God, however, represents much greater prominence of a universalistic deity compared with the very limited concern with a supreme being expressed in Xhosa tradition. Universalism is also evident in ideas about Christ as mediating 'ancestor spirit' for all peoples, which, however, reflect reinterpretation in terms of Xhosa ancestor beliefs, and leave room for their own ancestors as particularistic intermediary spirits beside Christ. This scheme of beliefs leaves little room for the Holy Spirit.

Christians' beliefs about the devil, demons, witches and sorcerers provide another example of the persistence of traditional Xhosa particularistic beliefs together with universalistic beliefs which in this case are altogether lacking in Xhosa tradition. The latter does not include belief in any single ultimate source of evil nor belief in a multitude of demons or malicious spirits acting independently of human beings. Human beings known as *amagqwira* or *abathakathi*, who maliciously harm their fellowmen by mystical means, are the main source of evil. Some are sorcerers using medicines, magical rites and spells, others are witches acting through familiars, some of which have sexual significance. Although familiars are thought of as occasionally acting on their own, they are generally the servants of witches.

Christians commonly identify witch familiars with the demons of which they read in the New Testament and, having fully accepted the idea of Satan as supreme devil, closely associate witches and sorcerers with him. 'That person who is a killer of the flesh [witch or sorcerer] – that is Satan. . . . Satan is a person who walks on two feet.' Thus the idea of a single devil with universal significance has been added to, and integrated with, particularistic Xhosa beliefs about witches and sorcerers.

Awareness of this particularism is evident from the attitude to medical services. Although Christians – and even many pagans – readily make use of the medical services at their disposal, diseases ascribed to witchcraft and sorcery are generally regarded as falling outside the scope of Western medicine. Many Christians say that a person with an illness caused by the witch-familiar known as *uThikoloshe* or *uHili* should consult a traditional Xhosa doctor, 'because white doctors know nothing about Hilis'. This recognition of the fact that the beliefs are limited to a restricted number of related peoples, and not shared by whites, for example, indicates particularism. But again the beliefs are also particularistic in the sense that the witches and sorcerers suspected of harming one are – for Christians also – usually certain kinsmen or affines or other persons within a limited spatial or social range.

Ideas about the abode of the dead are also relevant to our theme. Christians hold beliefs about heaven and hell as alternative destinations for all people after death, although going to heaven is accepted as a matter of course for almost everybody. Exceptionally evil people are believed to be denied entry even into hell, and are said to roam about at night as lights going on and off. They are known as *iziporo* (singular, *isiporo*), from the Afrikaans *spook* (ghost). At the same time rural Christians believe that their own ancestor spirits are present in their homesteads. Even urban Christians believe that their ancestors visit them in dreams, and some sacrifice to them in their urban yards, sometimes building a small temporary enclosure to represent the traditional cattle kraal. Ideas about the relation between earthly home and heaven are not very clear, but some people consider the spirits as alternating between two places, while others think that as spirits they can be in different places simultaneously.

Here again there are significant links with, and deviations from, Xhosa tradition. The latter includes a vague idea of a land of the dead considered by some to be below the earth, where the dead have a continued existence partly similar to the life of the living and partly different from it. But the ancestor spirits of a particular homestead are believed to be present in the homestead and their presence is particularly associated with the cattle kraal, where the homestead head is often buried and sacrificial animals are slaughtered, and with the rear portion of the hut, where sacrificial beer and portions of meat of sacrificial animals are left overnight for the benefit of the spirits.

These particularistic beliefs about a local abode of one's own ancestors are retained by Christians, but ideas about a universal heaven (and hell) have been added. Perhaps we may see the germs of universalism in traditional Xhosa ideas about a land of the dead 'down beneath', but Christian ideas about heaven, which have replaced them, are certainly much more explicitly universalistic.

Beliefs of non-orthodox Christians

Traditional Xhosa beliefs and rituals are less significant among the members of certain Pentecostalist and Sabbatarian–Baptist groups, but there is an element of particularism in a tendency among them to regard their own particular interpretation of Christianity and the Bible as the only valid one, and salvation as attainable only through their particular church. On the other hand they usually regard their message as relevant for all people. In this and in their attachment to the Bible, which often involves a tendency to identify themselves with the people of God or the church as portrayed in the Bible, we discern a universalistic element. The kind of particularism and universalism indicated here is, of course, not peculiar to churches among the Xhosa nor to African churches in general.

Part of the Biblicism of the Pentecostalists is a special concern with Pentecost and the Holy Spirit. This may be contrasted with the ideas of orthodox Christians in which God the Father takes a much more prominent place than Christ or the Holy Spirit. The numerous small independent groups known as *amaZiyoni* (Zionists) are characterised by a syncretism of this Pentecostalism and Nguni tradition. For them 'the Spirit' is the source of extraordinary powers manipulated by their prophets and healers.

In these independent Zionist groups traditional Xhosa beliefs are often openly recognised. Misfortune is commonly ascribed to forms of witchcraft or sorcery that conform to traditional ideas, but Zionists explicitly reject the services of traditional Xhosa diviners and medicine-men, which they replace with their own forms of prophecy and healing by laying on hands. The latter often has the intention of driving out witch-familiars or the effects of sorcery. Adaptations of traditional techniques, however, also occur, as in the use of salt water that has been prayed over or handled by the leader, taken as an emetic to rid a sick person of phlegm supposed to contain a sorcerer's medicine by which the sickness is caused. Leaders also interpret the experiences of members in terms of ancestor beliefs and advise them to perform rituals to propitiate their ancestors. Prophesying about members' complaints with reference to beliefs about ancestors, witches and sorcerers takes place during part of the regular service set aside for 'confessions' or 'testimonies' and healing. Thus, whereas the typical sectarian particularism tends to replace the particularism of Xhosa tradition in the other non-orthodox groups mentioned, the two kinds are combined in Zionism.

Universalism and particularism in relation to scale

That any Christians should hold universalistic beliefs is to be expected. The New Testament leaves no doubt about the intention that the gospel of God's salvation through Christ should be proclaimed to all peoples. Even the Old Testament writings, in which the particular relation between God and the people of Israel is a predominant theme, recognised all peoples as God's creatures. The call of Abraham to become the father of God's chosen people was accompanied by the promise that 'All the families on earth will pray to be blessed as you are blessed' (Genesis xii.3, *New English Bible*). In the New Testament, however, the universalism became much more explicit.[1] This happened at a time when peoples around the Mediterranean had experienced a marked increase in the range of political, economic and social relations compared with conditions during Old Testament times, and from this time onward the spread of Christianity has generally been associated with increase in scale. This does not imply that the spread of Christianity was merely the result of increase in scale. Among the Xhosa, as among many other peoples, Christian missionaries have been important 'agents of change' contributing to increase in scale.

In this context it is the particularistic beliefs of Xhosa Christians that call for explanation. I suggest that for orthodox Christians particularistic and universalistic beliefs are relevant in different social contexts. Orthodox churches, which individuals join of their own choice and which are usually organisations with wide-ranging international contacts, obviously represent the large-scale features of society and culture. Within these churches, therefore, the particularistic beliefs of Xhosa tradition have little relevance, and orthodox Christians preach

[1] Universalism here refers to beliefs considered to be relevant for all peoples, not to the belief, associated with the doctrine of *apokatastasis*, that all intelligent beings will ultimately attain salvation.

and pray in terms of universalistic ideas about God, Christ, Satan, heaven and hell. But in the daily life of rural Christians in their homesteads and in the community, among kinsmen and neighbours, where features of small-scale society are in evidence, particularistic beliefs are relevant. Hence beliefs about ancestors, witches and sorcerers persist, since orthodox Christianity has not supplied particularistic beliefs that could replace those of Xhosa tradition.

My own investigations indicate that the adherence to Xhosa beliefs about ancestors, witches and sorcery is somewhat less among urban orthodox Christians than among those in rural areas, but the difference is less than I expected. On the basis of an investigation of the interpretation of misfortune among Xhosa-speaking people in Grahamstown and in a rural area Hammond-Tooke concluded that the returns from the townspeople showed a distinct shift towards 'non-personal' and 'scientific' explanations, but the proportion citing mystical causes of Xhosa tradition was still significant (Hammond-Tooke 1970).

The continuing significance of such beliefs for townspeople is probably partly accounted for by a relatively low level of school education. Xhosa townspeople do have more school education than rural School people, but their average educational level is still considerably lower than that of South African whites, for example. Further, I suggest that the persistence of such particularistic beliefs is related in a general way to the considerable amount of personal face-to-face contact that Xhosa townspeople have with each other. For them city life is not all that impersonal and anonymous, and therefore not devoid of some affinity with small-scale society, which fosters the persistence of traditional particularistic beliefs or the acceptance of new ones.

Ancestor beliefs among urban Xhosa may specifically be related to the significance that kinship ties still have for them. Admittedly the members of townspeople's lineage groups are scattered, and lineage groups are not important in the urban social structure, but sufficient value is still attached to kinship ties to account for the persisting concern with immediate ancestors. Given certain small-scale features in urban society, the belief in witchcraft and sorcery persists and is further fostered by the competitive urban milieu. Neighbours, kinsmen, co-workers, business rivals and lovers accounted for a considerable proportion of accusations in Hammond-Tooke's urban sample (Hammond-Tooke 1970: 31).

'Sectarian' particularism seems to be directly related to the high degree of solidarity, group consciousness and intense interaction within the group, which are characteristic of many non-orthodox groups, and of Zionist groups in particular. 'The tiny Zionist groups which proliferate in South Africa achieve a very close-knit brotherhood, whose members, so far as is possible, interact only with one another. They preach no universal doctrine', although this should not be understood in an absolute sense, 'and their unity is achieved by exclusiveness' (Wilson 1971b: 121[1]). But even large urban groups in East London and Port Elizabeth, like the Assemblies of God, the Old Apostolic Church and the late Bishop Limba's Church of Christ, are characterised by the same kind of concentration of members' activities and social relations within the church group, sometimes in the context of neighbourhood clusters. In such groups 'the sort of pressures to conformity that exist in an isolated pre-literate community are matched in the modern world' (Wilson 1971b: 14). I argue that this, as well as the face-to-face personal relations within the groups, and their particularism account for a significant degree of affinity with small-scale society within the large-scale urban context.

Conclusions

Christianisation has resulted in a shift from the predominantly particularistic beliefs of Xhosa tradition towards more universalistic beliefs, as part of the process of increase in socio-cultural scale. But universalistic beliefs traditional to orthodox Christianity have been reinterpreted in terms of Xhosa tradition. This is evident, for example, in the tendency towards a unitarian conception of God, and in the view of Christ as ancestor of all peoples. The idea of heaven as the abode of all dead has a vaguely universalistic precedent in the traditional Xhosa belief in a general abode of the dead in an underworld.

Particularistic Xhosa beliefs in ancestors present in the homes of their descendants, and beliefs in witchcraft and sorcery, however, remain significant, and this may be partly related to the persistence of certain traditional small-scale features in rural as well as urban society. But here also there is adaptation in the very explicit view of the ancestors as intermediaries between the living and God, and in the association of witchcraft and sorcery with Satan and his demons.

Particularism is, however, not only expressed through the medium of Xhosa tradition; it also finds expression in a sectarian particularism typical of some groups of Christians throughout the Western world, usually characterised by close-knit, personal face-to-face relations reflecting a certain affinity with small-scale society.

[1] Cf. Kiernan 1974.

Archie Mafeje

RELIGION, CLASS AND IDEOLOGY IN SOUTH AFRICA

Theoretical setting and approach

One of the most profound and controversial questions in the episte-mology of the sociology of religion comes to us in the simple form of whether belief systems are a reflection of the world of experience or an expression of a transcendental inner self which is the incarnation of ultimate truth and bestower of meaning to all social existence. In its epi-stemology the transcendental viewpoint has combined two conflicting suppositions, a belief in the existence of an extra-societal source of meaning, and an unshakable faith in a positivist conception of science. This has prompted some a-religious critics to force a division between sociologists of religion and religious sociologists, an injunction which is given extra weight by a naive but general positivist belief in 'value-free' or non-partisan science.

Probably, such injunctions are nothing more than emotive noises which do not contribute to the discernment of the link between belief and practical experience. Even a comparison between such familiar writers as Durkheim and Weber shows that significant epistemo-logical distinctions are not to be made at the level of religiosity. What of the materialists who, though happy to abandon any search for meanings outside determinate social existence and willing to take the world of the individual as given, still have to contend with the problem of 'consciousness' and empirical history? It becomes apparent then that the problem of 'theodicy', as first formulated by Max Weber, is as serious for the positivist (whether Christian or not) as is the problem of 'consciousness' for the materialist.

Deriving from the predominance of the functionalist approach in the Anglo–Saxon world, South African sociology of religion has been confined to the study of churches, denominations, religious sects, tribal rites and their supposed functions in society. While this forms part of an heroic tradition, the preoccupation with institutions has meant a narrowing-down of context to a point where some of the more general ramifications of belief systems and some nascent forms of commitment are made to appear as something apart. I am referring to unorganised cosmic views and specific ideologies that underlie them and which might not only interpenetrate with confessed religious beliefs but might also transcend them. Secondly, the same functionalist organicism has led to the interpretation of 'social change' as a substitution of one set of institutions with another. At the descriptive level that might appear to be so but at the level of what we referred to as the problem of 'theodicy' or, alternatively, as the problem of 'consciousness' and history, it might be nothing more than ideological mystification by both onlooker and actors. What does it mean for an African to be a Christian? What does it mean for him to preach brotherhood in a world in which he is a victim of total alienation? Whatever the answer, could it mean the same thing for him as for his white fellow-Christian who is structurally and culturally distinct? A transcendentalist Christian, quite subjectively, would be inclined to say yes. But, analytically, the problem of linking meaning to meaning would still confront the sociologist of knowledge. In the totality of contrived Christian orthodoxy among some Africans, continued adherence to certain primeval African beliefs and, at times, a more blatant reversion to the pagan past by some, what does it mean for a positivist sociologist to assert 'social change'? Does 'social change' connote the same thing as historical transformation? Can it be supposed that the concept of 'social scale' is as critical in its analytical application as the concept of 'dialectics' in Hegelian–Marxian historiography?

Using my experience as a product of African Christian culture in South Africa and my rather limited researches into African religious beliefs as a functionalist neophyte, I shall endeavour to answer some of these questions. My method will be to diffuse 'sociology of religion' into sociology of knowledge. This will be achieved by deflating the religious, *qua* religious, by relating it more closely and more systematically than has been done so far to its material substratum, namely, class and ideology. The intention, as it might be supposed, will not be to debase the religious by denying it its own internal dialectic but rather to show that the permutations of the same dialetic derive from and contribute to other forms of social existence. Indeed, it is my conviction that this will enable us to comprehend the totality of South African history, without falling into that pious idealism which contents itself with bemoaning the contradictions and perversions of the South

African society, largely from the standpoint of a worn-out West European liberalism for which it offers no critique. Happily, for South Africa a worthy start has been made by B. G. M. Sundkler (himself a product of Scandinavian *social* democracy) in his classic *Bantu Prophets in South Africa.*

While substantively one may feel free to use Sundkler as a suitable point of departure, professionally it is still important to note that, of the two founders of modern sociology of religion, Emile Durkheim and Max Weber, the former has had a preponderant influence in South Africa which in its intensity was matched only by Malinowski's functionalism.[1] Durkheim's *Elementary Forms of Religious Life* formed the theoretical basis of the studies of rituals by an earlier generation of South African social anthropologists. For the anthropologists this was in keeping, as Durkheim was interested in the study of primitive societies. Secondly, Durkheim's proclaimed lack of concern with 'neither the truth nor the falsity' of religion had a tremendous appeal to those who had dedicated themselves to the development of a 'value-free' science of society. Thirdly, Durkheim's generalisations about the 'social significance' of religious expression and belief provided a convenient framework for comparative analysis to people who were working outside their societies. Finally, Durkheim's emphasis on the integrative value of religion seemed to receive immediate confirmation in the field,[2] and his general proposition that religious belief synchronised with the network of social relations in primitive society seemed to make sense.

In contrast, Max Weber, who wrote even more extensively on the sociology of religion than Durkheim, hardly appears in the reference lists of South African sociologists of religion.[3] Why? Is it because his main field was modern industrial societies? Max Weber was a radical liberal who had accepted the challenge from German materialists such as Karl Marx with all seriousness. While maintaining stoutly the neo-Hegelian idealism, he managed to transcend some of the positivist crudities espoused by Durkheim. He therefore provides an interesting counterpoint to South African intellectual liberalism, which is, in my

[1] Cf. E. J. and J. D. Krige 1943; G. and M. Wilson 1945; M. Wilson 1957, 1959a and 1971b; B. A. Pauw 1960; and a few minor works by the same authors. 'We, as sociologists, build on foundations laid by Tylor and Durkheim, Malinowski and Radcliffe-Brown' (G. and M. Wilson 1945: 83–4).

[2] Although his atheist heresy that the universal and external source of religion is society met with instant rejection from followers such as Monica Wilson (1971: 67).

[3] The only exception being his *Protestant Ethic and the Spirit of Capitalism*, used more as a reference than a source book.

view, essentially conservative and not dissimilar to that of the German Christian liberals under comparable circumstances in the inter-war period. However, this is a scenario which is best reserved for another occasion.

For our present purposes what needs to be brought into sharp focus is what is distinctive about Weber's sociology of religion. As is known, Weber was primarily interested in the ways in which different types of social experience, such as those attendant upon social class and status distinctions, were related to different modes of religious expression and belief. His approach was necessarily dynamic and his method distinctly historical. This was fully culminated in his *Protestant Ethic and the Spirit of Capitalism,* a *tour de force* with which he sought to illuminate the manner in which *rationalisations* of religious belief were employed to achieve consistency and rationality in relation to the contingencies and the problems of social life. One does not have to agree with Weber in order to appreciate the theoretical importance of questions such as: Did not Christianity, which started off as a doctrinal revolt of itinerant artisan journeymen, become vested by the middle ages in the infallible authority of popes? Did not the Protestants during the Reformation find doctrinal grounds for rebelling against the same authority?

Religion, class and ideology in Langa

In contrast, when I went to Langa to do fieldwork in 1961, I was armed with an essentially ahistoricist and overly functionalist question: Why and how do social groups cohere or split? Historically, it is necessary not to accuse myself of inanity but simply to acknowledge the fact that I should have known that ebbs and flows are the very movements of which the dialectic of history is made, and, as such, are permanent features of collective existence. But in the context of Langa what is collective existence? In Langa we enumerated thirty denominations, fifteen of which owed their origin to European mission churches and an equal number of Christian denominations created by the Africans themselves (Wilson and Mafeje 1963: 92–3). The latter are what have been referred to as 'independent African churches'. They readily fell into what Sundkler has categorised as 'Ethiopian' and 'Zionist' types. For Langa the history of these movements has already been given in the work cited. What remains for us in this presentation is to highlight some of the salient points.

Strange as it may sound, virtually everybody is *nominally* a Christian in Langa. The only exceptions are the pagan migrants who normally reside in the so-called 'barracks' and less frequently in the 'zones'. They live, not in isolation, but in the company of Christian fellow-migrants usually from the same district in the countryside. In this context the pagans are identified, albeit derogatorily, as *amaqaba* (those who paint themselves with red ochre). This is in contra-distinction to those who are variously identified as *abantu basesi-kolweni* (school people), *amagqoboka* (converts), *abantu becawe* (church people), *amakholwa* (believers) or, simply, *amakhumsha* (the civilised: literally, those who speak English). It is important to note that these terms sound a little archaic in Langa and that their use is more implicit than explicit. Perceptually, it is generally understood that those who have acquired European Christian culture and have been to school[1] are something apart from and above the pagans – an inevitable Christian teaching. Within this broad category further subtle distinctions are made. For instance, the younger generation in Langa, who in any case were born in the church, would not refer to themselves as *amagqoboka* (converts), *amakholwa* (believers), *abantu basesikolweni* (school people) or even *abantu becawe* (church people), except in jest. But they will readily confess Christianity and church attendance, 'when circumstances permit' (*xa imeko ivuma*) or 'when inspired' (*xa umoya uvuma*). For all that, they are largely indifferent to and even greatly disaffected from the church. The explanation will come later.

Religious piety seems to be the privilege of the old in Langa. It is the older generation who patronise the church and run its affairs. They are generally proud of their church affiliation and freely talk of themselves as *amaKrestu* (Christians), *abantu becawe*, *amakholwa*, *amagqo-boka* and the rest of the terms mentioned earlier. Any important positions that exist in the church are usually held by members of this group. Among priests there might be exceptions to this, but they are not thought of as being particularly fitting.

We have shown that within the rather broad category known as 'Christian', as opposed to pagan, in Langa there is a substantial section that is, in fact, irreligious, though socialised in the general Christian culture. Secondly, we observed that this varied according to generation. There remain two other important distinctions that are made in Langa, namely, the educated and the uneducated, the respec-table and the unrespectable. Xhosa is poor at expressing the status differentiations. In actual speech meanings get easily fused. Respondents referred to educated individuals as *ufundisiwe, akaloqaba* (he is

[1] Until 1953 African education in South Africa was the business of the missionaries.

educated, he is not a pagan, meaning that he is not raw or uncouth). They described migrant workers as *abafundiswanga, ngamaqaba* (they are uneducated, they are pagans – which was not necessarily true). But the association was clear. Education is equated with respectability and Christian civilisation (not being pagan). Lack of education is associated with lack of respectability and being uncivilised, irrespective of whether or not one is a Christian, as in the case of the migrants. Secondarily, education is associated with being well-off materially.

As people are described as 'educated' or 'uneducated' in Langa, so are churches divided into 'genuine' (*icawe yokwenyani*, a true/real church), and 'fake' (*oozenzele*, self-made).[1] At first sight, one would have thought that all the churches which owe their origin directly to white missionaries would automatically be classified as 'genuine', and yet not. On close inspection one soon discovered that the more Pentecostal denominations such as the Assemblies of God, Full Gospel, Jehovah's Witnesses, Seventh-Day Adventists and the Salvation Army did not qualify.[2] On the other hand, some of the African-led 'independent' churches such as the Presbyterian Church of Africa, the Ethiopian Church of South Africa, the Bantu Methodist Church and the African Ethiopian Baptist Church definitely qualified. Why?

Doctrinal considerations never entered our conversations with the people of Langa. Their arguments turned round style and perceived intellectual sophistication, particularly of the leadership and hence the clientele to which it appeals. Educated gentlemen and ladies are worthy African replicas of the original men of God and inheritors of the *true* House of God. This is the prevailing Christian *cultural* ethic and is realised in actual life. The clergy of the 'genuine' churches were found to be educated full-time ministers. Apart from the necessary theological training, all of them had completed primary school education, more than two-thirds had had secondary education and, at least three held university degrees. Also, having full-time clergy meant availability of funds in the church. It is true that the 'genuine' churches are wealthier and have proper facilities, including substantial buildings for worship. All of them enjoy financial support from white mother churches in South Africa or, in the case of some 'independent' churches, from affiliated organisations in America and Great Britain.

In sharp contrast, the 'fake' churches have neither full-time edu-

---

[1] In the Langa book we used 'real' and 'self-made', correct transations in themselves. But I think now that 'genuine' and 'fake' brings us closer to what is really meant.

[2] The Salvation Army has a rather ambiguous status. It has its own school grounds and building in Langa and reasonable funding, but it does not attract the respectable.

cated ministers, ladies and gentlemen in the membership, church buildings, nor creditable financial status. They draw their membership largely from uneducated pagan and semi-pagan migrants from the countryside. As unskilled black labourers these represent the poorest in society and, according to perceived categories, represent those least acculturated into white Christian civilisation. They are among those whom Langa residents readily recognise by their style of dress and gait. None of their leaders in Langa had had formal theological training, nor had any of them completed even primary school education. All the same, they styled themselves exactly the same as the other church leaders in Langa and elsewhere, 'Bishop', 'Moderator', 'Pastor', etc. A pathetic self-delusion but a datum of exceeding sociological import, if rationalisations are seen for what they are.

It is evident that Langa is pervaded by a Christian middle-class ideology which denigrates paganism and which places a premium on Christian education as a civilising influence and a source of respectability. The greater Christian world outside Langa and outside South Africa itself has, through its material and spiritual support, made sure that this remained not merely an ethical value but also an objective reality. Such is the logic of history and there is little point in quarrelling with it. But then the logic of history has its own dialectical contradictions. While the middle-class aspirants in Langa are willing to maintain and even articulate the difference between them and the uneducated *amaqaba*, they are not willing to be dominated by their supposedly more civilised white fellow-Christians. They then rationalise their subjective aspirations into a wider and more creditable moral and political value, rejection of 'white supremacy'. Perceptually, 'independent' African churches offer themselves as a structural solution. But, as is shown by the low rate of survival among breakaway African churches, 'independence' is hard to sustain financially and theologically, without white support – another reflection of the national and international contradiction between white and black. In the circumstances what does 'independent' mean? Personally, I would use '*independent*' churches only for those churches which have found a theoretical paradigm which transcends the peculiarly European 18th and 19th century middle-class Christian ethic. The gentlemen and ladies in Langa who are trying to approximate as closely as possible to these values and who are anxious not to debase the Christian ethic cannot be treated as potential subjects of such a process.

The antithesis of privilege is privation. Therefore, *logically*, one would look to the faked as the antithesis of the genuinely committed.

Are the Zionists and other 'primitive rebels' the answer to the problem? As has already been intimated, the members of the 'fake' churches are not averse to having Bishops, Moderators, Pastors and Archdeacons. Their problem is that they do not have the means for it. They rationalise their frustrations in an objectively white-dominated society by jumping on the 'independent' church band-wagon. They latch onto anti-whitism and proclaim that blacks will 'enjoy ascendancy over Europeans' or that when the Day of Judgement comes, 'whites will go a-begging to dip the tip of their finger in cool water but will get as a reply, "No, nobody can rule twice".' It is true that their version of Christian ideology emphasises those things which affect them directly, such as injustice, discrimination and material deprivation. But what they never confront is the black middle-class *Christian* ideology which emphasises 'respectability', 'orderliness' and Christian cultural indoctrination. Part of the reason for their inability is that, contrary to popular belief in Langa, they are as much products of Christianity as anybody else – an underdeveloped part of it, if you like. Their reliance on rituals which are similar to those of the pagans proper are to be seen as compensation for lack of what they aspire to and not as a reversion to paganism, as has been suggested by Bishop Sundkler (1961: 55). Their strenuous attempts to maintain a separate identity from pagans by a fanatical adherence to some of the Christian ritual taboos should be interpreted as making a virtue of necessity. Likewise their concern to 'combat the use of *inyanga*'s medicines' and to 'fight the diviner's demons of possession' (Sundkler 1961) is an assertion of moral superiority which they have in common with other Christians, irrespective of the weapons used. Far from being an 'escape into history', Zionist churches are, therefore, a stage in history. But the question to answer is: what stage in history?

The historical paradox

Christianity in South Africa has meant an encounter between very divergent systems of beliefs, an African pagan cosmos governed by ancestral spirits and shades (in Xhosa *izinyanya* and *amathongo*,[1] respectively), and a very ill-defined 'High God' (Xhosa *Thixo*, Zulu *uNkulunkulu*, Sotho *Modimo*, all of which have been bundled by Christians into an identical God, the Christian God) and a monotheist

[1] Although used interchangeably in ordinary speech, in Xhosa basic conceptions the two terms refer to two different orders of spiritual existence. While *amathongo* are guardian spirits in the same sense as *izinyanya*, the latter are never treated as objects of sacrificial offerings or ritual appropriation. (Cf. Wilson 1971: 26–8.)

European religion with a high level of theoretical self-consciousness, something which is required of any proselytising religion. As is shown by the predominance of personalised spirits, good or bad, at this time the African still depended on analogies for expressing mystical experience. The best reason that could be given for articulating one's mystical experience in terms of any given set of analogies was that that was how *individuals* had actually seen them in dreams or in other similarly dissociated states. The normatively compelling character of such visions was that they promised order in a potentially disorderly situation. *Amasiko* (customs) were nothing else but powerful media for channelling individual psychological and spiritual needs. But once again intellectual justification for their existence relied on a very simple and weak logic: 'This is the way things have always been and will always be.' In several interviews in Langa when it came to the crunch, I was solemnly reminded that '*amasiko ngamasiko*' (customs are customs). What is the significance of that in a township which has been described, approvingly, as having a 'Christian atmosphere'?

At its most basic level the problem is not one of mechanical increase in scale but rather one of continued clash between two cosmic world-views. Christian religion is equipped with a number of highly abstract and integrating concepts, which even the average European cannot pretend to understand fully.[1] Consequently, for its propagation it has had to rely on specialists for whom the African was no match. The reaction of the first generation of Christians was to swallow the whole thing at its most general *cultural* level, without feeling compelled, logically, to abandon its peculiarly African cosmic paradigms. What we see in Langa are different phases of the same self-contradictory motion. Whether Zionist or high-Anglican, all Africans in Langa share an implicit belief in ancestor-cult and have held on with varying tenacity to their *amasiko*. They conduct circumcision rites for their boys, birth rites for their babies (*idinara yomntwana*,[2] baby's dinner party, which, fortunately, coincides with baptism rites) and organise commemoration dinner parties for their departed heads of families.[3] Inhibition and even abstinence there are, but these should not be taken as signifying the absence of a lingering inner belief. Similarly, witchcraft beliefs persist in Langa, if in a hidden way, only to erupt

[1] Here I am reminded of the big difference in the level of awareness between theologians at a World Council of Churches conference and the Italian and Spanish peasants whom I observe at Christmas kissing away blindly at the feet of the statue of the Virgin Mary.

[2] Cf. the *ukulungisa* or *ukutyis' amasi* rites among the pagans in the countryside.

[3] Cf. *Ukuzila* rites among the pagans.

when individuals are in crisis.

The respectable Christians of Langa respond to these observations with a mixture of embarrassment and indignation because they necessarily detract from their civilised status as well as from their standing as Christians. And yet, by hiding this part of themselves to themselves, they have put themselves in an impossible situation, philosophically. They cannot be over-concerned to justify themselves to their *European* mentors and at the same time challenge them in the name of *African independence*. In their case, as a religious leadership, African independence will imply a radical synthesis which is both a resolution of the observable contradictions in their present spiritual lives and an affirmation of their self-denied Africanness. Perhaps, that would help them empathise with those whom they have been happy to call 'fakes' and to regard as unworthy 'debasements of Christianity'.

It is almost a platitude now among South African sociologists of religion to state that problems of mental and spiritual liberation cannot be comprehended independently of structural considerations. But in analysis there has been a greater emphasis on vertical cleavages, the so-called 'fissiparous tendencies' among African churches, than on horizontal cleavages such as we have described for Langa. European Christianity as much as European capitalism created a stratified society in South Africa in which mobility turned on education and race. Africans who embraced Christianity received education and had relative access to the good things of life – an access which was limited only by the existence of a white upper stratum. Within the church, it is the respectable Africans who are now asserting their equality at the cost of breaking away from their white mentors. But as they have come to appreciate the advantages – material and political – which are attendant on white association, they are careful not to rock the boat. So theirs should be seen more as the politics of accommodation than as an epistemological or ideological break. The fact that those of them who have actually broken away belong to the very few independent churches which were officially recognised is further evidence of the patterns of patronage. Bishop Sundkler has described this type of church as 'a right wing comprising churches which in their structure and outlook are 'carbon copies' of their parent Mission churches' (Sundkler 1961 : 54). At this level 'fissiparous tendencies', if so they be, mean ideological concordance.

As a dialectical opposite of the same motion, we should expect that those who have either no education or very little education would suffer frustration in a situation which is dominated by a specifically

European middle-class Christian ethic and which consciously denies the African ethic. Secondly, we should expect the frustration to be experienced irrespective of whether the domination is carried out by blacks or whites. We have already noted that the leaders of the 'fake' churches in Langa lack education on any significant scale. The second point was that none of them represented a rebellion against a white hierarchy in the church.

The clergy in the established churches in Langa are, in fact, black but strongly associated with white Christendom. Therefore, I suggest that the 'fake' churches are as much of a rebellion against racial domination as they are against class domination. The overwhelmingly anti-whitism in their rhetoric is partly a reflection of the ideology of the earlier independent African church movements such as Ethiopianism and partly an expression of resentment at the degradation of their African version of Christianity by white missionaries and white authorities. I see their obsession with high-sounding titles and insistence on the ritual uncleanliness of the whites as over-compensation for their rejection.

Lest we be accused of idealising the South African 'primitive rebels', let it be stated that there is both truth and falsity in the position of the 'fake' churches in Langa. The reverse side of their resentment of class domination is envy, as is shown by their internecine fights for position, power and glory. Some of them seek to exploit their followers and to mystify them into thinking that they are personifications of God Himself. Nationally, we have the supreme examples of Shembe, Lekganyane and Limba. Secondly, by insisting on antiquarian Christian values such as healing by 'Holy Ghost', 'prophesying', substituting gibberish for real, analytical communication, inducing deliberate hysteria among their followers, and placing a taboo on all sorts of food, they have not only reduced to a dangerous point their own sense of reality but are also fostering general false consciousness among their followers. Therefore, the fissiparous tendencies that have become endemic in these churches are no less an admission of weakness, impotence and lack of clear vision than they are an expression of frustration under white domination. Similarly, the three stages of initial secession, integration, and new crisis and secession, which Bishop Sundkler has postulated for them should be seen as a continuous process of fragmentation which is not compensated for by integration at *any* other level – the very definition of organisational weakness. They truly do not constitute an alternative to black middle-class (*petit-bourgeois*) orthodoxy, organisationally and theoretically.

Then we must declare along with the Bishop (Sundkler 1961:237) that:

The real clue to an understanding of the appeal of the Healing Message to South African natives is to be found in a social setting where ill-health, malnutrition and child mortality take a terrible toll. One may say in the changes and exigencies of modern times, the Zionist church wishes its message to function as an adaption of the Christian message to social needs of the African peoples. These healers are, however, a very definite threat to the progress of the African. ... They cannot by their methods bring the Africans out of the vicious circle of malnutrition—ill health—low wages—low social status—race hatred, but only serve to accelerate the downward plunge.

Finally, one cannot but agree with Sundkler that one could not expect to find radicals or even the politically conscious in these groups. But then how is that to be reconciled with his other view (p. 54) that they are a 'left-wing' movement?

Having dismissed both the 'right-wing' and the 'left-wing' churches in Langa, we seem to be heading for an ideological and theoretical impasse. It is only when we appreciate the significance of the statement that everybody is nominally a Christian in Langa that any hopes arise. In Langa Christianity is both an undeniable cultural affiliation and an implicit spiritual identity. We have already stated that in general the youth in Langa are indifferent to and even disaffected from the church.[1] They are ready to condemn Christianity as a diabolical scheme by the whites to enslave the black man and rob him of what legitimately belongs to him. They compare unfavourably the material well-being and greed of the whites with the misery, deprivation, exploitation and oppression of the blacks. Their feelings are genuine and they explode with anger and frustration. This is illustrated by an incident which occurred during the fieldwork, when a group of white university students from Stellenbosch came to sell Bibles in Langa. In the polemic that developed between them and some Langa young men the basic question that arose was whether they, as white South Africans who had betrayed every teaching in the Bible, dared to approach the Africans in the name of the same Bible? Not uncommonly among South African Christian liberals, the Stellenbosch visitors tried to get around the problem by dissociating religion from politics and by claiming that their sole concern was the scriptures. Nonetheless, more

[1] It is important to note that this excludes a small group, usually white-collar workers and members of the lower professions such as primary school teachers and nurses, whose devotion is as strong as that of the older generation, as attested by their members in organisations such as the Y.M.C.A. and the Y.W.C.A. They constitute the future leadership among laity in the respectable churches.

unpleasant questions and statements were hurled at them. Once again, typical of their kind, they sought to exonerate themselves on the ground that they, *personally*, were not party to the iniquities said to have been perpetrated by whites. That fell on deaf ears, and their accusers had the last word: 'The whites are the very people who have brought hell for us. We cannot be deceived any more, we have seen through the fraud of Christian religion. For years Christians have been preaching equality and mutual love amongst all people. But who is the first person to practise inequality? It is none other than the Christian himself.'

It is no exaggeration to report that such sentiments are universal among the militant radical youth in Langa and the not-so-young men of between 35 and 40. One often hears them being uttered at political meetings, debated hotly on buses and bruited about in the streets mainly to slight the pious. However, the seriousness of the matter can be judged by the fact that, during the worst political crisis in Langa and Sharpeville in 1960, three churches were burnt by the militants in Langa and an attempt made on a few more. As a further attack on the same symbols of respectability and collaborationist praxis, the municipal library was set on fire. It was obvious who the targets were, *the educated black Christian middle-class*, who are said to be prone to compromise with the white enemy.

It would be a very serious mistake if it were to be concluded from this account that the explicit rejection of Christianity by the younger generation implies a rejection of the idea of God itself. Apart from a tiny group of intellectuals and semi-intellectuals, among them university students, the younger generation cherish the idea of a God. When pressed in intimate discussion, they find it extremely difficult to justify existence without appealing to the concept of God. One of them, pushed to the ultimate logical end of his radicalism, suddenly said, 'I believe there is a God. But it is not something to be worshipped by me.' It was a good tension-releaser but it did not solve anybody's problem, as it failed to say what kind of God. For the younger generation, especially in the urban areas, the African God is a complete mystery, and the Christian God an anomaly. I watched this dilemma manifesting itself during one of the political rallies in 1960. One of the speakers made an impassioned speech, appealing to the 'African national God', which turned out to be 'the god of Moshoeshoe, the god of Hintsa, the god of Tshaka and the god of Tshekedi', in other words, the gods of the four most respected South African tribal chiefs. Is it hero-worshipping, or is it ancestor-cult? Obviously, the radical youth have not all the answers. But because they have rejected the *status quo* and have no wish or way of going back to the African past, they are destined to produce the necessary revolutionary paradigms, even for the unliberated African Christians. But, contrary to the expectations of the 'primitive rebels', who are their potential followers, the issue will be resolved neither in the church nor on Zion but in the wider society which the radicals have chosen as their terrain.

Religion, ideology and class permutations in rural communities

'Rural–urban continuum' theories have long postulated, to their discredit, a uni-directional tie between urban and rural communities. It is our intention in this section to reveal the dialectical link between the two sides. Shortly after my fieldwork in Langa, I had the opportunity to study two rural communities in the Transkei. It was then that it struck me that, sociologically understood, town and country are not polar opposites. If Langa is described as having a 'Christian atmosphere', All Saints, an Anglican mission station founded in the Engcobo District in 1859 could be described as possessed of an even greater Christian atmosphere. Everybody in All Saints mission is a Christian and is under direct pressure from the clergy and the elders to conform. Rural *mores* and self-interest make it possible. The mission controlled all the local schools – a primary, a secondary and a teacher-training school – until 1953 when the Bantu Education Act (47 of 1953) was passed by Parliament. It still controls the mission hospital and other social services. For such things as marriage and funeral rites and, of course, baptism which is an infallible entrée into mission life, the dependence of the residents is almost absolute.

The original village of *eNyanga* (from *eNtab'enyanga*) is now divided into a mission centre for the Christians and a periphery for the pagans – which is more than could be said of Langa. But, as in Langa, it is the members of the respectable Anglican Church who comprise the educated middle-class. However, unlike in Langa, their disregard for the pagans (*amaqaba*) is not complete and they refer to them, politely, as *abantu ababomvu* (red people) and in communication address them respectfully by their clan names. In the countryside the pagans are not necessarily poorer than the educated Christians and their political power is not any less than that of the Christians. In wider village affairs they participate on equal terms and often in concert with the Christians. This is not only because of their numerical strength but mainly because the terms of reference are *intrinsically* African, and not European. This is so much so that during the resistance movement in

Thembuland between 1959 and 1961 the pagans were in the forefront of the struggle.

The general impression gained during my field-trip and from my previous experience in other parts of the Transkei is that the pagans do not aspire to being Christians and are not concerned to be assimilated into Christian European culture. This puts them in an entirely different position, ideologically and spiritually, from those urban groups which are underprivileged and less educated, and which are so resentful and yet so desirous of being assimilated into the same Christian culture that has made pariahs of them. The conclusion is inescapable that the pagans by their militant conservatism have saved themselves from self-alienation. By the same token they might have helped their Christian fellow-villagers retain what has been lost to their urban counterparts. For instance, it was taken for granted in All Saints that when somebody's son or daughter was married the usual African marriage rites would be performed, over and above the Christian ceremony. Similarly, boys' circumcision rites and certain family cleansing rites after death were given full expression. The members did not feel any worse for it, nor did they feel called upon to make any recourse to 'those whites down there at the mission station, who know nothing about these things'. This is a reassertion of the African ethic, which is more militantly maintained by the pagans than the Christians. It becomes a curious logic of colonial history that the conservatives of yesterday have become the radicals of tomorrow. What is given to the pagans in the countryside is what is denied to the educated radical youth in towns and is what they seek to recapture by their impassioned invocation of an ill-perceived 'African God' as a reaction against Christian culture. Differences in level of theoretical self-consciousness there are, but the potential congruence between militant pagans and radical youth becomes the more real when we recall that since the beginning of the 'sixties they are the only two groups which have tried to fight white oppression bodily.[1]

At this point it becomes a question whether or not one is going to fasten on *self*-alienation or on white oppression and 'fissiparous tendencies' among Africans as a theoretical explanation. In All Saints, where white oppression is felt as much as anywhere else in South Africa, there are no independent African churches. Out of a total number of about 250 Christian homesteads in the village, the

[1] 1959–60 saw repeated revolts by peasants in Pondoland, Sekhukhuniland and Thembuland. 1960 was the year of the so-called *Poqo* campaign in the Rand, the Cape Peninsula and Queenstown.

Zionists, the Bhengu Church, Limba's Church, and Watch Tower collectively could boast of individual adherents from only eight families, whose sons had been to East London, Port Elizabeth or Cape Town as migrant workers.

At times such individuals are able to exert undue influence on their family members, as is shown by the following remark from one of the mothers: 'These things never used to exist during the time of our fathers. Even during our time they would not have existed, if it were not for our sons who go to the big cities only to bring us all sorts of things. Whether we like it or not, we have to follow, as we depend on them for financial support.' The same resistance against what are seen as alienating influences was shown by a younger woman, who expressed her scepticism by stating that she was not inclined to attend 'churches that meet in private houses' but, agnostically, concluded: 'I suppose that, though churches may be many and varied, they worship the same God. A man who has many cows does not milk them into different pails simply because they are unlike or because their milk tastes differently.' A friend of mine, a teacher and a warden in the local Anglican church, was not going to have any of this philosophical equivocation. Upon finding on his desk a batch of leaflets sent to him by Watch Tower, he groused angrily: 'What are the people going to think of me? What is this now? I do not like receiving these things, and I have been telling these people not to send me any of this stuff.' It was a violation of his Christian respectability as well as an unwelcome foreign intrusion. Compared to Langa, an important and subtle difference is that in All Saints pagans are accepted and accorded a higher status than Zionists and members of similar sects, who are seen as peddlers of a discreditable, alien influence. The fact that this kind of person tends to be a will-o'-the-wisp confirms the prejudices of the villagers. In the words of one of them 'Zionists are rootless, useless vagabonds' (ngoosithubeni abangenandlela).

Gubenxa, the pagan hinterland

Some thirty miles east of All Saints and up in the mountain fastnesses there is another village, Gubenxa – what one might call a God-forsaken hole. With more than 90 per cent of its population pagan, Gubenxa can be accurately described as the last bastion of paganism in the area. For all that, we can discern in Gubenxa permutations of the same pervasive historical dialectic as has been described for All Saints and Langa. In point of fact, it is an outpost of All Saints Anglicanism. The only primary school in the village was started by

All Saints missionaries. Consequently, the first few Christian families
in Gubenxa were emigrants from All Saints. Afterwards they were
joined by half a dozen young men who had been sent to All Saints for
their post-primary education, and by a local bigamist who had
decided to join the church with his two wives but was forced to
'divorce' one of them.[1] It is important to note that the young men so
converted continued to live as an integral part of their pagan families.
Those of them who had married by the time of the fieldwork in 1963
had taken ex-schoolgirls from the local or neighbouring Anglican
school as their wives and thus began to set up their own Christian
families. Otherwise, the rate of reversion to paganism among ex-
schoolchildren from pagan families was almost 100 per cent.

In other words, the pagans do not mind learning how to read and
write from the Christians but what they are not willing to do is to
alienate themselves by embracing Christian culture. The frequent
question I was asked by the girls was, 'Who will marry me, if I stay a
Christian?' Young men used to tell me, good-humouredly, 'It is not
fun to be a Christian.' In more serious discussions the older men
often remarked damningly, 'Mafeje's son, ours is a dead world. The
white man and educated Christians like you have made sure of that.'
Unlike the All Saints pagans, Gubenxa pagans had not yet learnt how
to live and struggle with the Christians. They were still isolated from
the militant movements which have become general throughout
Thembuland. Theirs was still a defensive and not a militant paganism.
However, those of them who have been to Cape Town, the preferred
city for employment, are beginning to change in their outlook.
Stories reach them about young Christian radicals such as Mapini
Lengisi,[2] the young guerilla who originally came from Gubenxa and
who was arrested and sentenced in 1972 for having tried to set up
military 'foci' in the Engcobo forests.

As part of the wider Christian community in South Africa, the
Christian community in Gubenxa, small as it is, exhibits the same
features as others. The few members of the Anglican Church and one
Methodist Church family formed the educated respectable upper
crust. But as in All Saints, they were not necessarily the wealthiest in
the community. In addition, there were the less respectable sects such
as the Baptists (amaBaptizi), the Sigxabayi sect and the Zionists. The

[1] Although he had scandalised his kinsmen by publicly agreeing to divorce his second
wife, privately it was understood that for local purposes she would remain his wife – an
expectation which he fulfilled.
[2] Nearly half of the Gubenxa residents belong to the Lengisi or Mvulane clan.

Baptists are more numerous than the Anglicans and Methodists combined. They come largely from established Lengisi families, which belong to the same minimal lineage as the original leader. Despite that, their pagan fellow-clansmen treat them as something apart, and perhaps as traitors, because they are very unaccommodating in their ritual behaviour. Apart from circumcision and some marriage rites, I cannot think of any traditional rituals they performed publicly. There were always apocryphal rumours circulating in the village that they did everything secretly (*egumbini*). Whatever the authenticity of these stories, they are sufficient indication of the general suspicion felt towards the Baptists. Next there was a Sigxabayi family, emigrants who did not belong to any of the Gubenxa clans. They were largely misfits in the village, and their addiction to the Book of Revelation, which one of their leaders used to proclaim on early Saturday mornings from the top of the mountains, before he finally lapsed into semi-paganism, contributed no less to their oddity. But their fluency of language, and the richness of the imagery conjured up to depict the golden past, reminded one of Ovid's *Metamorphoses*:

The earth herself, without compulsion, untouched by hoe or plowshare, of herself gave all things needful. And men, content with food that came with no one's seeking, gathered the arbute fruit, strawberries from the mountainsides, cornet cherries, berries hanging thick upon the prickly bramble, and acorns fallen from the spreading tree of Jove. . . .

These were primitive Christian romantics, and all they offered was the eternal gift of the gods. When asked about things of this world, one of them gazed at me and said, inquiringly, 'Mafeje, tell me. Why doesn't the government plant the whole country with orange trees and let the people eat?' No wonder the villagers found it difficult to take them seriously.

Finally, there came the Zionists, none of whom actually belonged to the village. They came from the neighbouring white farms to 'preach the Gospel' to the villagers. As in All Saints, they were regarded as vagabonds and referred to as *amaqheya* (degenerates), a term used of all farm squatters, who are believed to have completely forsaken African customs and traditions. Once again as in All Saints, the two founders of the movement were said to have come from Johannesburg and Cape Town. The villagers had no truck with them whatsoever and during the fieldwork they were discussing whether or not they should ban them from the village.

Conclusions

We thus see even in the remote and forlorn Gubenxa the same

stratification patterns emerging as were found in All Saints and Langa. In all three communities the Zionist and like movements appear at the bottom of the social heap, the educated from the established churches at the top; and the culturally militant, despite their varied social composition, fall somewhere in the middle and are more numerous than the other two groups. Similarly, the interpenetration and confrontation between Christian and African religious beliefs and ritual precepts are visible all round, but receive different interpretations. Likewise, the emerging class contradictions are being given different ideological rationalisations.

In the countryside as in town the usual South African racial ideology is pervasive. But within the church a specifically white liberal ideology[1] predominates and reproduces itself through missionary work and education, of which the missionaries were in charge from the very beginning. While at first this represented a *progressive* force, by introducing the arts of writing and universalising metaphysical concepts in small pre-literate societies which relied on simple theoretical paradigms for explanation, later it became *reactionary*, precisely by failing to come to terms with the contradiction of its own emergence in the peculiarly South African conditions. The tendency of the South African whites to impose totally on the blacks in the political, economic and social sphere coincided, even if inadvertently, with the insistence by the established churches of imposing totally white middle-class Christian values on the Africans. It was not just illiberal for the church to overrule completely the African ethic but, more importantly, it was *unprogressive* in that it destroyed the grounds for its own transformation in a new environment and unwittingly created grounds for the alienation of its converts.

When the first symptoms of alienation erupted towards the end of the 19th century, I believe that they were misunderstood by both white and black antagonists within the church. The black church leaders saw white domination as their basic problem in the church, while the white leaders, who belonged to a privileged group, could not dissociate themselves from that objective structural position. Therefore, both sides could only asseverate their consciences by agreeing to the principle of 'independent' African churches, preferably 'in communion with the mother church' – in itself an attenuation of the original spirit of Protestant liberalism. What the contenders did not see clearly were the forms of alienation intrinsic in the church ideology itself. While black and white middle-class protagonists were culturally

[1] This, perhaps, does not apply to the Calvinistic Dutch Reformed churches.

in communion and even able to agree on parallel development, the less educated and less acculturated African was feeling more and more out of communion with the established churches which *consciously* refused to give vent to his peculiarly African spiritual yearnings.

In the urban areas, where the pressure to approximate to European standards is particularly great and where the material base for African customs and traditions is weakest, the problem was bound to be chronic. This hypothesis is fully confirmed by the fact that religious protest movements originated from the cities – Johannesburg, Cape Town, Port Elizabeth and East London – and the various leaders in the countryside are often said to have come from there. They were protest movements of the dispossessed and quite distinct from the earlier 'independent' churches, which were led by educated black nationalists such as Tile, Mokone, Dwane, Mzimba, and others, who did not necessarily come from the cities. The 'primitive rebels' are a post-World War One phenomenon and, historically, they are both an affirmation and a repudiation of Protestant liberalism in South Africa. From the 'independent' African churches they inherited the principle of rebellion but from their experience with these churches they also discovered that their spiritual frustration was not attributable merely to the presence of whites but rather to a stifling religious orthodoxy which the whites held in common with the black respectables. Therefore, 'a plague upon both their houses'.

But as an indication of their *false consciousness*, along with their fellow-Christian liberal aplogists they proclaim the unity of man and imagine that the purity and felicity which man has not known since the primal fall in the Garden will be restored to the virtuous, namely, 'the children of Cush'. The sum effect is that they are unable to confront structure with structure but instead take refuge in self-induced halluci-nations. Nor could they rely on those who, at one and the same time, talk 'unity' and 'debasement'. In the circumstances their only hope might come from those who out of disillusionment see in Adam's fall a collapse into division and disharmony, and might conceivably surmise that, in the same way as Adam's soul was divided against itself by sin, so are all men divided against one another by selfishness, and that the envy of Cain bred murder and a world in which self-interest became the rule. This seems to have been the message of the disaffected radicals to the Stellenbosch Bible-sellers, and it frightened them.

In the countryside, as might have become apparent in our discussion of All Saints and Gubenxa, the problem of religious alienation is not as acute as in town, and the process of class differentiation is not as fast in the towns. Both Christian and pagan still join in common African rituals and in everyday life are still sustained by a common peasant culture. And in politics, religious affiliations are of no consequence. Economically, division of wealth cuts across the Christian/ pagan cleavages, and employer/employee relationships are still a rare phenomenon. This is in contrast to the cities, where status divisions are reinforced by definite production relations which are part and parcel of a capitalist mode of production. It then becomes evident that the so-called 'fissiparous tendencies' among African movements have resulted from deeper processes of alienation than can be deduced merely from racial tension.

We have identified the black 'carbon-copies' of white Christian orthodoxy in South Africa as among the sources. This change in perspective puts liberal theory in South Africa, which has always assumed its own progressiveness and that of its black followers, in an entirely different light. It may be asked: Does 'social change' or 'being civilised' mean, unambiguously, being assimilated into the white middle-class cosmic view? What will it take for that view to transcend itself? In answering this question it is well for sociologists of knowledge to remember that this was the final breaking-point of Weber's radicalism. Weber, having recognised the partiality of the German middle-class ideology, came to the conclusion that, since it was the fate of all ideologies to be both 'objective' and 'subjective', they could not be transcended. Therefore, the most that could be done was to endure them stoically. Thus he paid the price of being radical without being revolutionary.

Martin West

THE SHADES COME TO TOWN: ANCESTORS AND URBAN INDEPENDENT CHURCHES

Monica Wilson's work is known for its careful ethnography, clarity and precision. She has also been long interested in the processes of social change, particularly in ritual and belief. This contribution will attempt to give some precision to the complex of beliefs often referred to as 'ancestor worship', and will then deal with some aspects of belief in ancestors in Soweto, Johannesburg, with particular reference to the African independent churches that are so numerous there (West 1972b; 1975).[1]

The considerable literature on the subject of ancestors in Africa has brought with it some terminological and conceptual confusion, high-lighted in the term 'ancestor worship', which has survived, despite criticism, for nearly forty years. Those who have died are generally referred to as ancestors, although Monica Wilson has increasingly used the term shades. It is interesting to follow this terminological change and to suggest a reason for it. In her first work on the Pondo the term shades does not appear, but in her early books on the Nya-kyusa shades and ancestors are used simultaneously (1951a: 121–3; 1957: 4). The third book on the Nyakyusa refers only to shades (1959a), while a later work at one point refers to 'shades of their ancestors' (1971b: 4). Although no specific definitions of the two terms are given, close reading suggests that they make a useful distinction. Relatives who have died are referred to as ancestors, while the shades are more specifically dead people who are believed to affect the living directly. Hence Monica Wilson refers to the 'ancestors', and to the '*power* of the shades' (1951a: 121, my italics).

This distinction provides a basis for a more precise definition in an area of some complexity. We shall use *ancestors* as a general term for

[1] The fieldwork on which this paper is based was carried out in 1973. A grant from the Free University of Amsterdam is gratefully acknowledged. I have also profited from discussion with Dr. Michael Whisson and Professor B. A. Pauw.

dead lineal relatives, who may or may not be believed to be active, in the sense that they can affect their living relatives. *Shades* will refer more specifically to those dead people, irrespective of any descent rule, who are believed to be able to affect the living directly. Where the importance of descent is to be stressed in this category, we shall refer to *ancestral shades*. An important point to be made in relation to all three terms is that they refer in every case to people who were once living. This is a crucial distinction between ancestors and the supreme being, and we shall return to it later. Following this distinction between ancestors and shades, we may also make a useful distinction between belief and activity; thus there may be a general *belief* in the continued existence of ancestors, whether active or passive, but a *cult* of the ancestral shades who influence their living kinsmen. This distinction is conceptually as well as terminologically important, as we shall contend that in situations of social change the incidence of belief and activity may vary considerably.

This paper is restricted to ancestors and shades and their relationship with the living, but it is accepted that the line between the living and the dead is often arbitrarily drawn by ethnographers. In some cases what is termed an ancestor cult may also involve living elders. The argument for seeing ancestors as elders in Africa is admirably set out by Kopytoff (1971),[1] who praises Monica Wilson as being exceptional among ethnographers for referring to 'the power of the senior relatives, both living and dead, over their descendants' (Wilson 1957: 3).

The cults of the ancestral shades referred to in the ethnography generally involve their propitiation by living kinsmen to ensure their continued benevolence, or to stop punitive action. The belief and social action involved in this is often termed 'worship', and this term persists. An excellent article by J. H. Driberg, which has not had the attention it deserves, suggests that ancestors are 'intermediaries between man and the absolute Power – a function which brings them more into line with the saints of Christian hagiography than with pantheistically independent deities'. He suggests that the terms prayer and worship should more properly be reserved for this absolute power, and – long before Fortes – thought that *pietas* 'best describes the attitude of Africans to their dead ancestors, as to their living elders' (Driberg 1936: 6; cf. Fortes 1961).

While readers of 'A Beginner's Anthropology for District Officers

---

[1] Useful discussion and criticism of Kopytoff's paper dealing with shades and elders has been published in *Africa* (Brain 1973; Sangree 1974). Despite this, Kopytoff's point remains a useful one.

and Missionaries in Africa' were warned against the 'ancestor-worship fallacy' (Young 1947: 149–50), professional anthropologists have continued to use the term, and a number of writers have recently attacked its use. For example, Kopytoff suggests that one does not worship elders, living or dead, and cites Kenyatta's view that it is a misrepresentation to say that the Kikuyu 'worshipped' ancestors; 'communion with ancestors was preferred' (Kopytoff 1971: 137). A Zulu view of the relationship between the ancestors, *amadlozi*, and the living is similar: 'The early missionaries looked at the *amadlozi*–man relationship as worship; however it was a near fellowship' (Makhatini 1965: 155). A recent study of Zulu ideas and symbolism shows this clearly (Berglund 1972: 28):

Zulu are explicit that there is no *worship* of the shades in the sense that there is a veneration of them. If there is worship, then it is the veneration of the Lord-of-the-Sky. But with the shades there is an association, a togetherness which takes honour and respect of seniors for granted but allows for inti- macy and an atmosphere of mutual trust as expressed and experienced in the sharing of food. I maintain that there is no worship of the shades, neither is prayer addressed to them. On the other hand there is a speaking to them, a 'telling them everything' . . . .

While some are satisfied that worship is not an accurate term, others have re-defined it to mean something less than the commonly accepted definition. Goody, for example, offered the following: 'By worship I understand the sorts of activity to which Frazer referred when he defined religion as "a propitiation or conciliation of powers superior to man which are believed to direct and control the course and nature of human life" ' (1962: 379). Propitiation and conciliation, however, do not necessarily imply worship, which in our view implies elements of adoration, devotion and supplication of a superior power. We would therefore agree with Driberg that this term should be reserved for the supreme being, where relevant, and not used for cults of the ancestral shades. In this it is important to remember the distinction between superior powers who were once living (shades) and those which have always been spirits (supreme being): the former are in a different category from the latter, and this has been accentuated with the advent of Christianity.

The distinction above between belief and cult activity may be generally useful, but it is particularly important in dealing with situations of social change. Belief in ancestors may continue on one level in a situation of change, while on another level cults of the ancestral shades may decline or become modified. Failure to make this analytic distinction may result in an imperfect understanding of the processes at work. One problem in this has been that much anthropological attention has been focused merely on the transactional aspects of cult activity. This has led to a narrow view of the subject as dealing with propitiation and conciliation, punishment and benevolence, offering and prayer, with an emphasis on the interaction between the ancestral shades and their living corporate kin groups for their mutual and material benefit.

Typical of this approach is Fortes. While he has consolidated and extended our understanding of traditional cults (Fortes 1961, 1965), he has concentrated on ancestors and corporate kin groups with an emphasis on power and property relations in a rather material sense. This aspect is important, but it does not take into account such factors as morality and belief as intrinsic parts of the transactions.[1] While belief in ancestors continues to be expressed in a corporate cult of their shades, this approach may be adequate, but it has its limitations. By concentrating on unilineal descent groups and their relationships with their shades there is a tendency to lose sight of extra-descent group ancestors. McKnight (1967) has drawn attention to this subject. But the limitations are best shown up in situations of social change.

A useful analogy may be drawn here with the levels of kinship postulated by Barić in situations of change. Discussing change in Yugoslav kinship, she suggests that two levels operate – the 'substratum level of recognised kin outside the nuclear family' and the 'grouping of certain categories of kin into structured corporate units' (1967: 4). The former may remain, she contends, while the latter disappears, and this provides a framework in which to examine types of structural change. We can extend this argument to the ancestors. Belief in ancestors may remain as a 'substratum' on one level, while on another the cults of the ancestral shades of corporate groups may disappear. By preserving this distinction we have a useful tool in the analysis of change in this area.

Let us summarise at this point. It is important to take into account the beliefs and activities of *individuals* in relation to ancestors, and to be aware of the fact that the absence of overt cults does not necessarily imply the absence of belief in the existence of ancestors. It is important to remember that a belief in ancestors is not necessarily related exclusively to a descent principle, and that cults of the ancestral shades involve activities and attitudes not consonant with the term 'worship'. Shades are seen as elders who have died, rather than as gods. They are

[1] I am indebted to Dr. W. R. Huntington for useful discussion on this point.

often intermediaries between man and the supreme being. With this background we can now turn to the urban situation in South Africa.

The urban situation

Compared with the wealth of information on African rural areas, there is very little written on the importance of ancestors in urban areas. Much of what material there is comes from South Africa, and Pauw has recently provided a very adequate summary and analysis of findings to date (1974). The subject is usually dealt with briefly, or not at all, in most urban studies:[1] for example, the cult of the ancestral shades is dealt with for Red migrants in East London, but not for School people or settled townsmen (Mayer 1961: 150ff). In the study of Langa the shades are only briefly mentioned (Wilson and Mafeje 1963: 109–10, 112), and they are not discussed at all by Brandel-Syrier (1971). Where belief in ancestors is mentioned in relation to African townsmen, it is usually in the context of general religious beliefs. In this regard the evidence often points to belief in Christianity and the ancestors as existing side by side. This has been suggested in East London (Mayer 1961: 30; Pauw 1963a: 42) and stated specifically for Langa: 'Almost everyone believes in the existence of God . . . but belief in God is combined with a lively belief in the shades. The two are not felt to be incompatible' (Wilson and Mafeje 1963: 109). The evidence for Soweto, the large complex of African townships outside Johannesburg, is equally specific, as Möller (1972) and Hellmann (1971) have shown.

The majority of Soweto's population is Christian, but Ellen Hellmann, writing from her lengthy associations with the area, has stressed the importance of ancestors (1971: 11):

Soweto, today, it appears to me, is more conscious of the dead ancestors than it was twenty years ago. The degree of observance varies greatly, ranging from not more than a general awareness of the ancestors and the holding of a feast with meat purchased beforehand from a butcher on the occasion of a termination of mourning, to a recurrent and meticulous setting aside of home-brewed beer for the ancestors and sacrifice of goats on all the appropriate occasions . . . I would suggest that it has today become more general to regard the ancestors, who represent a limited social universe, as the intermediaries between the Christian God, who holds sway over all people, and the individual.

Hellmann's opinions are confirmed by the findings of others, not only in the compatibility of belief in Christianity and belief in ancestors, but

[1] A recent exception to this is the study by H. J. Möller (1972).

also in the wide range of beliefs one may encounter in the urban situation. Möller's sample in Soweto, for example, showed a high incidence of belief in ancestors with considerable variation in cult performance (Möller 1972: 46ff). In Soweto, therefore, we find people with beliefs ranging from the 'traditional' view of the importance of their shades to those of 'modern' persuasion who reject the notion of the influence of ancestors upon the living.

We now turn to a discussion of ancestors in relation to the African independent churches in Soweto. African independent churches have existed in southern Africa for nearly a hundred years, and present estimates suggest that there are about 3,000 individual groups in the country with a membership of approximately 25 per cent of the total African population. In Soweto alone, there are believed to be some 900 separate independent churches (West 1972b: 1–5). These churches in Soweto cover a wide range of types, but can for convenience be divided into two broad groupings, as first suggested by Sundkler: Zionist-type and Ethiopian-type (Sundkler 1961: 38–59; West 1972b: 26–33). Broadly speaking, the churches of Ethiopian-type remain very closely patterned on the Protestant churches from which they originally came (such denominations as Methodist, Presbyterian, Congregationalist, and others) while the churches of Zionist-type have their origins largely in American pentecostalism, and are syncretistic, healing movements which stress the power of the Holy Spirit. These two types show a marked difference in their official attitudes to beliefs in ancestors and to cults of the shades.

In general, Ethiopian-type independent churches have a negative attitude to belief in ancestors, and strongly condemn cult activity. Zionist-type churches, on the other hand, range from being neutral to approving such beliefs and activities. Leaders of both types of church, whatever their attitude to the subject, are strongly aware of the negative attitude of mission churches, and this factor often intrudes in discussion about the ancestors. As Pauw has pointed out (1963b: 34) the teachings of Protestant mission churches implied a complete rejection of belief in ancestors, and this has been the norm of most mission churches, although occasional missionaries took a more moderate stance.[1] This has led directly to a reluctance to admit neutral or positive attitudes to the ancestors by those of Western orientation, for fear of being regarded as 'primitive' or 'unChristian'.

A good example of this occurred during fieldwork in 1970. A leader of an Ethiopian-type church of Congregational origin stated cate-

[1] See Möller (1972: 53–4) for a contemporary example.

gorically that belief in the power of his shades was incompatible with Christianity, and that offerings to ancestral shades never took place in his church. After discussing the attitudes of missionaries to the ancestors, and when we had agreed that the cults had been misunderstood as worship, the leader suddenly said, 'I'd better tell you the truth.' He then described a dream, while on a journey, in which his father had appeared and looked hungry. He recounted this to his wife, who said that they would have to do something about it. When they returned to Soweto two sheep were slaughtered after a large church service, and a festival meal was held, ostensibly as a thanksgiving for the leader's safe return from his journey. Only close members of the family were informed of the real reason for the offering (West 1972b: 307–8). In discussing the ancestors with informants, a number of cases of similar initial reticence were encountered.

In dealing with the attitudes of independent churches to the ancestors the distinction between belief in ancestors and cults of the ancestral shades is also important. The strongest condemnation – mainly from Ethiopian-type churches – was reserved for activities surrounding cults: offerings of animals and beer in particular. Belief in ancestors, being a personal matter, was much more difficult to ascertain, and as it did not involve offerings redolent of pre-Christian times it did not pose any real threat to the church and its teachings. In this regard it should also be pointed out that beliefs and activities surrounding the ancestors did not necessarily have to impinge upon church activities. These were matters concerning either the individual or his family, and did not have to be brought to the attention of the church. It was thus possible to separate church affiliation from participation in a cult, and to entertain both successfully even if your church disapproved of such activity.

This seemed to be so in the Ethiopian-type churches. In general their leaders felt obliged to speak out against cults of the ancestral shades and to take action (generally expulsion) against members who transgressed the church rules, but in fact little was done unless specific cases were brought to their attention. In a small survey of churches in Soweto thirteen leaders were asked four questions about the ancestors: (1) Do you believe that your ancestors have power to help or harm you? (2) Do you believe that departed members of your church have power to help or harm your church? (3) Do you communicate with your ancestors? (4) Does your church communicate with the dead? Seven of the leaders belonged to Ethiopian-type churches, and all of them answered no to all four questions. There was, however, some discussion of the subject, with some leaders saying it was permissible to 'remember' ancestors while others said they would take action against anyone taking part in an offering to their shades (West 1972b: 312). Other leaders, who did not feel dogmatic about the ancestors, adopted a *laissez-faire* policy. The result in both cases was that a certain *de facto* latitude was allowed members of Ethiopian-type churches provided their beliefs and activities were not *seen* to break the rules. Available evidence would suggest – although accuracy is impossible – that a high percentage of Ethiopian-type church members had some belief in the existence of ancestors, and a varying belief in their power to help or harm. However, the incidence of cults of ancestral shades was fairly low, and at best sporadic.

The Zionist-type churches showed a different pattern. At no time during fieldwork was a Zionist-type leader encountered who actively spoke out against belief in the ancestors or cults of the ancestral shades. Six leaders of this type were asked the four questions mentioned above, and a variety of responses was encountered. Only one leader answered yes to all four questions, and in that instance he stated that these beliefs were personal matters and not the concern of the church. The other five leaders differed on details, and it is worth looking at these:

Leader 1 said that the ancestral shades were 'talked' to in church, when candles were lit. He distinguished between 'talking' and 'praying'. The shades were concerned about the church and had powers, but they were not prayed to; only God was prayed to.

Leaders 2 and 3 said that their churches communicated with the shades through offerings of animals and prayer.

Leader 4 said that communication was by offerings of meat and beer. Some members of his congregation were able to communicate with certain shades, and were occasionally able to receive instructions.

Leader 5 said that communication was through offerings and through dreams. Only five members of the church were able to communicate with their shades, and the church relied on them (West 1972b: 312–13).

In general the Zionist-type churches showed a much greater latitude in attitudes to the ancestors, and harboured members with beliefs ranging from the view that the ancestors were of no importance at all to those who maintained as many of the 'traditional' cults as was possible in the urban environment and in the absence of many family members. No evidence was found of variety of belief having any effect on standing in the church, and this was presumably in part because the subject of the ancestors was a private matter for most people. Activities regarding the ancestors would rarely take place in ordinary services, for example, and the only people whose relationship with their shades was at all important to their church were the prophets.

Zionist-type church prophets are people who are believed to have power to predict, divine and heal, with their healing activities being of paramount importance. I have described their activities more fully elsewhere (1972a: 52–5; 1972b: 152–211), but for the purposes of this paper it is important to note that there is a parallel between the training and activities of a prophet and a traditional diviner. The power of the diviner comes from his guiding shades; the power of the prophet comes from the Holy Spirit, but in some cases it comes via her shades (most Zionist prophets in Soweto were women), who have particular knowledge of the prophet and are specially concerned. In these cases the relationship between prophet and shades is important to the whole church, as the prophet is central to the healing activities which are vital to the existence and continued success of the church. The shades are likely to feature more prominently, therefore, in those Zionist-type churches that have important prophets who claim that their healing and predictive powers come from the Holy Spirit via their shades. In these cases their shades may be communicated with publicly in the presence of church members, as well as privately.

Most of the prophets encountered who stressed the importance of their shades communicated with them largely by means of dreams. Typically a guiding shade would appear in a dream with instructions or advice; on other occasions a mere appearance in a dream could be analysed to show that some particular form of behaviour was required. Dreams feature prominently in the work of most prophets, and analysis of dreams is usually a part of their training.

An interesting aspect of the importance of the shades in a healer's work is their part in calling the healer. All diviners, and one or two prophets, claim to be called to their work by guiding shades. The major difference is that with diviners their shades are the source of power, and with prophets they are intermediaries. In many cases encountered during fieldwork prophets stated that their first efforts to become healers had been directed by messages from their shades, who, being between God and man, were in a better position to see what was required of their living relatives, and to inform them accordingly. A relative thus approached would usually remain sick and troubled until the message was accepted and acted upon. After the normal training the new prophet would rely upon her shades to assist in the healing work, to give guidance in the techniques to use, and, in the words of one of the prophets, her shades would 'go and pray to God for the sick people'.

Evidence was also found in Soweto for a move on some scale from the traditional diviner, or *sangoma* to use the normal Soweto contraction, to Christian prophet. A number of Zionist-type prophets explained how they converted sangomas into prophets. This conversion was based on the permission of the diviner's shades. I encountered one case where permission was refused, but the general pattern was as follows. The prophet would become aware of the presence of a sangoma in the congregation, and would then suggest to the sangoma that as a Christian she should rather become a prophet. If the sangoma agreed, an animal would be offered to her shades, who would be asked to allow their relative to become a prophet. If permission was obtained, the prophet-novice would undergo purification, generally by immersion in a river, when the appurtenances of the sangoma would be ritually thrown away, and she would then undergo training as a prophet, after which she would be able to use the power of the Holy Spirit rather than just that of her shades. This added power would mean that the new prophet could now 'work with prayer and holy water and not with *muti*' (medicines). The shades would still be important to the new prophet, but they would now fulfil a lesser, intermediary role.

This view of the process would not be accepted by all diviners, however. One highly articulate sangoma with considerable knowledge of healers in Soweto had a different view of the process: 'Strictly speaking, 99 per cent of the Zionist Apostolic healers are originally sangomas – if you pin them down with questions on this point, some will tell you that they did not have the [financial] means to promote their powers as sangomas because it entails too much. So they performed certain ceremonies requesting their guidances [shades] to accept the Christian type which is less expensive. Others even have to undergo certain treatments by sangomas before their Christian powers can function, but the latter they generally hide.' This view was rejected by a number of Soweto prophets. However, the same sangoma felt that there was no basic conflict between the work of the traditional diviner and Christianity: 'The work of the sangoma, when undistorted, is very Christianised – there is nothing a sangoma can do under the direction of a guidance that would defeat the end of Christianity.' But her view of most independent church prophets was that what they regarded as the Holy Spirit was in fact the work of their guiding shades. Whatever the interpretation, the evidence points to a movement from sangoma to prophet, and some informants reported that even some non-Christian sangomas were beginning to use the techniques of the prophet, including the use of water and the laying on of hands.

Prophets vary considerably as to the incidence of their belief in the power of their shades, and also to activities surrounding them. The major public activity in Soweto appeared to be the propitiation of ancestral shades in terms of offerings of animals. Animals would sometimes be slaughtered for the shades at large church gatherings, but the intent would not always be explicit to all those attending. In some cases such an offering would have a dual function – for example as a thanksgiving both to God and to the shades for services rendered to the prophet. One church in Soweto had fairly regular thanksgiving offerings to God and to the shades who assisted the prophet in her work. These offerings were based on an Old Testament model which included the slaughtering of a sheep and the burning of certain parts of the body (according to Leviticus iii.6–11) on a fire. While the leader of the church and the prophet placed the offerings on the fire, the congregation moved in a circle round the fire, all holding candles and singing a hymn (West 1972*b*: 315–16).

Ancestral shades, therefore, are often seen as intermediaries by independent church prophets, but this role is not restricted to the church sphere. As already mentioned, Driberg (1936: 6) saw this as a characteristic of traditional cults and likened ancestral shades to saints. And speaking of secular Soweto, Ellen Hellmann (1971: 11) sees a similar role for the shades. Many independent church people saw their shades, where they regarded them as being important, as intermediaries, but few brought out the parallels, suggested by Driberg, between saints and shades. One informant was explicit on this point, and his position will be discussed as it also shows some of the general problems alluded to earlier.

The Revd. L had been a layman in the Methodist church for many years, and had risen to its highest council – the Conference. He held a responsible professional position in Soweto, and was a respected member of his church. During this time, however, he had not neglected his shades. He had continued to honour them, and to make offerings of animals to them. He knew this was against the teachings of his church and that he could be suspended or expelled if found out, but he felt that he had never been given a reasonable argument as to why he should no longer honour his shades in the traditional manner.

For a number of years, he said, he had continued in this manner,

and had experienced considerable conflict. On the one hand he felt
guilty for going against the teachings of his church; on the other he
felt he was doing no wrong and felt some resentment that he should
be put in this position. Over this period he worked out a specific
argument which he presented to certain of his ecclesiastical superiors.
In this he saw the offering of an animal as a purely cultural expression,
akin to the lighting of a candle, and prayer to specific shades to intercede on his behalf with God as the parallel of the Catholic petition to
a saint. In neither case were the objects of petition 'worshipped', and
the church's opposition to the shades was based on a faulty premise.
In his view he was given no satisfactory answer to this argument by his
church, and finally he decided to leave the church and join one where
his belief in the influence of his shades could be more open and above
board (West 1972b: 310–12).

This happened to be a man who left the Methodist church, but
similar cases were encountered of people leaving – or being forced to
leave – Ethiopian-type independent churches for their active belief
in their ancestral shades. Two particular cases were found where
women had been full members of an Ethiopian-type church, and were
then called to become prophets by their shades. In both cases the
women tried to combine their church membership with private healing
activities, but were expelled. They then formed their own churches,
based on the teachings of their former churches but with the important
addition of healing practices and a more flexible attitude to ancestors.

The attitude of Zionist-type leaders towards ancestors was generally
flexible, particularly with regard to the private activities of members of
their churches. The opinion of outside observers as well as of local
inhabitants was that the offering of animals to the shades was widespread in Soweto irrespective of whether or not one belonged to a
church. It was often pointed out that a large number of sheep and goats
were sold live in Soweto each week and suggested that many of these
were used in cult activities. In most cases these activities would be
restricted to the family, but it was noted that some independent church
members treated their fellow members as family in these situations.

This was seen particularly amongst the smaller Zionist-type
churches with their small congregations. It would be usual for the
whole congregation (and sometimes members of other congregations
of the same church) to be invited to important family occasions.
Weddings and funerals were the most common of these events, and
were the ones where the church leader would play an important role in
any case, but there were other instances of more private occasions,

some of which directly involved the shades: for example the raising of a tombstone of a dead relative, or a special thanksgiving to the shades.

On one occasion in Soweto, for example, the congregation of a church was invited by one of its members to attend a ritual involving the raising of a tombstone. This was interesting in that it was a family affair, involving six brothers. The eldest brother, who lived in Natal, had a dream in which he was instructed to raise a tombstone for his father, who had died thirteen years before, and was buried in Soweto. After a lengthy period of collecting money the ritual was held in Soweto. It involved a night of festivities and prayer at the house of the eldest brother living in Soweto, who was the church member mentioned, followed by the raising of the tombstone the next day. About fifty people, mainly church members, attended the ritual, which was marked by the slaughtering of a goat and cow and the propitiation of the shade of the father. The eldest brother took the leading role, being assisted by his other brothers and by the leader of the church.

A similar occasion involving members of another church had a rather different form. A senior member of the church, holding the rank of evangelist, held what he termed a 'thanksgiving' at his house. Although he would not specify the reason for the thanksgiving, others said that it was a propitiation of his ancestral shades. On this occasion, again, the whole congregation was invited, and a large tent was hired and erected behind the evangelist's house. This was the scene of a long church service which was dominated by the leader of the church, after which sheep were slaughtered and a communal meal held. During the service three male relatives of the evangelist, who were not churchgoers, drank beer at the front of the house and took no part in the proceedings. Unlike the first case where the senior brothers took charge with some help from the church leader, in this instance the church took full control to the exclusion of senior male relatives. And in a case mentioned earlier church members attended a feast but were unaware of the implications which it had for members of the church leader's family, who were making an offering to a particular shade.

We see therefore that some independent church members may be involved both privately and publicly in cults of their shades. Some rituals are performed at home before the family; others involve a wider circle of people and include members of the congregation. The church itself may play a varying role in these activities. We have also seen that the shades may be important within certain churches, particularly in relation to the work of prophets.

With all this there is clearly a considerable variation in belief and activity. Within the independent churches some people believe that ancestors are dead and buried and have no effect on the living; others feel very strongly that their ancestral shades are concerned about them and have some power to affect them. With this variation in belief goes a similar variation in cult activity; some believe in the power of their shades but make no offerings; some pray to and for their shades; some make offerings only at crisis situations, while others make regular offerings. One attempt to categorise this variety in Soweto has been made by Möller, who distinguishes according to the following typology: Strong belief/Reasonably strong belief/Weak belief/No belief (Möller 1972: 47f). This typology suffers from two faults, firstly that it does not take into account the belief-in-ancestors/cult-of-the-ancestral-shades distinction, and secondly – along with most typologies – that it artificially segments what is actually a continuum. Nevertheless it is an attempt to deal with a problem that is difficult to present. In this paper we shall present a few verbatim accounts by informants in Soweto of their attitudes to ancestors, which will show something of the variety as well as something of the individual conflict which exists when dealing with this subject.

The quotations below are taken from transcripts of tape-recordings made in January 1973 in Soweto. All the informants were people I had known for from three to four years prior to the recordings. We shall start with two cases of people who had a positive attitude towards their shades, and we shall then examine two cases where the individuals were more equivocal.

Case 1. Mr. M was a Zionist-type Christian healer of about 40, whose father and grandfather were Christian before him. He was of Zulu descent.

On the belief of churchgoers in their shades: 'I would say that 15 per cent still believe in the powers of *amadlozi*. The people who don't believe go in the way of the Western churches. They don't talk about spirits, it's something they hate – they feel it is backward. You see, they have been ill-informed, from the beginning, from the missionaries. .. Well, most of the Zionists believe in God. They believe God is great and that *amadlozi* get help from God. They pray to *amadlozi* to find the way for them, because they are nearer to Him. But some of them are still on the Western side – you can be on the Western side and still believe in *amadlozi*. But some people have been misled. They feel that the *amadlozi* are evil spirits. They are not. When you talk about a dead person they say you are talking about *amadlozi*. They have been ill-informed, they cannot distinguish between the dead and *amadlozi*. Some people go at night to *amadlozi*. Those people slaughter at night. They know it very well, but they don't want it in the open. It is very unfair, God doesn't accept that. . . .'

On the relationship between the shades and the saints: '*Amadlozi* are like – let me make this clear. The Virgin Mary was blessed . . . [People] worship her because she bore the child Christ. Mary was no God. Mary was a living virgin like any other person on earth. . . . The people who know Mary as a mother have taken her as an *idlozi*. Mary is an *idlozi* to her people, according to my information, but she is not God. . . .'

On his own shades and their powers: 'My power is assigned to me from my grandmother. She was a sangoma before. . . . Our belief is when people die we inherit from them, they go in you. They are what we call a guide in English. They guide you, they pick you from the family because of your good work, or because of the future they see ahead for you. Then they are always with you. The rest come and go, but you are ruled by one person – which is my grandmother. She helps me to see where to go and what to do. The only difference between this and the old beliefs is that I don't use medicines. My grandmother was not a churchgoer, but she directs me with the church and the word of God. She's never been to school, never spoken English. When she is in me and I start speaking people ask, "Has your guide ever been to school?" "No." She's a mystery, isn't she? . . . .'

On offerings to the shades: 'A few days back I saw my work going fine [reasonably well]. A goat came running in here, and they chased it away three times. It wouldn't go away. My little son came and said, "You know what, the *amadlozi* brought this – it must be a gift." So we took it and slaughtered it. And after that things went *very* well – it was wonderful. . . .'

In this interview, Mr. M was particularly clear on the misunderstanding of people of Western orientation in Soweto about the shades and the distinction between them and the dead (between ancestral shades and ancestors in our terminology). He was another of the few informants who themselves raised parallels between saints and shades, and was a good example of the general attitude of those who were open about their shades towards those who regarded the relationship with their shades as a surreptitious activity. Mr. M was also unusual for his explicit parallel between his activities as a prophet, and those of a traditional diviner.

Case 2. Bishop and Mrs. N were a Sotho couple in late middle age. He was leader of a Zionist-type church, and his wife was the senior prophet. Both their parents were Christian, but their grandparents were not. Both were present at the interview.

On Christianity and the shades: Bishop N: 'Although we are Christian in our religion we cannot forget *badimo* [Sotho: ancestors]. Those old people, parents of our parents, we do not believe that they have died – we believe that they are still alive, sleeping.' Mrs. N: 'In the New Testament, St. Paul said to the people of Thessalonia, I don't want you to worry about people who have passed away – they are sleeping. The *badimo* do help us.

They didn't know about the Bible, but they do the same things that the Bible says. They had God in their minds, and they were using God in other ways. You can't say I stand by *badimo* only. God can help me and *badimo* can help me. . . . Some *badimo* who were not Christian came to Father N in a dream and asked him to pray for them so that they could come out of jail where they had been sitting all the time. My forefather is always coming to me to ask me to pray for him because he was not a Christian. So I know that these people are as if in jail – you must bring them out with prayer. . . .' Bishop N: 'You see, in our nation *modimo* [God] and *badimo* are linked . . . I have to pray through *badimo* to *modimo*. They are our angels. In the same way you must put your word through Jesus Christ to God, then God will help you. Jesus said, I am not going to break any law. He didn't say we must drop everything of our nation – oh no. It is written in the Bible what people were doing before, and it can never be dropped. Some people say these are old things we cannot use any more, but it's in the Bible. But in some churches they want to break off with *badimo*. You know what they do? They cheat, they don't want people to know what they do. They take things to their house privately, and if you visit when they are busy with their family, they won't let you come in. That's not the right way.' Mrs. N: 'I didn't know *badimo* once. I was saying, how can I believe in *badimo* when we have Jesus Christ in our hearts? Then when God worked on me and gave me the Holy Spirit [to become a healer] and showed me things, then I understood.' Bishop N: 'Although we are Christian we cannot drop our old fathers. We cannot do it.'

This interview was interesting for the clear insistence that Christianity and traditional beliefs and practices were compatible, and in fact sanctioned by the Bible. Biblical justification was taken from both Old and New Testaments, with the authority for offerings, for example, coming from the accounts of Old Testament sacrifices. This was also another occasion where the secret practices of those who would not show their beliefs openly were criticised. This was also the only case of informants suggesting a two-way relationship with their shades: the shades could help them as intermediaries, and at the same time they could pray for and help those shades who were not Christian at the time of their death. Both informants believed very strongly in the power of their shades, and cited a number of circumstantial instances which showed the power of the shades at work – in one case, for example, a shade appeared in a dream to Mrs. N and showed her where she was buried; when Mrs. N awoke she found the site of the grave which she had been hitherto unable to find. In another case she had been ill until an animal had been offered to the shades, after which she recovered.

Case 3. Archbishop and Mrs. R were also a couple in late middle age. Like Mrs. N in the previous case, Mrs. R was the leading prophet in the church. Bishop R was of Zulu descent and Mrs. R was Xhosa; both their parents were Christian. Their church was of Zionist-type.

On the subject of the shades and offerings: Mrs. R: 'When I'm happy I want to make everyone happy. I just kill something to make everyone happy – like a party. Now other people call it *amadlozi* – no, it's not really *amadlozi*.'

On her relationship with her ancestral shades: 'I go every month to my mother's grave. This is not *amadlozi* – you see the white people do it. I used to work for an old lady and every week she used to take her children to the grave. And I also do that – I don't know why, it comes from my heart. My mother was not of *amadlozi*, she was a Christian. My father too, he was a preacher. The old people still believe in *amadlozi*, I pray for *amadlozi* to become Christian. . . . The right thing to do when you go to the grave is to pray for the people. You don't know if they are sleeping or what God is doing with them, you just pray for them. . . . When I didn't have the Holy Spirit I didn't know what was wrong with me. The *amadlozi* helped me to know what was what.'

On her mother (later in the interview): 'If my mother is of *amadlozi* then she is a Christian *idlozi*.'

Mrs. R on a recent operation and a dream before it: 'When I was going to have my first operation, I dreamed I saw my granny and my mother. My mother was a half-prophet; my granny was old and I didn't know her, I was too young. I saw my granny and my mother working in the hospital, and they took me to the hospital for my operation and I was all right afterwards. I dreamed this, but the operation was a success as I dreamed.

Bishop R on the shades, other churches, and his own views: 'Some believe in *amadlozi*, some believe in God. My father and mother were Christian. My mother was Dutch Reformed and they are not so strict. They can go to church and after church they can go and drink and do other things and nobody knows. My father believed in *amadlozi* that way. But if you don't believe in *amadlozi* and trust in God, then they can't help you. I don't trust in *amadlozi*. . . . Myself, I can't say I believe in *amadlozi*, but my father did. When I was a little boy I was in my father's church, the Dutch Reformed Church, and then I left that church and joined my brother's church. My father was always talking about *amadlozi*, but in my brother's church I never heard about them. Now I see that my father was a little bit wrong – he always used to talk about *amadlozi*. My brother read the Bible and never read about *amadlozi* – he read about God, Jesus Christ and angels. That's why I believe in God and don't worry about *amadlozi*. In some ways my father was a little bit wrong, hey? And my mother, too, she followed him. . . .'

The couple in this interview were both agreed that ancestors were not important; you prayed for them but they had no effect on you. They were adamant that they did not believe in *amadlozi*. The interview above, however, reveals something of Mrs. R's equivocal attitude. She stresses that visiting her mother's grave is nothing to do with the shades, but later says if her mother is a shade, then she is a Christian one. She admits at another point to having been troubled by her shades as a girl, and said on another occasion that the shades did have power to assist the sangomas in their work. The appearance of relatives in her dreams happened on a number of occasions, but she was always quick to point out that this had nothing to do with what she called *amadlozi*. We shall return to this point later. On the other hand, her husband took a more consistent line in denying any power or importance to ancestors.

Case 4. President W was a middle-aged leader of an Ethiopian-type church of Methodist origin. He was of Tsonga descent and his parents had not been Christians. He described his attitude to ancestors as follows: 'My father believed in God, *Xikwembu*. In old times God used to speak to them as he spoke to Moses. They spoke through *swikwembu* [shades] who were between [God and man]. When I was small I also did this. When I was 16 years old my father and mother were dead and I started to be a Christian. Then I didn't use *amadlozi* [now using the general Soweto word as opposed to the Tsonga word] any more. But I don't stop people if they want to do it. We pray for dead people. I don't know if they can help people – I don't know. I'm not sure, maybe. . . . We don't believe much in *amadlozi*, but we don't forget the dead people. We don't believe much, but still, in sickness. . . .'

On the place of the dead: 'Most of the Zionists still believe in *amadlozi*. Now I don't believe altogether, because a dead person is waiting in Hades, he can't come back. The Bible says he will sleep there for ever until the trumpet sounds, and then everyone will wake and the graves will be opened. . . .'

On those who do believe in their shades, and the origins of this: 'The Zionists are Christian – we don't disagree – but they are still holding to some of the old things. The time has changed now – it is not the old times. Before when most people believed in *amadlozi* there was no school. I think that when there was no school people didn't read the Bible. When I grew up there were very few Christians, but afterwards when people started going to school there were more Christians. . . . Even as a priest I can't just say "stop *amadlozi*". A man has to see how we work. You say "stop *amadlozi*" and you'll have nobody left in your church. I show them how I work. I don't say leave your *amadlozi* – that's not for me. God will tell them to leave *amadlozi*, not me. The spirit will change them, we don't force them. When I started this church I had fifteen sangomas. We didn't mind, we didn't chase them away, we only preached. Everybody must attend church and everybody must believe the name of Jesus. Then the sangomas left the church.'

In this case, President W had once been part of a cult of his ancestral shades, and had then changed and become a Christian. When asked directly he said that he did not believe his shades had any power to affect him. The interview above shows him musing on the subject, and wondering whether in fact they might have influence. His stated policy, unlike many other Ethiopian-type church leaders, was not to take a firm line one way or the other, but to allow people to make up their own minds on the subject.

Conclusions

Faced with this variety, we must make some attempt at understanding and explanation. As Pauw has shown, it is not sufficient to state that there is a general weakening of beliefs in urban areas, or a strengthening of beliefs in specific situations – for example to explain misfortune (Pauw 1974: 99). The typology of degrees of belief expounded by Möller (1972) and referred to above does not significantly increase our understanding of the observed variation or assist in explaining it. The standpoint adopted in this paper is that a necessary preliminary step to analysis is to distinguish the levels of belief and performance and to examine them in turn. We shall now look at these levels separately and then draw them together.

Let us examine the factor of belief first. In this category we refer to a range of attitudes regarding the continued existence, in whatever form, of people after they have died. The variety of belief encountered here is in the characteristics and importance of ancestors, not in their existence: no independent church member suggested the absence of life after death. Most Ethiopian-type church members who were interviewed stated that ancestors were not important or powerful – the standard view (as shown in case 4 above) was that ancestors were sleeping, waiting for Judgement Day – this did not mean that dead relatives were not remembered or prayed for, but that prayer for them did not involve any belief in their intercessory powers. It must be stressed again that this was an official attitude, and the view of a number of informants (see cases 1 and 2 above) was that some people would not publicly admit their belief in the power of their shades.

Another attitude found – again mainly in the Ethiopian-type churches – was that ancestors were not seen to be powerful, but that individuals did not rule out this possibility. Thus ancestors would not be important in everyday life, but a particular crisis might bring out a more specific attitude. We shall discuss this below when we come to performance of cult activity. Into this category would fall President W in case 4 above, who, although he himself did not feel his shades were important, would not prescribe the beliefs of others.

Some Zionist-type church members subscribed to the sort of views described above (see case 3), but in general they had a more specific view of the importance of their shades in their lives, and of their power to help and harm. This view included their own shades but, as has been suggested, would be strengthened by the presence in the church of a successful prophet who stressed the importance of her own shades in her healing work. In this category attitudes towards the shades included a belief in the power of the shades to influence the living as well as a belief in the importance of shades as intermediaries and intercessors between God and man.

An interesting distinction sometimes made was between shades who had been Christian while alive, and those who had not. This was shown clearly in Mrs. R's testimony in case 3: she was at pains to point out that the people who had appeared to her in a dream were in fact Christian – they were not *amadlozi*. This confusion may perhaps be traced to the view of some missionaries that the shades and Christianity were incompatible. Mrs. R therefore equated *amadlozi* with pagan beliefs; others in Soweto, as has been shown, felt that belief in ancestors and Christianity were compatible, if not compulsory (see case 2). A number of those whose shades were not Christian stressed that their work was not anti-Christian (see cases 1 and 2). The shades, as Mrs. N said, 'had God in their minds'.

With this variety in belief went a variety in actual performance. Generally those who had no strong belief in the power of their shades made no offerings to them. Exceptions to this might occur, however, in crisis situations where people would turn to any possible help. One Ethiopian-type leader who did not believe in the power of ancestors or the work of prophets, explained the behaviour of those who did in the following terms, 'My people do these things because they are suffering – if a man is suffering he will try anything to get better.' He held the view that many people made offerings to their shades more in hope than in faith. This might have been the case with some, but others were encountered during fieldwork who, although retaining a belief in the potential power of the shades, made no offerings except under exceptional circumstances. One such case was described above where an Ethiopian-type leader made a secret offering to his father only after an important dream. And others would neglect their shades until some misfortune befell them.

Those with strong beliefs in the influence of their shades tended to express this regularly in some form of activity. This activity varied considerably: for some it involved regular offerings of animals in the traditional manner, and the setting aside of beer. For others the emphasis was on prayer, with or without the occasional offering. Offerings varied too, from the traditional to a more modern form. Pauw, for example, refers (1974: 105) to the change among Xhosa people from the traditional *idini* sacrifice to a Western-type meal, *idinara*, which is associated with ancestor beliefs. Other adaptations are linked to the Bible, for example the offering described above, which was based on an Old Testament form. Thus incidence and type of performance vary considerably in people who maintain a belief in their shades and their influences.

The question which remains to be answered is how the incidence of beliefs and the incidence of performance are related to one another. From what we know of the traditional situation it would seem that the two were dependent variables, but this is no longer necessarily the case in a situation of change such as is seen in Soweto. We shall now try to examine the different possible relationships between these two aspects.

Clearly, a decrease in belief in the importance of shades may lead to a decrease in performance. This would be a standard response, but may not occur in all cases; for example a person may begin to lose faith in the influence of his shades but yet keep up his performance for the sake of appearances. And we have seen that a decrease in belief may be coupled with occasional performance at crisis periods. But in general the tendency would be towards a decrease in performance.

People who retain a firm belief in the influence of their ancestral shades may vary in degree of performance. Those who come to town, for example, may decrease their performance because they are away from their rural homes, traditionally the place of their shades. Others may continue the normal offerings in town, setting aside a suitable place for them (cf. Pauw 1974: 105-6). One or two cases were encountered in Soweto where people neglected their offerings to their shades on coming to town, and then fell sick. They recovered only after they had performed the necessary rites and propitiated their shades. On the other hand, one may encounter an increase in performance on coming to town. This may arise in a situation where the individual becomes more dependent on a guiding shade in the urban situation, and communicates regularly. This may be so particularly of people who have difficulty in adjusting to a new situation; their troubles are often diagnosed by a prophet or diviner as coming from their shades. Others, as we have seen, increasingly use their shades as intermediaries with God.

This raises a third situation: where people still believe in the importance of their shades, but where their belief in the *nature* of the importance changes. This is seen in the increasing idea of personal guides (Pauw 1974: 108), but is clearest in those who accept the teachings of Christianity. For these people the shades are not all-powerful. They may have influence on the lives of their living relatives, but they are also subservient to God. In this relationship their importance may change as their role as intermediaries becomes more pronounced. A good example of this is the process already described whereby diviners depending on their shades are changed into Christian prophets.

It should also be pointed out that not only the incidence of performance may vary, but also the type of activity. We have seen that the range extends from the traditional offerings of animals and setting aside of beer, to modifications of this including Western-type meals. The multi-ethnic situation in Soweto has also seen to it that specifically 'tribal' customs change – thus Nguni people in Soweto may slaughter sheep and goats where before only goats were permissible. Propitiation of the shades, however, is no longer only expressed in offerings. In the independent churches prayer has also become important – prayer both to and for the shades. In some isolated cases encountered, prayer had become the only specific activity involving the shades, but in most cases offerings were also important.

To conclude, we have looked at beliefs and activities surrounding the ancestors in general terms, and suggested a terminological and conceptual distinction between ancestors and shades, leading to an analytical distinction between belief in ancestors (on a cognitive level) and cults of the ancestral shades (on an operational level). We have tried to show that this distinction is useful in situations of change, and have looked specifically at the independent churches in Soweto to see the considerable independent variation of the two levels. The influence of the urban environment and of Christianity has caused important modifications at both levels and we suggest that the basic distinction made between belief and performance is important to a fuller understanding of the social processes involved.

THE PUBLISHED WORKS OF MONICA AND GODFREY WILSON

MONICA WILSON (BORN HUNTER)

1932   'Results of Culture Contact on the Pondo and Xosa Family', *South African Journal of Science* 29.
1933   'Effects of Contact with Europeans on the Status of Pondo Women', *Africa* 6.
1934   'Methods of Study of Culture Contact', *Africa* 7 (reprinted as 'Contact between Europeans . . .', see 1938 below).
1936   *Reaction to Conquest*. London: Oxford University Press (2 ed., 1961).
1937   'An African Christian Morality', *Africa* 10.
1937   'The Bantu on European-owned Farms' in I. Schapera (ed.), *The Bantu-Speaking Tribes of South Africa*. Cape Town: Maskew Miller.
1938   'Contact between Europeans and Natives in South Africa, I: In Pondoland' (publisher's title), *Methods for the Study of Culture Contact in Africa*. Memorandum XV, International African Institute.
1942   'Contemporary European–Bantu Relations in South Africa' in A. le R. Locke and B. J. Stern (eds.), *When Peoples Meet*. New York: Progressive Education Association.
1948   *Some Possibilities and Limitations of Anthropological Research* (Inaugural Lecture as Professor of Social Anthropology). Grahamstown: Rhodes University.
1949   'The Pondo and Pondomise' in A. M. Duggan-Cronin (ed.), *The Bantu Tribes of South Africa*, vol. 3. Cambridge University Press.
1949   'Nyakyusa Age-Villages', *Journal of the Royal Anthropological Institute* 79.
1950   'Nyakyusa Kinship' in A. R. Radcliffe-Brown and D. Forde (eds.), *African Systems of Kinship and Marriage*. London: Oxford University Press.
1951   *Good Company; A Study of Nyakyusa Age Villages*. London: Oxford University Press (reprinted Boston: Beacon Press, 1963).

1951   'Witch Beliefs and Social Structure', *American Journal of Sociology* 56.

1952   (with Kaplan, Maki and Walton) *Social Structure* (Keiskammahoek Rural Survey, vol. 3). Pietermaritzburg: Shuter and Shooter.

1952   (with Elton-Mills) *Land Tenure* (Keiskammahoek Rural Survey, vol. 4). Pietermaritzburg: Shuter and Shooter.

1954   'Nyakyusa Ritual and Symbolism', *American Anthropologist* 56.

1954   'Conditions in the Ciskei', *Race Relations Journal* 21.

1955   'Development in Anthropology', *Race Relations Journal* 22.

1956   'An Anthropologist's View of the Tomlinson Report', *Race Relations Journal* 23.

1956   'To whom do they pray?' *The Listener* 56, no. 1440.

1956   'An Urban Community' (East London) in *Social Implications of Industrialization and Urbanization in Africa South of the Sahara*. Paris: UNESCO.

1957   *Rituals of Kinship among the Nyakyusa*. London: Oxford University Press.

1957   'Joking Relationships in Central Africa', *Man* 57.

1958   *The Peoples of the Nyasa–Tanganyika Corridor*, Communications from the School of African Studies, University of Cape Town.

1959   *Communal Rituals of the Nyakyusa*. London: Oxford University Press.

1959   *Divine Kings and the Breath of Men* (The Frazer Lecture). Cambridge University Press.

1959   'The Early History of the Transkei and Ciskei', *African Studies* 18.

1960   'Myths of Precedence' in A. Dubb (ed.), *Myth in Modern Africa*. Grahamstown: Institute of Social and Economic Research, Rhodes University.

1961   'South Africa', *International Social Science Journal* 13. Paris: UNESCO.

1962   'The Principle of Maintaining the Reserves for Africans', *Race Relations Journal* 29.

1963   'Effects on the Xhosa and Nyakyusa of Scarcity of Land' in D. Biebuyck (ed.), *African Agrarian Systems*. London: Oxford University Press.

1963   (with Archie Mafeje) *Langa: A Study of Social Groups in an African Township*. Cape Town: Oxford University Press.

1964   'The Coherence of Groups' in J. F. Holleman *et al.* (eds.), *Problems of Transition*. Durban: University of Natal.

1964   *Let No Man Put Asunder*. Cape Town: Brian MacKenzie.

1964   'Traditional Art among the Nyakyusa', *South African Archaeological Bulletin* 19.

1965   'Freedom to Teach', *South African Outlook*, September. (Also in F. Wilson and D. Perrot, eds., *Outlook on a Century*.

Johannesburg: Lovedale and Spro-cas.)

1966   'The Implications of the Gospel in South African Society', *South African Outlook* 96.

1966   'Urban Revolution in South Africa' in Egbert de Vries (ed.), *Man in Community*. New York: Association Press.

1967   'Nyakyusa Ritual and Symbolism' in John Middleton (ed.), *Myth and Cosmos*. New York: Natural History Press.

1967   'Nyakyusa Age-Villages' in Ronald Cohen and John Middleton (eds.), *Comparative Political Systems*. New York: Natural History Press.

1967 · 'Scale' in P. Bohannan and F. Plog (eds.), *Beyond the Frontier: Social Process and Cultural Change*. New York: Natural History Press.

1968   'Ritual in Local Politics' in M. J. Swartz (ed.), *Local-level Politics: Social and Cultural Perspectives*. Chicago: Aldine.

1968   'Z. K. Matthews: A Man for Reconciliation', *South African Outlook*, July. (Also in F. Wilson and D. Perrot, eds., *Outlook on a Century*. Johannesburg: Lovedale and Spro-cas.)

1969   'Changes in Sócial Structure in Southern Africa: The Relevance of Kinship Studies to the Historian' in L. Thompson (ed.), *African Societies in Southern Africa*. London: Heinemann.

1969   'The Changing Society' in *The Church Crossing Frontiers*. Uppsala: Almqvist and Wiksell.

1969   'Co-operation and Conflict: The Eastern Cape Frontier' in M. Wilson and L. Thompson (eds.), *The Oxford History of South Africa*, vol. 1. Oxford: Clarendon Press.

1969   'The Hunters and Herders' in M. Wilson and L. Thompson (eds.), *The Oxford History of South Africa*, vol 1. Oxford: Clarendon Press.

1969   'The Nguni People' in M. Wilson and L. Thompson (eds.), *The Oxford History of South Africa*, vol. 1. Oxford: Clarendon Press.

1969   'The Sotho, Venda, and Tsonga' in M. Wilson and L. Thompson (eds.), *The Oxford History of South Africa*, vol. 1. Oxford: Clarendon Press.

1969 &   (ed. with Leonard Thompson) *The Oxford History of South Africa*, vols. 1 and 2. Oxford: Clarendon Press.
1971

1970   *The Thousand Years before van Riebeeck* (Raymond Dart Lecture). Johannesburg: Witwatersrand University Press.

1971   'The Growth of Peasant Communities' in M. Wilson and L. Thompson (eds.), *The Oxford History of South Africa*, vol. 2. Oxford: Clarendon Press.

1971   *Religion and the Transformation of Society* (The Scott Holland Lectures). Cambridge University Press.

1971   'Problems for Research in Tswana History', *Botswana Notes and Records* 3.

1972   'Lovedale, Instrument of Peace' in F. Wilson and D. Perrot (eds.), *Outlook on a Century*. Johannesburg: Lovedale and Spro-cas.

1972   *The Interpreters* (The Third Dugmore Memorial Lecture). Grahamstown: The 1820 Settler National Monument Foundation.

1972   'Reflections on the Early History of North Malawi' in B. Pachai (ed.), *The Early History of Malawi*. London: Longmans.

1972   'The Wedding Cakes: A Study of Ritual Change' in J. S. La Fontaine (ed.), *The Interpretation of Ritual*. London: Tavistock.

1974   *The Changing Status of African Women* (5th Bertha Solomon Memorial Lecture). Cape Town: National Council of Women.

1974   'Problems for Research in Frontier History' in C. Saunders and R. Derricourt (eds.), *Beyond the Cape Frontier*. London: Longman.

GODFREY AND MONICA WILSON

1939   *The Study of African Society*. Rhodes–Livingstone Papers 2.
1945   *The Analysis of Social Change*. Cambridge University Press.

GODFREY WILSON

1936   'An African Morality', *Africa* 9.
1936   'An Introduction to Nyakyusa Society', *Bantu Studies* 10.
1937   'Introduction to Nyakyusa Law', *Africa* 10.
1938   *The Land Rights of Individuals among the Nyakyusa*. Rhodes–Livingstone Papers 1.
1939   *The Constitution of Ngonde*. Rhodes–Livingstone Papers 3.
1939   'Nyakyusa Conventions of Burial', *Bantu Studies* 13.
1940   'Anthropology as a Public Service', *Africa* 13.
1941–42   *An Essay on the Economics of Detribalization in Northern Rhodesia*. Rhodes–Livingstone Papers 5 and 6.

BIBLIOGRAPHY

Adams, R. N. (1960) 'An Enquiry into the Nature of the Family' in G. E. Dole and R. L. Carneiro (eds.), *Essays in the Science of Culture*. New York: Croswell.

Anon. (1832) *History of the Civilization and Christianization of South Africa*. Edinburgh: Waugh and Innes.

Ardener, E. (1971) 'The New Anthropology and Its Critics', *Man* 6.

Ashton, E. H. (1943) *Medicine, Magic and Sorcery among the Southern Sotho*, Communications from the School of African Studies, University of Cape Town.

Ashton, E. H. (1952) *The Basuto*. London: Oxford University Press for the International African Institute.

Barić, L. (1967) 'Levels of Change in Yugoslav Kinship' in M. Freedman (ed.), *Social Organisation: Essays Presented to Raymond Firth*. London: Cass.

Beach, D. N. (1973) 'The Initial Impact of Christianity on the Shona' in A. J. Dachs (ed.), *Christianity South of the Zambesi*. Gwelo: Mambo Press.

Beattie, J. M., and J. Middleton (1969) *Spirit Mediumship and Society in Africa*. London: Routledge and Kegan Paul.

Beaver, R. P. (1970) 'Comity' in S. C. Neill *et al.*, *Concise Dictionary of the Christian World Mission*. London: Lutterworth.

Berger, J. (1971) 'Animal World', *New Society*, 25 November 1943.

Berger, P., and T. Luckmann (1972) *The Social Construction of Reality*. Harmondsworth: Penguin University Books.

Berglund, A.-I. (1972) 'Zulu Ideas and Symbolism.' Ph.D. thesis, University of Cape Town.

Bradbury, R. E. (1966) 'Fathers, Elders and Ghosts in Edo Religion' in M. Banton (ed.), *Anthropological Approaches to the Study of Religion*. London: Tavistock.

Brain, J. L. (1973) 'Ancestors as Elders – Further Thoughts', *Africa* 43.

Bryant, A. T. (1949) *The Zulu People*. Pietermaritzburg: Shuter and Shooter.

Bryant, A. T. (1970) *Zulu Medicine and Medicine-Men*. Cape Town: C. Struik.

Bulmer, R. (1967) 'Why is the cassowary not a bird? A Problem of Zoological Taxonomy among the Karam of the New Guinea Highlands',

Man 2.

Burton, Richard F. (1964) *Personal Narrative of a Pilgrimage to Al Madinah and Meccah*, 2 vols. Memorial ed. New York: Dover Publications (first published 1893).

Callaway, H. (1868) *Izinganekwane: Nursery Tales, Traditions, and Histories of the Zulus*. Springvale, Natal: J. A. Blair.

Carstens, W. Peter (1961) 'The Community of Steinkopf: An Ethnographic Study and an Analysis of Social Change in Namaqualand.' Ph.D. thesis, University of Cape Town.

Carstens, W. Peter (1966) *The Social Structure of a Cape Coloured Reserve: A Study of Racial Integration and Segregation in South Africa*. Cape Town: Oxford University Press.

Carstens, W. Peter (1969) 'Some Aspects of Khoikhoi (Hottentot) Settlement Patterns' in *Contributions to Anthropology: Ecological Essays*. Ottawa: National Museums of Canada.

Christian, William A., Jr. (1972) *Person and God in a Spanish Valley*. New York and London: Seminar Press.

Cook, P. A. W. (1930) *Social Organization and Ceremonial Institutions of the Bomvana*. Cape Town: Juta.

Cory, G. E., (ed.) (1926) *The Diary of the Rev. Francis Owen, Missionary with Dingaan in 1837–1838*. Cape Town: Van Riebeeck Society.

Daneel, M. L. (1972) *Old and New in Southern Shona Independent Churches*. The Hague: Mouton.

Dapper, O., *et al.* (1933) *The Early Cape Hottentots*. Cape Town: Van Riebeeck Society.

de Jager, E. J., and V. Z. Gitywa (1963) 'A Xhosa *Umhlwayelelo* Ceremony in the Ciskei', *African Studies* 22.

de Jouvenel, B. (1967) *The Art of Conjecture*. New York: Basic Books.

Doke, C. M., and B. W. Vilakazi (1948) *Zulu–English Dictionary*. Johannesburg: Witwatersrand University Press.

Douglas, M. (1957) 'Animals in Lele Religious Symbolism', *Africa* 27.

Douglas, M. (1966) *Purity and Danger*. London: Routledge and Kegan Paul.

Douglas, M. (1968) 'The Social Control of Cognition: Some Factors in Joke Perception', *Man* 3.

Driberg, J. H. (1936) 'The Secular Aspect of Ancestor Worship', supplement to *Journal of the Royal African Society* 25, no. 138.

Durkheim, E. (1915) *The Elementary Forms of the Religious Life*. London: Allen and Unwin.

Ellenberger, D. F., and J. C. Macgregor (1969) *History of the Basuto, Ancient and Modern*. New York: Negro Universities Press (originally published 1912).

Evans-Pritchard, E. (1951) *Kinship and Marriage among the Nuer*. Oxford: Clarendon Press.

Evans-Pritchard, E. (1956) *Nuer Religion*. Oxford: Clarendon Press.

Farmer, Leslie (1944) *We Saw the Holy City*. London: Epworth.

Farrant, J. (1966) *Mashonaland Martyr: Bernard Mizeki and the Pioneer Church*. Cape Town: Oxford University Press.

Firth, R. (1963) 'Offering and Sacrifice: Problems of Organisation', *Journal of the Royal Anthropological Institute* 93.

Firth, R. (1964) *Essays in Social Organisation and Values*. London: Athlone Press.

Firth, R., J. Hubert, and A. Forge (1964) *Families and Their Relatives: Kinship in a Middle-class Sector of London*. London: Routledge.

Firth, R., (ed.) (1965) *Two Studies of Kinship in London*. London: Athlone Press.

Fortes, M. (1949) 'Time and Social Structure' in Fortes (ed.), *Social Structure: Studies Presented to A. R. Radcliffe-Brown*. Oxford: Clarendon Press.

Fortes, M. (1961) 'Pietas in Ancestor Worship', *Journal of the Royal Anthropological Institute* 91.

Fortes, M. (1965) 'Some Reflections on Ancestor Worship in Africa' in M. Fortes and G. Dieterlen (eds.), *African Systems of Thought*. London: Oxford University Press.

Fripp, C. E., and V. W. Hiller (1949) *Gold and the Gospel in Mashonaland 1888*. London: Chatto and Windus.

Geertz, Clifford (1966) 'Religion as a Cultural System' in M. Banton (ed.), *Anthropological Approaches to the Study of Religion*. London: Tavistock.

Gluckman, M. (1955) *Custom and Conflict in Africa*. Oxford: Blackwell.

Gluckman, M. (1972) 'Moral Crises: Magical and Secular Solutions' in M. Gluckman (ed.), *The Allocation of Responsibility*. Manchester University Press.

Goodall, N. (1954) *A History of the London Missionary Society 1895–1945*. Oxford University Press.

Goode, W. J. (1963) *World Revolution and Family Patterns*. Glencoe: Free Press.

Goody, Jack, (ed.) (1958) *The Developmental Cycle of Domestic Groups*. Cambridge University Press.

Goody, J. (1962) *Death, Property and the Ancestors*. London: Tavistock.

Goody, J., (ed.) (1971) *Kinship*. Harmondsworth: Penguin Books.

Goody, J., (ed.) (1973) *The Character of Kinship*. London: Cambridge University Press.

Groves, C. P. (1954) *The Planting of Christianity in Africa*, vol. 2. London: Lutterworth Press.

Guillarmod, A. Jacot (1971) *Flora of Lesotho*. J. Cramer.

Hahn, T. (1881) *Tsuni-//Goam: The Supreme Being of the Khoikhoi*. London: Trubner.

Hammond-Tooke, W. D. (1962) *Bhaca Society*. Cape Town: Oxford University Press.

Hammond-Tooke, W. D. (1965) 'Segmentation and Fission in Cape Nguni Political Units', *Africa* 35.

Hammond-Tooke, W. D. (1968) 'The Morphology of Mpondomise Descent Groups', *Africa* 38.

Hammond-Tooke, W. D. (1969) 'The Other Side of Frontier History: A Model of Cape Nguni Political Process' in L. Thompson (ed.), *African Societies in Southern Africa*. London: Heinemann.

Hammond-Tooke, W. D. (1970) 'Urbanization and the Interpretation of

Misfortune: A Quantitative Analysis', *Africa* 40.

Hammond-Tooke, W. D. (1974*a*) 'The Cape Nguni Witch Familiar as a Mediatory Construct', *Man* 9.

Hammond-Tooke, W. D. (1974*b*) 'World-view: A System of Beliefs' in W. D. Hammond-Tooke (ed.), *The Bantu-speaking Peoples of Southern Africa*. London: Routledge and Kegan Paul.

Harris, Marvin (1968) *The Rise of Anthropological Theory*. New York: Thomas Y. Crowell.

Hellmann, E. (1948) *Rooiyard: A Sociological Survey of an Urban Slumyard*. Cape Town: Oxford University Press for Rhodes–Livingstone Institute.

Hellmann, E. (1971) *Soweto – Johannesburg's African City*. Johannesburg: S.A. Institute of Race Relations.

Hemmy, Gysbert (1767) *De Promontorio Bonae Spei* (*The Cape of Good Hope*) (translated and ed. K. D. White, 1959). Cape Town: South African Public Library.

Hoernlé, A. W. (*née* Tucker) (1913) Journal. Unpublished.

Hoernlé, A. W. (1918) 'Certain Rites of Transition among the Hottentots', *Harvard African Studies* 2.

Hoernlé, A. W. (1922) 'A Hottentot Rain Ceremony', *Bantu Studies* 1.

Hoernlé, A. W. (1923) 'The Expression of the Social Value of Water among the Naman of South West Africa', *S.A. Journal of Science* 20.

Horton, R. (1962) 'The Kalabari Worldview', *Africa* 32.

Horton, R. (1970) 'A Hundred Years of Change in Kalabari Religion' in J. Middleton (ed.), *Black Africa: Its Peoples and Cultures Today*. London: Macmillan.

Horton, R. (1971) 'African Conversion', *Africa* 41.

Houghton, D. Hobart, and E. M. Walton (1952) *The Economy of a Native Reserve* (Keiskammahoek Rural Survey, vol. 2). Pietermaritzburg: Shuter and Shooter.

Hunter, M. (1936) *Reaction to Conquest*. London: Oxford University Press.

Jenkinson, T. B. (1882) *Amazulu: The Zulus, their Past History, Manners, Customs and Language*. London: Allen.

Jopp, W. (1960) Die Frühen Deutschen Berichte über das Kapland und die Hottentotten bis 1750. Ph.D. thesis, University of Göttingen.

Junod, H. A. (1927) *The Life of a South African Tribe*. London: Macmillan.

Kiernan, J. P. (1974) 'Where Zionists Draw the Line: A Study of Religious Exclusiveness in an African Township', *African Studies* 33.

King, Georgiana Goddard (1920) *The Way of St. James*. New York and London: Putnam.

Kitchingman, J. (1820) Diary (ms.).

Knight-Bruce, G. W. H. (1970) *Memories of Mashonaland* (Rhodesiana Reprint Library 13).

Knock Shrine Annual (1968) Knock, Ireland: Knock Shrine Society.

Kohler, M. (1941) *The Izangoma Diviners* (Ethnological Publications 9). Pretoria: Department of Native Affairs.

Kolb, Peter (1731) *The Present State of the Cape of Good Hope*, vol. 1. New York and London: Johnson, 1968.

Kopytoff, I. (1971) 'Ancestors as Elders in Africa', *Africa* 41.

Krige, E. J. (1936) *The Social Structure of the Zulus.* Pietermaritzburg: Shuter and Shooter.

Krige, E. J. and J. D. (1943) *The Realm of a Rain Queen.* London: Oxford University Press.

Krige, E. J. (1964) 'Property, Cross-cousin Marriage and the Family Cycle among the Lovedu' in R. F. Gray and P. Gulliver (eds.), *The Family Estate in Africa.* London: Routledge and Kegan Paul.

Krige, E. J. (1974) 'Woman-marriage with Special Reference to the Lovedu – Its Significance for the Definition of Marriage', *Africa* 44.

Laslett, P., (ed.) (1972) *Household and Family in Past Time.* Cambridge University Press.

Laubscher, B. J. F. (1937) *Sex, Custom and Psychopathology.* London: Routledge and Kegan Paul.

Laydevant, F. (1952) *The Basuto.* Roma: Social Centre, St. Michael's Mission.

Lee, S. G. (1950) 'Some Zulu Concepts of Psychogenic Disorder', *Journal of Social Science.*

Lee, S. G. (1969) 'Spirit Possession among the Zulu' in J. Beattie and J. Middleton (eds.), *Spirit Mediumship and Society in Africa.* London: Routledge and Kegan Paul.

Levin, R. (1947) *Marriage in Langa Native Location,* Communications from the School of African Studies, University of Cape Town.

Lévi-Strauss, C. (1955) *Tristes Tropiques.* Paris: Plon.

Lévi-Strauss, C. (1964) *Mythologiques: Le Cru et le Cuit.* Paris: Plon.

Lévi-Strauss, C. (1969) *Totemism.* Harmondsworth: Penguin Books.

Lewis, I. M. (1971) *Ecstatic Religion.* Harmondsworth: Penguin Books.

Loudon, J. B. (1959) 'Psychogenic Disorder and Social Conflict among the Zulu' in M. K. Opler (ed.), *Culture and Mental Health.* New York: Macmillan.

Loudon, J. B. (1965) 'Social Aspects of Ideas about Treatment' in A. V. S. van Reuch and R. Porter (eds.), *Ciba Foundation Symposium on Transcultural Psychiatry.* London: J. and A. Churchill.

Mabille, A., and H. Dieterlen (1961) *Southern Sotho–English Dictionary.* Morija: Sesuto Book Depot.

Madala, A. (1965) *Amavo Amafutshane.* Cape Town: Oxford University Press.

Makhatini, D. L. (1965) 'Ancestors, uMoya, Angels' in Missiological Institute, *Our Approach to the Independent Church Movement in South Africa.* Mapumulo: Lutheran Theological College.

Marwick, B. A. (1966) *The Swazi.* London and Edinburgh: Nelson.

Mashonaland Paper, no. III (1893). London: S.P.G.

Mayer, P. (1954) *Witches.* Grahamstown: Rhodes University.

Mayer, P. (1961) *Townsmen or Tribesmen.* Cape Town: Oxford University Press.

McFeat, T. (1974) *Small-group Cultures.* Toronto: Pergamon Press.

McKnight, J. D. (1967) 'Extra-descent Group Ancestor Cults in African Societies', *Africa* 36.

McLaren, J. (1944) *A Xhosa Grammar* (ed. G. H. Welsh). London: Longmans.

Möller, H. J. (1972) *God en die Voorouergeeste in die Lewe van die Stedelike Bantoe* (Stedelike Bantoe en die Kerk, vol. 2). Pretoria: Human Sciences Research Council.

Murdock, G. P. (1949) *Social Structure*. New York: Macmillan.

Pauw, B. A. (1960) *Religion in a Tswana Chiefdom*. London: Oxford University Press.

Pauw, B. A. (1963a) *The Second Generation*. Cape Town: Oxford University Press.

Pauw, B. A. (1963b) 'African Christians and Their Ancestors' in V. E. W. Hayward (ed.), *African Independent Church Movements*. London: Edinburgh House Press.

Pauw, B. A. (1974) 'Ancestor Beliefs and Rituals among Urban Africans', *African Studies* 33.

Pauw, B. A. (1975) *Christianity and Xhosa Tradition*. Cape Town: Oxford University Press.

Peacock, J. L., and A. T. Kirsch (1970) *The Human Direction*. New York: Appleton-Century-Crofts.

Pike, K. (1954) *Language in Relation to a Unified Theory of the Structure of Human Behaviour*, vol. 1. Glendale: Summer Institute of Linguistics.

Radcliffe-Brown, A. R. (1957) *A Natural Science of Society*. Glencoe: Free Press.

Raum, O. (1973) *The Social Functions of Avoidances and Taboo among the Zulu*. Berlin: Walter de Gruyter.

Redfield, R. (1960) *The Little Community* (first published 1955) in one volume with *Peasant Society and Culture*. University of Chicago Press.

Richards, A. I. (1956) *Chisungu*. London: Faber.

Richards, A. I. (1963) 'The Pragmatic Value of Magic in Primitive Societies', *Proceedings of the Royal Institution of Great Britain* 39.

Richards, A. I. (1970) 'Socialisation and Contemporary British Anthropology' in P. Mayer (ed.), *Socialisation and the Approach from Social Anthropology*. London: Tavistock.

Rigby, P. (1971) 'The Symbolic Role of Cattle in Gogo Ritual' in T. O. Beidelman (ed.), *The Translation of Culture*. London: Tavistock.

Roussel, Romain (1954) *Les Pélerinages à travers les Siècles*. Paris: Payot.

Sangree, W. H. (1974) 'Youths as Elders and Infants as Ancestors: The Complementarity of Alternate Generations, both Living and Dead, in Tiriki, Kenya, and Irigwe, Nigeria', *Africa* 44.

Sapir, E. (1927) 'Anthropology and Sociology' in W. F. Ogburn, and A. Goldenweiser (eds.), *The Social Sciences and Their Interrelation*. Boston: Houghton Mifflin.

Schapera, I. (1930) *The Khoisan Peoples of South Africa*. London: Routledge and Kegan Paul.

Schapera, I. (1956) *Government and Politics in Tribal Societies*. London: Watts.

Schultze, L. (1907) *Aus Namaland und Kalahari*. Jena: Fischer.

Sekese, A. (1970) *Mekhoa ea Basotho*. Morija: Sesuto Book Depot (originally published 1893).

Setiloane, G. (1973) 'Modimo: God, among the Sotho–Tswana', *Journal of Theology for Southern Africa* 4.

Soga, J. H. (1930) *The South-Eastern Bantu*. Johannesburg: Witwatersrand University Press.

Soga, J. H. (1931) *The Ama-Xosa: Life and Customs*. Lovedale: Lovedale Press.

Spiro, M. (1966) 'Religion: Problems of Definition and Explanation' in M. Banton (ed.), *Anthropological Approaches to the Study of Religion*. London: Tavistock.

Starkie, Walter (1965) *The Road to Santiago*. Berkeley and Los Angeles: University of California Press.

Stow, George W. (1905) *The Native Races of South Africa*. London: Swan Sonnenschein.

Strathern, A. and M. (1968) 'Marsupials and Magic: A Study of Spell Symbolism among the Mbowamb' in E. R. Leach (ed.), *Dialectic in Practical Religion*. Cambridge University Press.

Sundkler, B. G. M. (1961) *Bantu Prophets in South Africa*. London: Oxford University Press.

Tambiah, S. J. (1969) 'Animals are good to eat and good to prohibit', *Ethnology* 8.

Tau, M. N. (1972) 'Some Medical, Magic and Edible Plants of Lesotho', *Lesotho* 9. Maseru: Lesotho Scientific Association.

Turner, V. W. (1964) 'Symbols in Ndembu Ritual' in M. Gluckman (ed.), *Open Systems and Closed Minds*. Chicago: Aldine.

Turner, V. W. (1967) *The Forest of Symbols*. Ithaca: Cornell University Press.

van der Merwe, W. J. (1952) *Sendinggenade in Mashonaland*. Cape Town: N.G. Kerk Uitgewers van S.A.

Vedder, H. (1928) 'The Nama' in *The Native Tribes of South West Africa*. Cape Town: Cape Times.

Walsh, M. (1957) *Knock: The Shrine of the Pilgrim People of God*. Tuam: St. Jarlath's College.

Weber, Max (1904–5) *The Protestant Ethic and the Spirit of Capitalism* (translated by Talcott Parsons and reprinted in 1958). New York: Scribner.

West, M. E. (1972a) 'Thérapie et Changement Sociale dans les Églises Urbaines d'Afrique du Sud', *Social Compass* 19.

West, M. E. (1972b) 'African Independent Churches in Soweto.' Ph.D. thesis, University of Cape Town.

West, M. E. (1975) *Bishops and Prophets in a Black City: African Independent Churches in Soweto, Johannesburg*. Cape Town: David Philip. London: Rex Collings.

Whisson, M. G. (1964) 'Some Aspects of Functional Disorders among the Kenya Luo' in A. Kiev (ed.), *Magic, Faith and Healing*. London: Glencoe Free Press.

Willis, R. (1974) *Man and Beast*. Bungay: Chaucer Press.

Wilson, G (1939) *The Study of African Society*. Rhodes–Livingstone Papers 2.

Wilson, G. and M. (1945) *The Analysis of Social Change*. Cambridge University Press.

Wilson, M. (1951*a*) *Good Company: A Study of Nyakyusa Age Villages*. London: Oxford University Press (reprinted Beacon Press, 1963).

Wilson, M. (1951*b*) 'Witch Beliefs and Social Structure', *American Journal of Sociology* 56.

Wilson, M. (1952) (with Kaplan, Maki and Walton) *Social Structure* (Keiskammahoek Rural Survey, vol. 3). Pietermaritzburg: Shuter and Shooter.

Wilson, M. (1957) *Rituals of Kinship among the Nyakyusa*. London: Oxford University Press.

Wilson, M. (1959*a*) *Communal Rituals of the Nyakyusa*. London: Oxford University Press.

Wilson, M. (1959*b*) *Divine Kings and the Breath of Men* (The Frazer Lecture). Cambridge University Press.

Wilson, M. (1963*a*) 'Effects on the Xhosa and Nyakyusa of Scarcity of Land' in D. Biebuyck (ed.), *African Agrarian Systems*. London: Oxford University Press.

Wilson, M. (1963*b*) (with Archie Mafeje) *Langa: A Study of Social Groups in an African Township*. Cape Town: Oxford University Press.

Wilson, M. (1969) 'The Nguni People' and 'The Sotho, Venda, and Tsonga' in M. Wilson and L. Thompson (eds.), *The Oxford History of South Africa*, vol. 1. Oxford: Clarendon Press.

Wilson, M. (1971*a*) 'The Growth of Peasant Communities' in M. Wilson and L. Thompson (eds.), *The Oxford History of South Africa*, vol. 2. Oxford: Clarendon Press.

Wilson, M. (1971*b*) *Religion and the Transformation of Society* (The Scott Holland Lectures). Cambridge University Press.

Young, C. (1947) *Contemporary Ancestors – A Beginner's Anthropology for District Officers and Missionaries in Africa*. London: Lutterworth.

Young, M., and P. Wilmot (1966) *Family and Kinship in East London*. Harmondsworth: Pelican Books (first published by Routledge and Kegan Paul, 1957).

INDEX

Adams, R. N., 146
Amsterdam, Free University of, 185n
ancestors, 16, 18, 20–2, 24, 25, 32, 48, 49, 51, 59, 74, 111, 117, 156–62, 184–206; cult, 17–19, 83, 156, 172, 176; hero, 82–4, 94
Anglo–Boer War, 105
Anglo–Saxon, 164
Argyle, Professor W. J., 145
Ashanti, 137
Ashton, E. H., 61n, 62, 66n, 71n, 72n
Aztecan, 122
Bantu Prophets in South Africa, 166
Barić, L., 188
Beach, D. N., 105
Beattie, J., and J. Middleton, 71n
Beaver, R. P., 101
Bechuanaland, 101
beer, 15, 64, 69, 71, 130, 160, 191, 197, 205, 206
Belingwe, 105
Bemba, 3–5, 9, 10
Berger, J., 27
Berglund, A.-I., vii, ix, x, 19, 34–48, 187
Bhaca, 15n, 19, 21, 25, 27, 153, 156
Bhebe, N. M. B., 97n
Blake, W., 111, 112
Bloemfontein, Bishop of, 99, 100
Botha's Hill, 48
Bradbury, R. E., 18
Brain, J. L., 186n
Brandel–Syrier, M., 189
Britain, 56
British South Africa Company, 103
Brittany, 122
Broken Hill, 4, 5
Brown, Gordon, 3
Bryant, A. T., 48, 52
Buddhism, 113
Bulmer, R., 27
Bulawayo, 98
Bunyakyusa, see Nyakyusa
Bunyan, J., 116
Burridge, K., 8n
Burton, Sir Richard, 107
Callaway, H., 19
Calvinist, 87–9, 93, see also church
Cambridge University, 2, 3
Campbell, A. C., 21

Cape, Dutch frontiersmen, 86; Peninsula, 178n; Province, x, 13, 15n, 129, 153; see also Nguni, Cape
Cape Town, 1, 106, 179–81, 183; Bishop of, 98; University of, ix, 1, 13
Carnegie, David, 99–102
Carstens, Peter, vii, x, 78–95
cattle, 15, 23–5, 28–31, 45, 70, 71, 79, 132, 135; keeping, 6, 12, 20, 35, 155; marriage payments in, 61–3, 133, 134; see also sacrifice
Ceza mountain, 37, 40
Chaucer, G., 116
chiefs, 23, 32, 33, 67, 69, 85, 102, 104, 156
chiefship, 6, 32, 67, 157
child-rearing, 2, 6, 58, 75
chisungu, 9, 10
Christian, 10, 13, 17, 66, 78, 80, 86, 107, 110, 129–206
Christian, William A., Jr., 122
Christianity, xi, 12, 93–106, 107–27, 153–63; see also Christian, church, missionary, missions, religion, ritual
church, 86, 92, 93, 97–106, 130, 155, 157, 158, 160, 164, 167–9, 179, 182, 185–206; African Ethiopian Baptist, 169; Anglican, 102, 103, 154, 172, 177, 179–81; Assemblies of God, 163, 169; Baptists, 180, 181; Bhengu, 179; Bishop Limba's Church of Christ, 163, 179; Catholic, 112–14, 119–21, 124, 126, 154, 196; Congregationalist, 190; Dutch Reformed, 154, 182, 201; Ethiopian, 167, 174, 190–2, 196, 202–4; Ethiopian Church of South Africa, 169; European mission, 167, 190; Full Gospel, 169; history, 97–106, 170; Independent, 51, 167–84, 190–206; Jehovah's Witnesses (Watch Tower), 169, 179; Lutheran, 105, 154; Methodist, 88, 102, 103, 105, 154, 157, 180, 181, 190, 195, 196, 202; Methodist, Bantu, 169; Old Apostolic, 163; Pentecostal, 55, 154, 160; Presbyterian, 154, 190; Presbyterian Church of Africa, 169; Protestant, 167, 183, 190; Reformed, 93; Sabbatarian-Baptist, 154, 160; Salvation Army, 169; Seventh Day Adventist, 169; Sigxabayi, 180, 181; Zion Christian Church, 105; Zionist, 55, 105, 130, 160, 161, 163, 167,

222 INDEX